THE LAST
CHRISTMAS SHOW

Maison Blanche, North Africa, 1943. (U. S. Army)

THE LAST CHRISTMAS SHOW

by BOB HOPE

as told to Pete Martin

1974

DOUBLEDAY & COMPANY, INC., GARDEN CITY, NEW YORK

Other books by Bob Hope

FIVE WOMEN I LOVE:
BOB HOPE'S VIETNAM STORY

I OWE RUSSIA $1200

I NEVER LEFT HOME

HAVE TUX, WILL TRAVEL

ISBN: 0-385-07263-5
Library of Congress Catalog Card Number 74–16384
9 8 7 6 5 4 3 2

Dedicated
to
The Men and Women of the Armed Forces
and
to those who also served
by worrying and waiting

ACKNOWLEDGMENTS

For the many pictures in this book we are deeply grateful to the fine photographers of *Stars and Stripes*, the Associated Press, UPI, *Time*, *Life*, and *Newsweek*, the many and varied members of the Defense Department, and to our very loyal and talented lensmen at NBC: Gary Null, Paul Bailey, Herb Ball, Frank Carroll, Fred Sabine, and Jerry Smith. Thank you, thank you.

B.H.

Contents

EDITOR'S NOTE

The following article was originally printed in the New York *Herald Tribune* and was datelined London, July 20, 1943. It tells a lot about the author—what he does—how he does it—and gives an insight into why he does it. I felt it was important to this book and have taken the liberty of including it.

FERRIS MACK
Editor, Doubleday

JOHN STEINBECK

Laughter for men who need it

When the time for recognition of service to the nation in wartime comes to be considered, Bob Hope should be high on the list. This man drives himself and is driven. It is impossible to see how he can do so much, can cover so much ground, can work so hard and can be so effective.

Moving about the country in camps, airfields, billets, supply depots and hospitals, you hear one thing consistently: Bob Hope is coming, or Bob Hope has been here.

He has caught the soldier's imagination. He gets laughter wherever he goes from men who need laughter.

His wit is topical, both broad and caustic, but it is never aimed at people, but at conditions and at ideas. Where he goes men roar with laughter and repeat his cracks for days afterward.

Hope does four, sometimes five shows a day. In some camps the men must come in shifts because they can't all hear him at the same time. Then he jumps into a car and rushes to the next post. Because he broadcasts, and because everyone listens to each broadcast, he can't use the same show more than a few times.

In the midst of his rushing and playing he must build new shows constantly. If he did this for a while, then stopped and took a rest, it would be remarkable. But he never rests. His energy is boundless.

Hope takes his shows all over, not only to the big camps. You hear the same thing in little groups on special duty, "Bob Hope is coming Thursday." They know weeks in advance that he's coming. It would be a terrible thing if he didn't show up.

The battalion of men who are moving halftracks from one place to another, doing a job that gets no headlines, no public notices, but which must be done if there is to be a victory, are forgotten and they feel forgotten. But Bob Hope is in the country. Will he come to them, or won't he?

And then one day they get a notice that he is coming. Then they feel remembered. In some way the man has become that kind of a bridge. It goes beyond how funny he can be or how well his No. 1 songbird sings. He has become a symbol.

Probably the most difficult, the most tearing thing of all is to be funny in a hospital. The long, low buildings are dispersed in case they should be attacked. Working in the gardens or reading in the lounge rooms are the ambulatory cases in maroon bathrobes. But in the wards, in the long aisles of pain, the men lie, with their eyes turned inward on themselves, and on their people.

Time drags. It hangs very long. Letters, even if they come every day, seem weeks apart. Everything that can be done is done, but medicine cannot get at the lonesomeness and the weakness of men who have been strong.

Bob Hope and his company come into this quiet, inward, lonesome place, gently pull the minds outward and catch the interest, and finally bring laughter up out of the black water.

There is a job.

It hurts many of the men to laugh. It hurts their knitting bones, it strains their sutured incisions, yet their laughter is a great medicine.

The story is told in one of those nameless hospitals that must be kept safe from bombs. Hope and company had worked until gradually they got leaden eyes to sparkling, had planted and nurtured and coaxed laughter to life.

A gunner, who had a stomach wound, was gasping softly with laughter. A railroad casualty slapped the cast on his left hand with his right hand by way of applause. And once the laughter was alive, the men laughed even before the punch line and it had to be repeated so they could laugh again.

Finally, it came time for Frances Langford to sing. The men asked for "As Time Goes By." She stood up beside the little GI piano and started to sing. Her voice was a little hoarse and strained. She has been working too hard and too long.

She got through eight bars and was into the bridge when a boy with a head wound began to cry. She stopped, and then went on. But her voice wouldn't work any more. She finished the song whispering. Then she walked out, so no one could see her, and broke down. The ward was quiet. No one applauded.

Then Hope walked into the aisle between the beds and he said seriously: "Fellows, the folks at home are having a terrible time about eggs. They can't get any powdered eggs at all. They've got to use the old-fashioned kind you break open."

There's a man for you . . . There is *really* a man.

Laughter for men who need it

THE LAST
CHRISTMAS SHOW

Bing Crosby, Max Baer, Governor Olson (California), and Babe Ruth at Mather Field, Sacramento, California, 1940. (Photo by Bob Handsaker)

The last Christmas show

CHAPTER 1

Is this trip necessary?

It was 1941 and Pearl Harbor was still dozing in the Pacific sun. The Japanese were trying to carve off large chunks of Asia and the British were rattling their teacups and trying to keep the Nazis at bay.

I was in Hollywood and it was the third year of my radio show for Pepsodent. After a slow start we had suddenly climbed to the top of the ratings and we had it made. Radio . . . what a delicious con! It was fifteen minutes from the house to NBC in Hollywood, no make-up, no costumes, no holding in your stomach. Just pick up a script . . . have a ball with the audience . . . drop the script in the ash can and off to the golf course.

As a matter of fact, I was making my run for the golf course when Cappy Capstaff, the producer of our radio show, stopped me in the parking lot and asked if I'd take the show to Riverside, California, for the Army Air Force at March Field.

"What for?" I asked. "Why don't you bring them here?"

"We can't handle a crowd like that." Cappy screamed. I had closed his hand in the window and was driving toward the exit.

"What kind of crowd are you talking about?"

"Probably a thousand people."

A thousand people! I'd carry a camel a mile to hear ten people laugh. A hundred people is a symphony to me. But a thousand people . . . sheer fantasy.

"You're sure . . . a thousand?"

"Maybe two."

"You mean a captive audience . . . with military police guarding the gates so they can't get out?"

He said yes and I said yes and it was one of the happiest yeses in my life.

If I had said no I would have missed twenty-five of the greatest road shows any performer ever got to make, a quarter century of overseas trips to entertain U.S. servicemen around the world, a chance to work with some of the most talented and beautiful artists in the business.

That yes made it possible for me to get to meet a few million of our service guys in person and to get to know men like Ike Eisenhower, Omar Bradley, Jimmy Doolittle, William "Westy" Westmoreland, George Patton, and Emmett "Rosy" O'Donnell.

It made it possible for me to stand before the Army Chief of Staff at the Pentagon and receive the Medal of Merit from General Eisenhower in 1946. It made it possible for me to stand in the Rose Garden at the White House and receive a congressional gold medal from President Kennedy with all the senators in attendance. And there was the Medal of Freedom from the President, the USO Gold Medal, the Sylvanus Thayer Award, and the George C. Marshall Medal from the Army, the Navy Medal of Honor, and the Spiked Helmet Award from the Marines.

I've got roomfuls of souvenirs, plaques, awards, and commendations for the shows we've done. I've also had my share of criticism, flak, and hostility from some who accused me of being a "war lover." Of course that was just during the Vietnam stalemate. During World War II and Korea I was just a straight lover.

A couple of years ago in front of Will Right's Ice Cream Parlor in Van Nuys a good-looking hippie kid—you know what I mean—the long hair, torn T-shirt, a beat-up pair of jeans, and a lot of bare feet hanging out below—stopped me. "Hey, Bob . . . it's you . . . how you been . . . how's the eye?"

I did a lot of "fine . . . fine . . . thank you." And then the kid really blew my mind. He said, "Hey, did you sponsor the war in Vietnam?"

I couldn't believe it. "Where did you get that?"

"I heard it at a meeting. A couple of guys told me you sponsored the war." Wow . . . how do you answer that?

I felt like the veteran Hollywood actor who toured small towns in a Shakespeare recital. He had nothing in common with Hamlet. He came out on stage and declaimed, "To be or not to be . . . that is the question." And the boos started. And the further he went the more boos and catcalls there were. Finally he couldn't take it any longer and he stepped forward, "Now just a damn minute," he said. "This ain't my fault . . . I didn't write this crap, you know."

And I didn't write the Vietnam War. I never did understand it. If you're going to fight, then fight. If not, everybody pick up their bullets and go home. But nine years of hesitation is a lot of pain and a terrifying waste of lives.

But I don't mind the flak and I don't feel I owe anybody an apology. The cheers and the applause outweighed all the slings and arrows. We went—not just me, but scores of entertainers—because there were kids there who needed a show.

And television gave us a chance to do something that hadn't been done before. It made it possible for us to show the faces of thousands of kids in combat areas to the families back home—mothers, fathers, wives, and children. To prove to them that their kids were alive and not too skinny and best of all still capable of laughter. I'm not sure I'm too happy about this, but a lot of reviewers said that the faces of the audiences were the best part of the shows.

And if you're going to be in show business or in politics you're bound to be a target. And that's especially true if you're involved with controversial current events. One side is bound to hate you . . . and that's if you're lucky.

Back in 1954, when Senator Joseph McCarthy was on his famous witch hunt, we got a lot of copy for one of our television specials:

"Senator McCarthy was out here for a visit but he couldn't stay. He'd been gone almost a week and he doesn't trust even the Republicans with Washington that long.

"Senator McCarthy has disputed the leadership of our country, and a lot of people are wondering just how much longer Walter Winchell is going to stand for it.

"But I have it on good authority that McCarthy is going to disclose the names of two million Communists; he just got his hands on a Moscow telephone book. These days, you can't open a newspaper without reading about McCarthy. Yesterday there was a headline: MCCARTHY TIES SHOELACES; ARMY CLAIMS HE TIED LEFT ONE FIRST. Even President Eisenhower is careful what he says on the air these days because McCarthy may demand equal time in the White House."

After I did that routine, a judge in Appleton, Wisconsin, McCarthy's home town, wrote a letter to the local paper saying I must be a Communist because I was picking on McCarthy. That's about the same as some draft dodger saying that I must love war because I went to Vietnam to entertain the troops.

And lest there be any confusion I want to make it clear that I wasn't the only one. Johnny Grant and Roscoe Ates maneuvered their troupes all over Korea. And, of course, Georgie Jessel was a regular visitor and one of the troops' favorites. In fact, he was wounded under fire. The details of this are somewhat obscure. They're not sure whether he was hit by a piece of flak while flying at low level or if he pulled a ligament while bending over to plant a tree.

And certainly every GI has seen (or at least heard of) Martha Raye, who was the only entertainer to have a billboard on the Ho Chi Minh Trail; also, Charlton Heston, John Wayne, and Bill Holden. Sid Marion and his crew crossed sled tracks with us in Alaska.

Lionel Hampton thrilled the GIs in the Far East on five different trips. He's got the kind of act that's a show stopper in any language. And one of the hot items of our show business scene today is Sammy Davis, Jr., who made a very successful trip to Vietnam. They cheered and cheered.

The great coach of Ohio State, Woody Hayes, always jumped to Vietnam right after the Rose Bowl with films of the outstanding football games and

Victor Mature at Naval Hospital, San Diego, California, 1942. (U. S. Navy)

delighted the guys at so many spots. And don't forget all the National Football League players who went over on handshaking tours. Joe Scibelli of the Rams, Larry Csonka of the Dolphins, Tom Matte of the Colts, Marlin McKeever of the Rams, John Fuqua of the Steelers, Bill Curry of the Colts, Bill Kilmer of the Redskins, Archie Manning of the Saints, Cliff Harris of the Cowboys, John Gilliam of the Vikings, Franco Harris of the Steelers, Bill Munson of the Lions, Jim Mandich of the Dolphins, Diron Talbert of the Redskins, Jack Youngblood of the Rams—to name just a few.

They all volunteered. Some of them didn't even want to know where they were going. They soon learned that nothing can ever quite match the 28,000 volts of electricity you get when you step out and find 28,000 kids from the 3rd Marine Amphibious Wing sitting there in the rain at Da Nang, waiting for you. Or the excitement that can run through an audience of lonely GIs when a beautiful package of woman like Joey Heatherton, Raquel Welch, Anita Ekberg, Jill St. John, or Jayne Mansfield steps before them.

Tony Romano, Frances Langford, Jack Pepper at P-38 base, North Africa, 1943.

We had our share of excitement and kicks, but we also had our share of hairy, anxious moments: On our first trip, when the weather got so thick that they ordered us into Mae West life jackets and parachutes, and the only thing that got us down was one anti-aircraft searchlight that managed to pierce the storm. The time we had to crash-land in a Navy flying boat between Brisbane and Sydney, Australia. The time in 1958 they put the wrong kind of fuel in our plane in Morón, Spain, and it wasn't discovered until the last minute. The time when the Vietcong tried to blow us up in Saigon in 1964. And the time the Cong managed to put a few holes in our plane in 1966.

I was lucky. But the luckiest thing about the trips was the chance to meet those men in uniform who served in seas of mud and blazing suns and endured the kind of humidity that mildews your feet right through your shoes. That's called jungle rot; I still get a touch of it myself on hot, moist days.

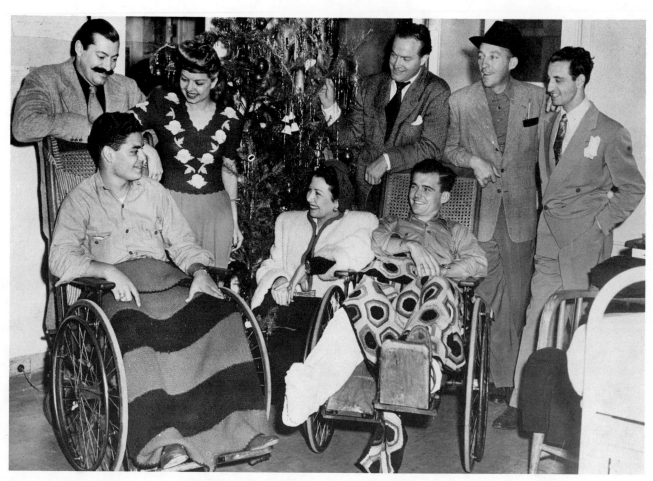

From left to right, Jerry Colonna, Frances Langford, Barbara Jo Allen, Bing Crosby, Tony Romano, San Diego, California, 1944. (U. S. Navy)

A lot of those guys tried to repay me for what I did, which is, to say the least, embarrassing. One kid in Germany actually gave me a diamond ring. Where he got it I don't know, but he insisted on shoving it into my hand. He said, "I just want you to have it."

All of us could have stayed home, worked paying audiences, and had things a lot easier. But you had to face those audiences and hear the reactions of laughs and cheers to realize how we were paid off. I saw so many places the Commies have tried to squeeze us out of. There was Cuba, where they tried to set up missiles armed with nuclear warheads, and President Kennedy called their bluff. There was the squeeze play in Korea, when Harry Truman told them no.

Let no one tell you that when JFK and LBJ sent Americans to Vietnam it wasn't to keep all of Indochina from toppling over like a row of dominoes. Let no one kid you that Communist China and Russia weren't our real reason for being there.

The last Christmas show

Things were different when we made our first trip to Alaska in 1942. In those days Germany and Japan were the black hats and China and Russia were the kids in the white hats in a bloody war that involved all the countries of the world.

We'd been planning all summer to head north for our first offshore trip but at the last moment we received a telegram saying we wouldn't have time to make the trip and get back in time for our first Pepsodent show of the 1942–43 season.

So I sent a wire to Major General Simon Buckner, who was in command of all the troops in the North Pacific, "Four thespians, bags packed with songs and witty sayings, ready to tour your territory, have been informed, due to lack of time, trip is off. Please let us make trip and will take our chances. Best regards. (Signed) Frances Langford, Tony Romano, Jerry Colonna, and Bob Hope."

In about twelve hours we received this answer: "You leave Thursday. (Signed) General Buckner."

This was the first of many trips we made to the "Great White Way" and in 1942 we played all the glamour spots—White Horse, Anchorage, Annette, Cordova, Nome, Naknek, Unimak, and Cold Bay.

There were only the four of us touring. We didn't have much in the way of sequins—no big band sound and no line of show girls. But to those kids "hunkered" down in those Quonset huts any sign from home was welcome.

They'd had plenty of those signs in the previous eighteen months. Edgar Bergen and Charlie McCarthy, Joe E. Brown, Al Jolson, and lots of other USO units with young performers, pretty girl singers, and budding young comics had been up there.

And while I'm on the subject of entertainers in the arctic, old Gravel Gullet, Andy Devine, did a tour up through Greenland and Labrador and up around the Hudson Bay country. Andy's unit was a little three-piece combo featuring a young singer named Mary Elliott and a piano player named Sergeant Chuck Broadhurs whom they picked up in the Far Northeast.

We played to a lot of troops—not only to the American GIs but to a lot of Russians. In Fairbanks we were training their pilots and giving them DC-3s and C-47s to fly back to Russia. They all seemed like giants fresh off the tractor. They were fearless flyers and they loved American booze. They'd trade you their boots for a bottle, which is logical—they like anything that'll take them straight up.

And we ran into the Russians again, this time their Navy, at Cold Bay, where we were training the Russian crews in the handling of LCIs (Landing Craft Infantry) and LCTs (Landing Craft Tanks) in preparation for the landing against Japan. It was all ultra top secret. Once the training was completed the boats were decommissioned from the United States Navy and then became a part of the Russian fleet. The American crews were sent back to Seattle with the word that their ships had been torpedoed. If I were sure that Zanuck wouldn't sue I'd make a movie out of this called *The Coldest Day*.

We almost had a very cold night on one of our last stops. We finished gigs at Annette and Cordova and were anxious to get back to Anchorage. We'd promised ourselves never to fly at night in Alaska. The weather is treacherous and constantly changing. However, our pilots, First Lieutenant Marvin Setzer of Pomona, California, and Second Lieutenant Bob Gates of Aberdeen, South Dakota, checked with Weather and received the report that the weather looked okay.

We'd only been up about ten minutes when the sleet and hail started hitting us. We tried to fly out of it. It kept getting worse and worse and then over Anchorage our radio went out.

We were about thirteen or fourteen thousand feet in the air. So were the mountains. Anchorage lies in a sort of saucer. After we'd been cruising around in this soup for about twenty minutes, Marvin Setzer called, "Dubowsky!" He was the crew chief.

Dubowsky went forward and whispered with the pilots for a minute, then came back and pointed toward Frances and said, "Come here."

Frances walked forward, and Dubowsky handed her a Mae West and a parachute. "Put these on," he said. "If we have to abandon ship, pull this. If you land in water, pull this!"

I turned to Captain Don Adler, the Special Services officer who was with us, and asked, "What about this?"

"Doesn't look good," he said.

Why is it that in the most tense situations the talk is dullest?

One by one Dubowsky gave us Mae Wests, parachutes, and instructions. I thought of all the lousy parachute gags I'd pulled, and suddenly none of them seemed funny.

To make it worse, another plane was also trying to get into Anchorage. Once we felt its prop wash. That's how close we came to colliding. Tony sat there, a delicate shade of chartreuse, and said, "This sort of thing isn't good for a guitar."

Colonna stroked his mustache and said, "I'll bet they'll forget to have the station wagon pick us up."

Frances said nothing, but later confessed she was hoping we'd have to jump.

At that point only a miracle could save us. There was no visual way we could find the field through the sleet and without radio they couldn't talk us down into the field. The miracle was the plane that came so close we felt its prop wash. When that plane landed they reported the incident to Operations. Operations had our departure from Cordova and knew we were in trouble. General Buckner ordered every searchlight in the area turned on. They made

The last Christmas show

WAVE *training school at Milledgeville, Georgia, 1944.*

a cone of light which pierced the sleet. We caught it on our fifteenth pass over the field and we rode right down the beam of lights onto the field.

When we staggered out of the plane, Colonna and I kissed the ground, which was frozen solid—that'll give you an idea how hysterical we were. You know how it is when you come through a close one, how you have this exhilarating love of life and the need to drink and shout and dance. Well, we went over to General Buckner's and played ping-pong. Sorry about that.

Is this trip necessary?   9

Gary Cooper and Joe Foss (r.), first World War II ace, at Santa Barbara Marine Air Base, January 4, 1944.

The last Christmas show

CHAPTER 2

"You remember World War II—it was in all the papers"

The week after that first remote radio show from March Field in 1941, we went down to Camp Pendleton, then up to Camp Roberts, and then to the San Diego Naval Training Base. Our sponsor, Pepsodent, noticed a big jump in sales immediately and started encouraging us with more travel money. For the next five years, from 1941 to 1946, we broadcast from military bases every week.

We had practically every Hollywood celebrity as guest star during those five years—Gary Cooper, Edward G. Robinson, Walter Pidgeon, Victor Mature, Betty Hutton, June Haver, Claudette Colbert, Marilyn Monroe, Rosalind Russell, Linda Darnell, Frank Sinatra, Hedy Lamarr, Madeleine Carroll, and scores of others who will call to remind me as soon as this book is published.

Our first trip to a combat area was in 1943, when we visited England, Africa, Sicily, and Iceland—only because we got weathered in.

At that stage of the war we were winning the battle of the bombers, we were mopping up in Africa, and we had just landed in Sicily. Rommel the Desert Fox had shed his tan and was wearing a derby, hoping to pass for David Niven. And the general of the hour was Patton, who was writing an Academy Award movie but didn't know it at the time.

Langford, Jack Pepper, Tony Romano, and I crossed the Atlantic in a Pan Am Clipper. You remember the Pan Am Clippers? They were half plane, half boat. And if your pilot was a coward you trolled all the way to England.

We were over the Atlantic about nine hundred miles out when suddenly the plane seemed to be turning in a wide arc. I called to my friend the steward, "Hey, O'Toole, what's cookin'?"

"We're going back," he said.

"Going back? What makes you think so?"

"We're turning around."

"Why?"

"I was so busy making you a sandwich the captain didn't want to disturb me to explain."

When I asked Captain Vaughn why we were going back, he wasn't too busy to explain. He said, "The wind's against us."

I told him the wind was against me playing golf, but I didn't give up.

He pointed out that a Clipper with about thirty-two people on board is entitled to more care than a golf ball. "When the Clipper gets a certain distance out over the ocean," Captain Vaughn explained, "we check the gasoline supply, and then the whole crew decides whether we'll go on or turn back."

"We're supposed to hit the other side with a five-hundred-mile reserve of gasoline," Captain Vaughn went on. "That's in case we overshoot the field or if it's closed in. After checking the head winds we can expect from here to Ireland against our present position, we decided we could only make it with a two-hundred-mile reserve of gas, so we're turning back."

I said, "Thank you."

He said, "Not at all. I value my life as much as you value yours."

Do you think that's possible?

Our first show in England was at an Army Air Force base called Sharpington. I guess that was the name. They were still worrying about an invasion and everything was a secret in London. The road signs were all missing . . . the bases were all called by different names . . . even the food was called by strange names, or maybe that was the food. We did four to five shows a day. Sometimes in hangars, sometimes in officers' clubs or enlisted men's clubs, sometimes off the back of a truck. Most of the time they waited for us . . . sometimes we chased them.

On the way back from Sharpington we heard a tremendous noise. The sky was black with B-19s. We dashed back to the base and asked where the pilots would go first.

A young lieutenant offered to take us to the place where they'd be interrogated. The planes were coming in one after another, kicking up clouds of dust, filling the whole countryside with the powerful vibrations of victory. Pretty soon trucks and jeeps full of fliers began rolling in. The men were excited and deliriously happy. When they saw us they began to cry and laugh and shout. They grabbed Frances and hugged her and kissed her. They kept screaming, "You brought us luck, you brought us luck." To show you how brave those guys were, they even hugged me. How was it, we asked? "A milk run," a kid grinned. "Eighteen went out and eighteen came back. Isn't that sensational?"

It made us feel great too. Suddenly we realized that all day long each of us had been thinking about those guys. We hadn't said anything about it to each other, just worried quietly. "We've been thinking about you guys all afternoon

Pat O'Brien at naval station, Terminal Island, California, 1945. (Official U. S. Navy)

The last Christmas show

The Andrews Sisters, Santa Ana, California, 1944. (U. S. Air Force)

and sort of sweating you in." One kid in the back hollered, "You been sweating *us?*" When Colonel Bert Solero was in the States sometime after that trip he told me of one mission in which twenty-one bombers from one base went out and only one came limping home.

We left Great Britain from Prestwick and took off on the road to Morocco. What a reception we got in Marrakech! The greetings we'd received when we landed in England and at all the different spots we'd played in the British Isles had made us kind of used to receptions. But I'm not kidding when I say we certainly weren't prepared for what we got in Marrakech. You can't imagine it.

But to put it into the fewest words possible, not a soul was there to meet us.

It turned out we arrived in Marrakech three days late because of having played extra shows in Prestwick. So our little group staggered into the airport cafe with our eyes half closed from lack of sleep and started to look for the Travelers Aid desk.

All of a sudden a lieutenant came up and said, "When did you get in? We didn't think you were going to make it!" It was a man who used to be a cop in St. Louis and now was Lieutenant Frank Choury, head Provost Marshal of Marrakech. That means he ran the Military Police. Frank and the officer with him, Lieutenant Bruce Pinter, took us over to a hotel and got us some breakfast and a place to clean up a little. He then told us that General Doolittle had had a B-17 waiting at Marrakech for two days to take us to Tunis. But when we didn't show, they thought the trip had been called off. This made us feel a little better.

From there we went on a tour of places that only Humphrey Bogart had heard of: Tunis, Algiers, Mateur. We worked in the desert all day and hid from bombers all night.

Ferryville was a good example.

This is a town sort of around the bay from Bizerte. It lies in about the same relative position that Bay Meadows does to San Francisco, or that Yonkers does to New York, or Gary, Indiana, to Chicago. If you happen to live in Council Bluffs you're on your own.

At Ferryville we did a show for about seventy-five hundred guys and gals. It was the most mixed audience we played to, except in a theater. All kinds of uniforms were there—soldiers, sailors, WACs—about the only fighting uniform not represented was the Brooklyn Dodgers.

Just as I stepped up to the microphone to start the show, a light tank came shoving through the crowd like a fat woman making for a seat in a crowded subway car. People gave way in all directions. A tank commands plenty of respect. I thought it was out of control. It looked as if the thing was going to mow us right down, and I was getting ready to jump off the platform when suddenly, right in front of me, it stopped.

The top flew open and a guy crawled out wearing a tanker's crash helmet and enough grease on his face to sing "Mammy." He was dragging a folding chair, which he set up on top of the tank. He sat down, smiled at me, and said, "Okay, Bob, start the show."

Three days after Messina, Sicily, fell, we'd landed and were driving into Palermo to do a show for the men who'd been injured in the assault.

But as we drove into Palermo, it didn't look much like Sicily to us. The countryside could have been around San Bernardino or Santa Barbara, California, depending on whether you were looking toward the hills or the ocean. And the road was jammed solid both ways with the American Army going to and from Messina.

There were about sixteen thousand guys jammed into the Palermo soccer field. When I came on and did my monologue they were just so excited not a sound came out of them. Then I introduced Tony and Jack, and they cheered

At naval station, San Pedro,
California, 1945. (U. S. Navy)

Frances Langford and General Jimmy
Doolittle at Carthage, North Africa, 1943.

North Africa, 1943. (Signal Corps)

16   The last Christmas show

like mad. When I brought Langford on those sixteen thousand guys whistled as one man and blew me right off the platform.

While Frances was singing, General Patton's aide came to invite us to have supper with the general, up at his headquarters at the King's palace in Palermo and I said, "Gee, that's a shame, because we have already ordered spaghetti and meat balls that Tony is going to make at the Excelsior, and he's got all the stuff ready and we're gonna go down there." And he just let me talk myself out, then looked at me and said, "Look, General Patton wants you for dinner and if you don't go it's my ass and yours too."

We were led into the main hall of the King's palace where they had the big banquets and there we were with a little table and the four of us eating and Patton who had eaten earlier just sitting there kind of talking to us. And after we finished I said, "Well, General, I know you didn't have a chance to see the show so we'll just give you a rough idea of what we do."

I got up and told a couple of monologue jokes, introduced Tony, who played one number, and Frances, who sang one. We did the Ink Spots. We did our finale and I said, "That will give you a rough idea."

And he said, "That's fine. Just fine." Then we took a picture.

And I said, "Well, we better get along because I know you're busy and have a lot of things to do."

And he said, "I want to speak to you," and he took me over in the corner and put his arm around me and said, "You know you can do a lot for me when you get back home."

And here was our hero saying this to me and I looked up at him and said, "What do you mean?"

And he said, "I want you to tell the people that I love my men. See."

I looked at this guy and I thought he was suffering from some kind of battle fatigue. And I said, "You're the biggest general in our country. You're in the headlines all the time . . . you don't have to worry about anything."

He said, "No, I want you to go on radio when you get back. I want the people to know that I love my men."

When we got back to the Excelsior Hotel in Palermo, Ernie Pyle—the famous newspaper columnist—was waiting for us. And I said that we'd just come from the King's palace and he said, "How did you like that son of a bitch?"

I said, "What?"

And he said, "Didn't you hear about it?" and he told us all about Patton slapping a kid in the hospital.

Sunday night in Palermo I hit the pad about eleven-thirty and the next thing I knew I was sitting up, looking around. There was a distant voom! and I saw a tracer bullet go scooting across the sky. When I heard the drone of Ju-88s, I knew we were in for it.

The docks, which were naturally the target for the raid, were only about

Bizerte, North Africa, 1943.

two blocks away. And two blocks isn't very far as the bomb flies. If I ever get into the diplomatic service I'll suggest an agreement among all nations to put their best hotels farther away from the docks and railway stations . . . maybe even in another town.

They say when you're drowning, your whole life flashes before your eyes. I don't know about you, but with me it's the same way with bombing. I thought of my first professional tour in vaudeville. I went twenty miles from Cleveland to East Palestine, Ohio. I remember wondering at that time what it would be like really to go on the road . . . maybe even to Chicago. As I

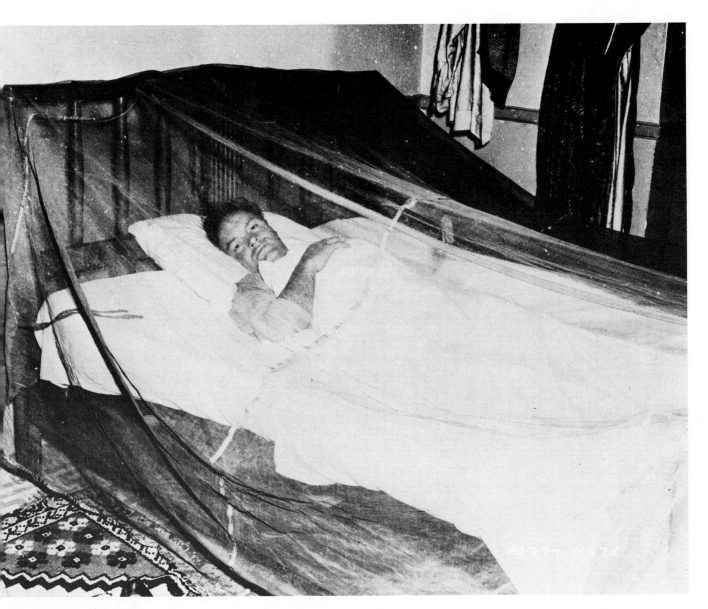

Tunis, North Africa, 1943.

thought of East Palestine, and the distance I'd traveled to get to the Excelsior Hotel in Palermo, I listened to the 500-pounders blowing the docks to bits, and I wished sincerely that I was back in East Palestine.

I thought of doing everything in the world but going to the bomb shelter in the basement. I began to talk to myself:

"Should I put my helmet on?"

"That would look silly."

"Who's gonna see?"

"Maybe I should get under the bed."

"That's ridiculous. It's bad enough to be bombed, but with your arms around a pee pot?"

"What about the closet?"

"Forget it. It's not a husband coming home. It's a bomb."

"You're right."

"And suppose the bomb misses the closet and hits the bed. Then how would you feel?"

"Stupid and terribly dead."

"I got it. What about the bathroom?"

"Too late."

This dialogue was interrupted when a great big hunk of red-hot flak sailed past my window and the Germans started dive-bombing. One Nazi, obviously aiming for my room, also let go with all his machine guns on his way down. Between the strafing and the screeching of the Stukas as they dived, you've got a noise that I'd trade any day for a record of Crosby. And the Germans weren't making it all themselves. We were throwing plenty of stuff at them, too. I joined in. I threw up my dinner.

From Palermo the Air Force flew us back to Algiers and we headed for the Aletti Hotel for a change of laundry. In the hall I met John Steinbeck, who said, "Do you want to see something great?" I nodded. He said, "Come on. The first consul has a big double room. Two weeks ago Quentin Reynolds dropped in for a drink, went out, came back with four friends and they've all been living there since."

John was right. The consul's digs looked like Ratso's room in *Midnight Cowboy*. The consul was in one bed, Bruce Cabot had passed out in another, Clark Lee was on a cot nursing an ulcerated tooth, H. R. Knickerbocker was sleeping on the floor, and Quentin Reynolds was directing the snoring and was on guard over the scotch supply—which explains why they were all sharing the room with the consul . . . somehow, some way, he had enough juice to get some juice.

After he issued us our ration of grog I asked Quent what to do in case of bombing. He said, "Bombing?" looking at me as though I'd lost my mind.

I said, "Yeah, you know, those things that kill! Do you go down to the bomb shelter?"

He said, "Oh . . . no, no. If you're not hit there's nothing to worry about . . . and if you are, you ride down to the shelter in your bed!"

We drank to that.

The next morning, Hal Bloch and I and a small hangover went over to the Red Cross building to get ready for a radio broadcast. We were auditioning some GIs. Tony was working on arrangements and Frances was breaking in a new tonsil. In walked a Major Hill. He said, "Pardon me, Bob, could I talk to you for a minute?"

Ernie Pyle at Palermo, Sicily, 1943.

"You remember World War II—it was in all the papers"   21

Hal Bloch, Jack Pepper, General George S. Patton, Frances Langford, and Tony Romano at King's palace, Palermo, Sicily, 1943. (U. S. Army)

I said, "You can talk to me any time but not today. We've got a radio show to do here tonight."

He said, "I'm General Eisenhower's aide. And the general would like to see you right away."

I said, "I've got all day."

So we dropped our scripts on the floor and went to meet Ike. He was marvelous. It was like meeting your father. He had a wonderful warm, simple

Jack Pepper, Clark Gable, Frances Langford, Tony Romano at Polebrook Air Force Base, England, 1943.

quality. We told him about being bombed in Bizerte and Palermo and he said, "You're perfectly safe here in Algiers. We haven't had a bombing in three months. You can really get some rest here."

Before we left, we asked Ike for a picture and he pulled out three of them, pointed to one of them, and said, "Take that one. It's the best one, isn't it?" I loved it . . . a four-star with a little ham bone.

That afternoon we did a show and that night we did the radio broadcast.

Nouméa, New Caledonia, 1944.

Sometime—a long time after midnight—we finally sacked out. Hal Bloch and I had the beds, Bill Lange of *Time* magazine had his choice of floor. About four-twenty I heard Pepper pounding on my door yelling, "Air raid!"

I yelled, "Get Langford and Romano," and we all ran for the air raid shelter, which in this case was a wine cellar. We sat there in the wine cellar testing for loose corks. We could hear the anti-aircraft guns being fired from the roof of the hotel and the bombs falling in the distance. We shook to-

The last Christmas show

gether for about twenty minutes when suddenly a strange apparition walked in. It was a barrage balloon in pajama striping which turned out to be Stubby Kaye. We didn't know he was anyplace in that part of the world. By the time we finished hugging and kissing and lying about how well we were doing, the air raid was over.

Quent Reynolds and the guys never got out of bed. I doubt if they ever woke up.

But I did send General Eisenhower a wire the next day: "Thanks for the rest. Here's your picture back."

The last time I saw our General Eisenhower was at Walter Reed Hospital just before he left us. We were discussing the movie *Patton* and he reminded me what a great soldier Patton was. And, of course, Ike proved it when he brought General Patton back to lead a division in the Battle of the Bulge. All Patton wanted to do was to get to Berlin. He was quoted as saying, "I won't stop until I piss in the Rhine."

Maurice Evans at Honolulu, 1944.

CHAPTER 3

South Pacific—not the musical

In 1944 the emphasis on the war shifted to the South Pacific. And so did we. The "we" this outing included Mama Langford again; Stash Colonna, who in preparation for the trip took a four-week course on how to shave under fire; our lovely tap-dancing Patty Thomas; Tony Romano and guitar; and Bing's straight man, a shy little charmer named Barney Dean.

I thought I'd seen the most rugged kind of warfare in North Africa and Sicily until I got a gander at what those guys in the Pacific were up against. Just keeping alive on most of those jungle islands was a man-sized struggle against almost man-sized bugs.

The plane they flew us to Hawaii in that summer of 1944 was a C-54 litter plane en route to Saipan to pick up some wounded. That meant for the trip to Pearl Harbor we were able to lie down and take it easy instead of sitting up for hours on end. And by "on end" I mean in one of those bucket seats. They may be all right for some people. But it's silly to ask a bucket to do a washtub job.

In those days the Hawaiian Islands were the Manhattan Transfer of the Pacific. They kept pumping men and supplies eastward and back. Along the same line of supply came the battle-scarred fighters to rest and recuperate in the many hospitals and playgrounds planned to wipe out some of the memory of the horror and grim monotony of Pacific Patrol.

We played the whole Pineapple Circuit. Honolulu, Kwajalein, Eniwetok, Milne Bay where we did a show in a volcano, the Treasury Islands, Wendy Island—where we saw Jack Kennedy and his torpedo boat crew. Of course, I didn't know who he was at the time—a fact that he enjoyed reminding me of at the White House when he was President and I was a taxpayer.

On most of these islands we had only a small perimeter. And in Biak, New Guinea, the perimeter was about a mile and everybody had a gun in his hand and my first line was: "Hello, everybody. Thank you very much. Thank you for the applause and point your guns the other way please." Because they

Tarawa, South Pacific, 1944.

were sitting carelessly with their guns. Half of them were pointing up toward the stage. I'm sure that wasn't their intention.

We opened in Hollandia. Our first show was for the Sixth Army—General Eichelberger and twenty thousand troops. And our microphone was terrible. And, of course, with a bad microphone I'm dead. My stock in trade is words, and let's be honest, if you can't hear me there isn't a lot to look at. Somehow we got through the show. I forced it a little and the audience laughed and applauded mostly out of courtesy.

After the show they had a reception for all the cast and the brass and all the people who set up the show. I met General Eichelberger and he congratulated us on a great show. I said, "General, it's nice of you to say that, but for me it was a rotten show. That public address system was terrible."

He said, "Come to think of it, it was a little fuzzy."

I said, "It's a shame to bring these entertainers twenty thousand miles and not have these guys hear anything."

General Eichelberger looked me in the eyes and said, "You're right, Bob, and it will never happen again." And from then on he had the Signal Corps testing microphones on islands all over the South Pacific a day ahead of us.

They'd be shouting, "Testing . . . one . . . two . . . three . . . four . . ."

And the Japanese would be peering out from the trees saying, "Must be new kind of booby trap."

In later years we never had to worry about being heard. We had Dave Forrest with us to mix our sound in the field and Johnny Pawlek on our public address system—two of the greatest sound men in the world. In fact, in some of the bases we played in Africa the monkeys are still reciting jokes.

In Hollandia we lived up on a hill where General MacArthur had his headquarters. It was about three quarters of a mile up and pretty steep. And the GIs had to build a road to get up there. It was a historic road. Somebody had written to a congressman about it and there was a lot of controversy surrounding it . . . the GIs hated it.

Every time we'd drive up the road the kids would hiss us, thinking it was MacArthur—then they'd find out it was us and they'd turn around and wave. There's another possibility: they were booing me and cheering Frances Langford. I like the MacArthur story better.

Our second show was for the Seabees in a natural amphitheater very close to the beach. And there were about five thousand Seabees and I'll never forget this because it was a beautiful night. We did a moonlight show—and Langford stepped out and she sang "I'm in the Mood for Love" and a guy in the middle of the house said, "You've come to the right place, honey." You've never heard a laugh that big.

And when I got back up, I said, "Are you the Seabees that build the roads the Marines land on?"

And this guy said, "No, we're the Seabees that build the roads the Japs retreat on."

In the New Guinea area at Hollandia, which could have been called Bulldozer Junction, we got a load of how those mechanical Martha Rayes renovated the town. The Seabees did a terrific job of clearing the way for those essential supplies that had to keep moving toward the front. When we played the hospital, we met Lew Ayres as well as Bud Ward, the national amateur golf champion, who was then in the Air Force. Lew wouldn't come up on the stage and take a bow even when his own gang gave him a terrific ovation. Dr. Kildare in khaki was strictly a soldier. And a good one.

On Munda we did some shows with the help of Clark Dennis, who used

Captain E. W. Lethers, Guadalcanal, 1944.

to tenor for Paul Whiteman, and Billy Sherman, of Cleveland, who warbled for Abe Lyman.

And we did one show in that area that wasn't scheduled. Our little band of gypsies flew over to the island of Pavuvu, in Piper Cubs, to do a show for the men of the 1st Marine Division, then training for the invasion of Palau.

They had to take us in Pipers because the island had no regular air strip. We had to land on the road. And as we buzzed the baseball field it was the most exciting thing that happened on the trip to see those fifteen thousand guys all looking up and cheering each little plane as she came in. Forty per cent of those Marines were never seen again. And I ran into a bunch of the "lucky" 60 per cent in a hospital in Oakland. I happened to be going through a ward when a guy suddenly hollered, "Pavuvu!"

Owl Island, New Guinea, 1944.

After working Mensa Island, we flew down to Brisbane and from there we were going to go to Sydney. And I was flying a Navy Catalina. It can be told now. Lieutenant Ferguson, who lived down the block from me in North Hollywood, let me fly this thing and I was up there all alone and the left motor started to sputter. He ran up to the cockpit and said, "Get out of here." I flew out of there and Ferguson took over the controls, feathered the prop, and said, "Jettison everything on this plane."

So I pulled Barney Dean out of a bunk and I said, "Come on, Barney, we've gotta jettison everything."

And he said, "Stop kidding around." Because Barney hated flying and I was always putting him on about forced landings and disasters. To convince him I pulled him out of the sack and I pulled him up to the blister and showed him the feathered prop and I said, "That's supposed to be going around, you know."

And he said, "Spare me the technical crap. How long have we got to live?"

We threw everything overboard but the plane wouldn't hold altitude. We were over a sleepy little resort called Laureton which naturally had no airport. So we strapped ourselves in and with fingers crossed made a forced landing in a lake. The plane skipped twice, hit a sand bar, and lurched to a stop.

We all climbed out on the wing and hugged each other. Colonna started singing, "Oh, I love life—and I want to live." At about that point a native Aussie rowed out from the shore in a beat-up boat, looked up at us on the wing, and said, "I say there, do you have any American cigarettes?" At this point we were so high, we gave him two packs, but only after he rowed us ashore.

By the time we got to Sydney, we'd been missing for an hour and we were quite a news event. There were ten thousand people in Sydney waiting for us. And we stayed there three days and the Australian people were marvelous to us. And all the artists held a big breakfast for us—a dance—at the Roosevelt nightclub.

We were at the Empress Hotel. And we needed it too. We'd been in the jungle for three or four days. And we finally got washed up and got our pits all scrubbed.

Then we took off for Hollandia and we landed and standing there waiting for the plane door to open was Corporal Henry MacLamore, one of the great syndicated writers and a very funny guy who was well known around my golf club, Lakeside in North Hollywood. And he didn't say "Hello," he said, "Have you got any booze on board?"

And I said, "Yeah. We picked some up in Sydney. A couple of cases of Black Label." So he stayed with us for two weeks until the Black Label was gone and he was a riot.

We were doing a show in Noemfoor, where they had the Black Widow planes—that was one of those night fighter things. And we were having lunch with the general after the show when a guy came in and handed him a communiqué. The general read it; it said, "They killed a Jap two hundred yards from the stage during the show."

And we all kind of gulped and Henry said, "Was he coming or going?"

CHAPTER 4

Four jills and three jerks

In 1945 half the war had been won when once more the USO beckoned and we headed for England, France, and Germany.

This time we boarded the *Queen Mary*. Today she's just another immigrant who's settled down in Long Beach, California, to collect social security, but in those days she was a gallant broad plying her trade back and forth across the North Atlantic.

At that time our little Unit 676 consisted of Jerry Colonna, the Stash; Gale Robbins, the Thrush; June Bruner, pianist and crooner; Ruth Denas, who also sang and pumped a squeeze box; Patty Thomas, who wore a small costume and danced; Roger Price, who did everything, including our laundry; and Jack Pepper, the ballast from Dallas who spent most of his time in some mess hall, making a big man of himself—a troupe of troupers never too tired to do another show and always willing, eager, and able to steal a scene or a laugh from guess who.

We did a very polite show the first night out for the other civilians aboard the ship, the officers, and the Army brass, in the Grand Salon.

Then we did a second show in the dining saloon for the enlisted personnel, who like an extra *o* in their salon. Naturally, we had to do a third show for the guys who were on duty and couldn't catch the second show. Then we found out that there were a bunch of men aboard for whom we'd played in Honolulu and they hadn't been asked to see the show. So we did a special show for them. We practically did a show in every cabin on the boat, a whole week of vaudeville booking at sea.

In London we did a big Fourth of July show in Albert Hall for ten thousand GIs. Albert Hall is like Carnegie Hall in New York, only more so. They usually hold only concerts and esoteric lectures there, so the manager was worried about our kind of show going on in his hall. I heard him arguing with an MP, but he finally let us do the show when he was told that the United States Army would pay half of the fumigating expenses.

At USO headquarters at Chatou near Paris, it looked as if Central Casting had opened an overseas branch.

In five minutes I met Alfred Lunt, Lynn Fontanne, and Bozo Snyder. Everyone wore the same uniform, of course, but naturally Lynn Fontanne looked better in hers than Bozo Snyder. And everyone lined up for chow, which, of course, looked better in Bozo Snyder.

There were really so many actors around the place that the breeze from bowing kept the joint air-conditioned.

I had luncheon with Reginald Gardiner, Clifton Fadiman, John Kieran, and Franklin P. Adams, the group from "Information, Please!" I couldn't even get my nickel back.

Also on hand were Bea Lillie, entertaining soldiers and trying to forget the son she lost, Billy Van, Constance Dowling, Broadway Harry Rose, Artie Conroy, Cliff Hall, Pat Lane, Harriet Page, Joy Hodges, Charlie Steward, and an old friend, Josephine Del Mar. Josephine had been peddling laughs to the men around the U.K. for twenty-six months. Then she hit the beach at Normandy right after D-Day and had been in France ever since. A big morale booster.

Really, in spite of what you see in your bookstores, a lot of men and women made offshore trips and never said a word about it. So different from you-know-who. The mighty head of the William Morris office, Abe Lastfogel, spent most of the war years getting entertainers off their duffs and out into the combat areas. I don't know how many tours Jack Benny made all together and I try not to find out. But I do know that he was all over the European Theater of Operations with Larry Adler and Ingrid Bergman, and he covered the South Pacific with the beautiful Carole Landis, Martha Tilton, and June Bruner.

Fred Astaire saved the USO a fortune on transportation. He tap-danced from base to base. And then there was Bing Crosby, whoever he is—a crooner of dubious voice and limited charm who was sent overseas to let our GIs know the kind of hardships the people at home were enduring.

Bing has a great story about how he first met General Eisenhower.

> "We were in Paris and wheels were really a problem. Paris had just been liberated and nobody had any automobiles. We were staying at the Ritz Hotel, which was run by the Army then, and you'd see a colonel drive up in a jeep, get out, take a piece of chain about six feet long, wrap it around a wheel and then wrap it around a hydrant and put a great big lock on it.
>
> "We went up to Eisenhower's headquarters at Versailles to do a show for him and all his staff. And afterward we went over to have lunch at his quarters. The grape was flowing and we got to singing barbershop quartets, having a big time.

Bing Crosby, Fred Astaire, near
Paris, 1945.

Jerry Colonna, Billy Conn, Roger Price, Jack Pepper, June Bruner, Ruth Denas, Gale
Robbins on V-E Day, Mannheim, Germany, 1945.

Four jills and three jerks   35

"We finally finished up and it was time to go and Ike said, 'Anything I can do for you?'

"And I said, 'Well, yes. We'd like some wheels. I'd like a car of some description. We're going to be in Paris for a week and the only time we get a car is when we're brought to work.'

"He said, 'Take my car.'

"'What about a driver?'

"'Take my driver, Sergeant Day.'

"I said, 'When do you want it back?'

"He said, 'When you're finished with it.'

"So we took it for a week and that car with its five stars was parked in front of some very questionable places. Bill Hearst was in town and Fred Astaire and Broderick Crawford, and we were going to parties all the time.

"I finally brought it back to Ike after this week in Paris. I apologized for keeping it for so long and said, 'Is there anything I can do for you?'

"He said, 'Yes. Yes, you can. Send me some grits. Hominy grits. I love hominy grits and there's no way I can get them.'

"We went back and when we landed in New York we had a press conference and they wanted to know who we'd seen. And I told them Bradley and everybody . . . and Eisenhower. They wanted to know how he was and I said fine. And I mentioned to the reporters that Ike needed some grits. They put it in the papers, the wire service picked it up, and about a month later I got a cablegram: 'Call off the grits!!!' "

There were a lot of gypsies out there. Jim Cagney, Al Jolson, Gary Cooper, Ann Sheridan, Lanny Ross, the famous Chicago Bears coach George Halas, Bill Gargan, who went to the China-Burma-India theater with Paulette Goddard—and who wouldn't.

Even Ed Gardner, the star of that fine radio show "Duffy's Tavern," the only guy in radio who prided himself on being more illiterate than I am, didn't write a book. And he really had a book to get off his chest after touring the ETO being billed as "Jinx Falkenburg and Company." Jinx also went to the Caribbean, South America, and the CBI theater with Pat O'Brien. Pat killed 'em with those stories of his and "Shake hands with your Uncle Mike."

From Paris we ducked over to Amiens to cross sneers with the men of the 438th Troop Carrier Group, the boys who went in first at Normandy, spearheading the airborne infantry and paratroopers. I couldn't write about all these names of outfits and places during the war. In those days the censors

Chief of Staff Dwight D. Eisenhower at the Pentagon, 1946. (U. S. Army)

Four jills and three jerks   37

were so careful about security that every time I laid an egg, a second lieutenant ran out and candled it.

One of our last shows in France was a big all-star benefit in Nice. Sitting in the audience was an old friend from Paramount—Maurice Chevalier. A major, whose name I conveniently forget, said, "Don't introduce him. He's suspected of being a collaborator."

I said, "I don't know anything about that. I'm not a judge and jury, I'm just an emcee and this guy's one hell of an entertainer." I introduced him and he walked out there in a white turtleneck sweater and bright red pants and the audience cheered.

Of course, he sang "Louise" as only he could and at the end of his act he got a standing ovation. Later that night up at the chateau where we were staying he said, "I will never forget what you have done for me in the ball park in Nice." And he kissed me—on both cheeks. Nothing freaky.

Our first show in Germany was at the General Ike Stadium, a race track and athletic field on the edge of Bremen. Our audience was eight thousand guys from the 29th Division, all combat men, and 90 per cent wore the Purple Heart. They were pretty cocky and had a right to be. What an outfit!

I had played for them in England in 1943, when they were training for the invasion. But there weren't many left who could remember that.

These guys had landed at Normandy at a cost of about 21,000 men, fought their way up through northern France, at Aachen, St.-Lô, in the Bulge, and across Germany. They were a great audience. Their motto was "Let's Go!" And they kept hollering it all during my show.

It was in Bremen that we began to get used to a new kind of audience. The last time we'd played the ETO the men who'd seen our shows had been all hopped up with anticipation of impending combat and they wanted to like everything. But in 1945 they listened to our routines while packing.

Literally, every place we went we got the same farewell when the show was over and we were trying to sneak out of town. It wasn't "Good-by" and it wasn't "See you again!" To a man, the guys hollered, "Take us with you!"

On our way to Munich to do a broadcast we were forced down at Kassel. We finally made Munich about three in the afternoon, thinking our broadcast was scheduled for seven. What we found out was that they had an audience waiting at the Prinzregenten Theater for us. So we piled into some cars and rushed to the theater, trying to work out a few routines on the way. But what we put on could have brought back the crystal set.

The control booth at the theater turned out to be a broom closet full of captured German equipment and manned by engineers who didn't understand English. We went on the air before our baggage arrived, and Ruth Denas found she couldn't make an accordion out of matchboxes and Kleenex. On top of that, I told five jokes and the microphone went dead. Either

The last Christmas show

Dust Bowl, Marseilles, France, 1945. (U. S. Army)

those engineers were lying that they couldn't understand English, or it's the first time I was ever criticized by the electrical system.

Fortunately, Captain Sandy Cummings, of the Armed Forces Network, helped us sweat it out. Really nothing stopped those AFN boys. Sandy told me that once in Frankfurt they'd scheduled a concert by Glenn Miller's band, but they couldn't get the equipment to carry the music to the sending stations. So they plugged it into the local telephone system, and for an hour, when some *Hausfrau* called the butcher for wieners, she got "The Chattanooga Choo-Choo."

From Munich we hopped up to Nuremberg for the GI Olympics. The town was really muscle-bound. Soldiers and sailors from all over the ETO filled Soldiers' Field, nee the Nuremberg stadium, battling each other on the cinders or cheering their favorites. It was one of the greatest days of my life, in spite of the fact that it was raining and everyone was too interested in the track events to ask me to say a few words. Here's why.

Four jills and three jerks 39

It was during the GI Olympic meet that they announced Japan had offered to surrender. The whole stadium full of guys seemed to rise twenty-five feet in the air. Nothing could compare with that moment. It's pretty tough to upstage peace.

The rain had killed all chances of doing the big show we had scheduled for that evening in the stadium, so we did two little shows at the opera house. The only difference was that the opera house roof was so full of holes you got soaked with filtered water. The audience couldn't really applaud but they splashed loudly.

The GI Olympics attracted a lot of *types* to the area. *Type*, that's the French version of our word "character," meaning the unique denizen of show business and Broadway who made a rich man out of Damon Runyon. The watchword of these Broadway boys in the Army was, "Don't knock the street." And when they gathered in my room, it could have passed for one of the smaller tables at Lindy's.

The hecklers included Sergeant Jimmy Cannon and Private Dave Gordon of *Stars and Stripes*; Corporal Billy Conn, who was a champion for thirteen rounds; Allan Jackson, the INS man (that's a news syndicate, not a branch of the Army); Sergeant Harold Grey; Colonel Swede Larson, ex-Navy football coach, then in the Marines; and Major Torchy Torrance, also of the Marines, who was at the meet with an eye to promoting a similar one in the Pacific theater.

We'd just finished two evening shows at the Heidelberg Capitol Theater for the Seventh Army HQ and 84th Division boys, and I was playing ping-pong with Pfc Stanley Weise in our billet at the Schloss Hotel, when Pfc Bonner F. Jennings, of Washington, D.C., suddenly burst in hollering, "It's finished! The war's over!"

Gale Robbins, whose husband was with the Air Force in the Pacific, gave out the first scream. Weise, whom the boys called "Brooklyn," just laid his paddle down and said softly, "Now I can go back to God's country, Flatbush."

And back we went each to our own God's country for what we naïvely figured would be forever.

CHAPTER 5

The airlift and the air secretary

My first cold-war Christmas show started in 1948 with a worried phone call from Stu Symington, then President Truman's Secretary of the Air Force. Stu was concerned about the morale of the Air Force boys who were teamed up in Europe trying to make something called Operation Vittles work. He wanted me to go along with him to some of our air bases to spread a little Christmas cheer. While I was at it, he wondered, how about stopping off in the Azores and Newfoundland along the way? I said I'd be glad to.

Some Frenchman once said that the more things change, the more they are the same. He had something there. The Russians had us in a crack and were trying to squeeze us out of Berlin. They had thrown a blockade around the city, deep inside East Germany. The East German Reds had closed off the road and rail corridors into the city and had stopped the shipment of food and fuel.

We took to the air to keep Berlin from starving. The Air Force was flying shuttle flights round the clock, from Wiesbaden in West Germany to Berlin and back again. A couple of years before, most of these pilots had been carrying cargoes of high explosives. But none of the payloads were more important to the welfare of the free world than the bags of coal, sacks of flour, and cases of canned food that filled the bellies of those C-47s. Every plane was loaded above its usual weight limit. The only time one would go out of service was when it was flown to Burtonwood Air Base, near Liverpool, England, for maintenance.

One of the bright things about Operation Vittles was that it not only lifted the morale of the German people, it also helped lift the smog of hatred that had existed between them and us since World War I.

The Berlin weather presented a problem that only experienced pilots could handle. Blind takeoffs and landings were no novelty to the magicians who flew that corridor into Berlin. It was a running gag with our flyboys that instruments were needed just to walk along a Berlin street without bumping into somebody. The routine of battling the weather and flying the same route over and over turned what could have been considered heroics into drudgery.

Once in a while a Russian MIG fighter pilot broke the monotony by zooming up, buzzing one of the American planes, and taking a look at the food on board. Then he drooled all the way to the ground. The Russians flew so close that our boys could almost hear them singing "Red Christmas." But our pilots didn't have time to listen. They were trying to keep 2.5 million Germans from freezing and starving to death.

Despite its importance, the monotony of Operation Vittles was beginning to wear on the nerves of the American airmen, and a lot of the gung-ho feeling of World War II was gone. As Stu says: "Morale is always lower during a non-war or a no-win war than during a fighting war."

That 1948 Christmas tour was memorable for a lot of reasons, not the least of which was the company I was keeping. Vice-President Alben Barkley, the original Veep, was on our plane. Also along were Irving and Ellen Berlin, Jinx Falkenburg and her husband Tex McCrary. In those days the McCrarys had a Mr.-and-Mrs. breakfast radio show in New York. Remember when young actresses used to get married? Hy Averback was a great straight man and announcer. He worked with me for two years. He was the Carl Reiner of radio. After two years with me he gave up radio forever and became a director. I hope it was nothing I said. Irene Ryan was with us too. Later she became a star as Granny on "Beverly Hillbillies." Irene was a doll. She had that vaudeville training and she made it work for her all of her career. Our chanteuse was Jane Harvey, a lovely gal with a great voice who had an allergy to performing. Just before she'd go on and just after, she'd break out in a rash, she'd start to itch all over and have to rub against everybody. That's the story I told Dolores and that's the story I'm going to stay with. And then there was Elmer Davis, the news commentator, writer, and former head of the Office of War Information, and "Thirty Seconds over Tokyo" General Jimmy Doolittle. We all went over in Stu's plane.

Alben was a fast man with a quip. When he went to bed on the plane he looked at Dolores and said, with a muffled sob in his voice, "Oh, well, I guess I'll go and bunk down in my hopeless bed."

We did a brief gig in the Azores, then headed for Burtonwood. Stu says that when we flew over London, where I was born, I peered down and said, "Look at all those roofs. They don't give much of a landing place. Think how the stork must have felt lugging me. I hope he was in a holding pattern."

When we landed, one of the colonels at Burtonwood came up to Stu and said, "The spirit on this base is the worst I've ever seen." Stu toured the base with that colonel. He was in uniform, of course, but nobody stood up when he walked into a barracks. That was bad. No respect, no morale. Stu went over to one of the boys who was sitting on a cot and said, "Hello, I'm with the Air Force too."

Jane Harvey, Hy Averback, Tony Romano, Irene Ryan, Tex McCrary, Jinx Falkenburg,
Billy Farrell, Irving Berlin at mike in Wiesbaden, Germany, 1948.

The kid just looked at him.

"What's the matter with you?" Stu asked.

The kid stared at him a long time. Then he said, "I ain't got any teeth. I was in a truck accident and my teeth were knocked out. When I go into town everybody laughs at me." All of a sudden the kid began to cry.

"Get me the base dentist," Stu said to the colonel. When the dentist arrived, he said, "Mr. Secretary, I'm the only dentist here. There are six thousand men on this base. Taking care of the teeth of six thousand men is not easy. In fact, it's impossible."

The personnel at Burtonwood were living in Quonset huts, eighteen to a hut. The only heat came from one small stove in the middle of each Quonset. The floors were bare concrete. When it's cold in England, it's very cold. There was no hot water either. If anybody wanted a shower, he had to take it in an open courtyard and run the risk of freezing solid.

The airlift and the air secretary   43

There were two freight cars full of Christmas gifts waiting for the men on the base, but the British wouldn't unload them. They said our men would sell them on the black market if they did.

Stu flew to London to the Air Ministry and said, "If you don't release those two cars immediately, I'll make sure ·that Liverpool and any other towns with any American Air Force nearby are put off bounds. No American will be allowed to go into such towns, spend money, have a drink, or do anything else."

They said to him, "You wouldn't do that."

Stu said, "Just try me."

Those freight cars were released right away.

Back at Burtonwood, Stu called a meeting of all the men on the base. He climbed up on a platform and said, "I'll be coming back here with Bob Hope and his troupe on our way home from Germany. I'm going to leave a big empty oil drum. I want everybody to write down what he doesn't like about conditions here and put it in that barrel. Don't be timid. Don't hold back. Nobody will read your complaints except me."

We flew from Burtonwood to Wiesbaden via Brussels. Twenty minutes after we were on the ground we were doing our first show. The GIs had been sitting in that hall all day waiting for us, and we weren't going to keep them waiting any longer even if it meant not eating. My spot with singer Joy Nichols consisted of four musical numbers (chosen especially to suit the American palate) plus an ad-lib love scene. Its title was obvious: "I'm in the Mood for Love."

You can imagine the byplay and fooling around that went with that little opus of ours. I remember having my arm around her, looking at the GIs, and saying, "But fellas, she's so *young*," and then giving a guttural wolf bark.

At Wiesbaden, conditions were so bleak and everybody was so poor it was really kind of frightening. Dolores remembers that she had some tissue paper wrapped around her clothes; as she unwrapped them at the hotel, she started to throw the paper away. The hotel people watching her begged her, "No, no, no, no." They took it away and folded it up carefully because they had nothing like it at the time.

General Lucius Clay was our Berlin commandant in those days, and he and his wife flew out to welcome us. On Christmas Eve the Clays threw a party for all of us at Wiesbaden Air Force headquarters. I remember that in the middle of the party I went over to Dolores and said, "I'm going to have to leave now. The weather's so bad they're afraid I won't get into Berlin unless I do. In case both planes can't make it, they'd like to have at least half of us there for tomorrow's show. They'll take you and the rest of the gang in the second plane tomorrow."

Dolores just had time to say, "Don't miss midnight Mass." I'm not a

The last Christmas show

Catholic, but I've always gone to Mass with my family on Christmas Day or Christmas Eve and on Easter Sunday.

Then I left, with Irving Berlin and Jinx. All at once we were on a cargo plane loaded with sacks of coal. I remarked to the crew chief, "The weather is a little soupy." He replied, "Soup I'd settle for—but this stuff has noodles in it. Even the birds here check with the control tower before they take off."

Our show Christmas Day was at the huge Tatania Palast Theater, an old vaudeville house that we were well acquainted with. I last played there when the Allies first occupied Berlin in 1945. It was a brutally cold Christmas Day but a wonderfully warm audience from the first monologue joke on.

How do you do, everybody. This is Bob "here in Berlin to entertain the men in the airlift" Hope saying I'm here with Swan soap in lots . . . Meet me tonight in Potsdamer Platz.

We had a nice trip in from America. We had good company on the plane . . . Irving Berlin was along. He didn't help our morale any. All the way across he kept singing, "How Deep Is the Ocean?"

This certainly has been an unusual experience flying into Berlin. It's the first time I ever was in a corridor and didn't have to worry about the house detectives.

As we arrived over Berlin several Soviet planes started to buzz us, but the first Russian pilot took one look at me and said, "They're okay, look at the hammer head and sickle."

And the good old Air Force hasn't changed . . . They make you spend an hour getting into a parachute, then fly so low you wouldn't have time to open a parasol.

They really fly low . . . In fact, one pilot flew so low over a farm, milk started forming on the wings. Lucky the cow was bowlegged.

And the people over here really know me. Whenever I walk down the streets of Berlin, everybody follows me yelling and cheering. Any of you fellows know what Schweinehund means?

After the monologue I introduced Jimmy Doolittle and then brought on Irene Ryan, one of the greatest comediennes I ever worked with.

BOB: Fellows, right here I'd like you to meet a gal who's a new addition to our Swan Show this year. The folks back home have really latched onto her and I'm sure you'll agree with them when you meet Miss Irene Ryan. (*applause*)

The airlift and the air secretary   45

IRENE: Thank you, Mr. Hope . . . It was wonderful of you to bring me on this trip. You know, I've met some of your boys.

BOB: Isn't that sort of thing for the younger girls?

IRENE: Well, I'm not as old as I look . . . You may not think so, but I'm just arriving at my early thirties.

BOB: Arriving at your thirties?

IRENE: Yes.

BOB: Didn't you buck a head wind most of the way? Tell me, Miss Ryan, did you enjoy our stopover in Paris?

IRENE: Oh yes. I went shopping and I got a complete new outfit . . . I bought an off-the-shoulder blouse, one of those long skirts that trail the ground, then I had my hair done in spit curls, and then I put on one of those French berets . . . they stopped me at the border.

BOB: They did?

IRENE: Yes . . . the MPs shined a light in my face and said, "Who are you?" I told them I was a girl from the United States that came in with the last shipment . . . He said, "That's the trouble with those steamship lines . . . they let things lie around the dock too long." Well, I got to go now . . . good-by.

(*applause*)

When we first started on the trip we used to bring out Tex McCrary and his wife Jinx Falkenburg together and they'd talk to the guys and hit tennis balls to the audience. And I'm going to be honest with you, there have been more successful acts. After two or three disasters it finally occurred to me that there were probably more thrilling sights for an all-male audience than the good-looking civilian husband of a gal like Jinx.

A lot of people would be a little nervous about telling somebody the size of Tex that he'd been cut from the show, but it didn't bother me. I had Hy Averback tell him.

By the time we got to the Tatania the act had evolved into something like this:

BOB: And now, fellows, it's a real pleasure to bring you a Hollywood gal who flew here with us so she could be with all you guys on Christmas Day . . . One of America's leading beauties . . . Miss Jinx Falkenburg.

JINX: Thanks, Bob, and thanks a lot, gang.

BOB: Jinx, it's fun having you here. You know, I always listen to your breakfast program with your husband Tex McCrary back in the States.

JINX: Thank you, Bob. You know, we do the show right from our breakfast table.

BOB: Well, they were going to do a broadcast like that from the mess hall here, but it didn't work out.

JINX: Why not?

BOB: Before they could get started, a chowhound peeled the microphone and ate it for an artichoke. But I'm sure glad we got a chance to see this Christmas celebration over here. The Army really treats these fellows royally.

JINX: Different than the rest of the year, huh?

BOB: Oh yes . . . on Christmas morning each enlisted man is wakened by a gentle tug on his shoulder, and when he looks up from his bunk, twelve MPs are standing there singing "Jingle Bells" . . . and after the MPs carry the men piggyback into the mess hall, the cook runs in with a flit gun full of beans, and shoots them on the plate so that they spell out "Happy Temporary Duty."

   (*applause*)

General Lucius D. Clay and Secretary of War Kenneth C. Royall at Berlin, Germany, airlift, 1948. (U. S. Army)

The airlift and the air secretary   47

Another note of honesty. Irving Berlin doesn't have the best voice in the world. He sounds like a rusty hinge in search of a can of 3-in-1 oil. But it couldn't have mattered less. He sang some of his hits: "This Is the Army, Mr. Jones," "White Christmas," "Easter Parade," and they gave him a standing ovation. The best part is that Irving loved the way he sang, he loved doing it, and if you called him on the phone from anywhere in the world, any time of the day or night, he'd put the receiver to his Steinway and play his heart out.

While we were playing Berlin on Christmas Day, Major Robert Kelso dropped in to see me. "I'm a disc jockey," he said. "I play records for everybody in the European Theater of Operations. I'd like you to come over to the studio and maybe say a few words on my show."

"I'll try to do that," I promised.

That night the Clays invited us to dinner at their home in Berlin. In the group was Kenneth Royall, Secretary of War, and his wife. Stu Symington and the Irving Berlins were there too. I remember that the Clays had a beautiful Christmas tree with lovely German-type natural candles on it.

Just before we went in to dinner, a man and woman came in. They looked like orphans of the storm or like people being chased across the ice by bloodhounds, like Eliza in *Uncle Tom's Cabin*. They turned out to be the U.S. ambassador to Moscow, Walter Bedell ("Beadle") Smith, and his wife. They had just got out of Russia, and it had been touch and go: they hadn't known whether they were going to make it or not.

Beadle swore he'd never go back to Russia. He said he'd had enough of Moscow and his job. Mrs. Smith was even more emphatic about it. She was fed up with the whole thing. They had been completely isolated; it seemed that Stalin's boys had even cut off milk for the children of the embassy staff. To be back in American company meant a lot to her.

After the dinner at the Clays, Dolores and I started back to the hotel. It was about two in the morning, but I thought of something. "I hate to disappoint that disc jockey," I said to Dolores. "Why don't we go over there and pay him a call?"

We had his address jotted down on a scrap of paper, so we borrowed an Army jeep and started. Fuel-saving regulations were on in Berlin then, and we drove only five blocks before we ran out of gas. We walked the rest of the way through grim Berlin streets with only a flashlight to guide us. It was a pretty weird little stroll. The streets had been bombed out, and there were still people buried beneath the rubble. There was a distinctive whiff of death in the air.

When we found the radio station where the boy was working, he was all by himself. I walked in and he almost fell out of his chair. "No, no," he said. "I can't believe it!"

Then he turned back to his mike. "Hey, guys! I've got news for you! Here's Bob Hope. I'm turning the mike over to him!"

I started to talk. Then I looked around. The disc jockey was gone. The program was all mine. He'd gone to wake up the other guys who manned the station. He knew they wouldn't believe him in the morning when he told them I'd dropped in at 2:30 A.M. to see him. So I held the fort until he came back.

When we headed out of Berlin bound for Burtonwood, the weather was even worse, if possible. We were held up for four hours by ice on the runways at Wiesbaden; when we got to Burtonwood three thousand men were waiting for us in a hangar and a barrelful of complaints was waiting for Stu Symington. I washed and shaved, then yakked with those three thousand guys while the band and other members of our troupe unloaded from the plane that had followed us in.

Stu sat with a group of generals in the commanding officer's quarters and read those letters of complaint. Then he asked the CO, "How much will it cost to clean this damned place up and make it livable?" The answer was several hundred thousand dollars.

"I'll authorize it right now," Stu said. "You get to work."

Before my show was over, Stu showed up onstage and told the men that some of their beefs were already being taken care of. Two thousand coal stoves were being delivered, so there would be plenty of heat. Fifty-six thousand square yards of linoleum were being ordered to cover bare concrete floors in barracks rooms. There had been two lights in each hut; from then on there would be eight lights in each bunkhouse. Stu also promised central heating for all the Burtonwood mess halls. Extra doctors and dentists were assigned.

Believe me, we left Burtonwood a much happier place than we found it. We did our bit in Newfoundland on our way back to the States; then Stu dropped us off in New York and headed for Washington. He reported what he'd done at Burtonwood to President Truman. And President Truman was really thrilled. He said, "I'm delighted you did it, Stu. You're a great Secretary of Air. But now let's get to the nitty-gritty; the next time Bob Hope takes Jane Harvey instead of Margaret, you've had it."

And that's how Stu Symington became a senator.

General Nate Twining, crew, Air Force Secretary Stuart Symington, Geoff Clarkson, Jimmy Wakely, Dolores Hope, Patty Thomas, rest of crew, Elmendorf Field, Anchorage, Alaska, 1949.

50   *The last Christmas show*

CHAPTER 6

America's icebox

In addition to being a great public relations man, Stu Symington was the best booking agent any stand-up comedian ever had. He was also the most persuasive. In 1949 he called me in Hollywood to talk about another morale problem—this time in Alaska. "Our people up there are a long way from home," he said. "They get homesick; they don't like the bitter cold. I'm thinking about going up there and looking things over. If I go, will you come too?"

"I'd figured on spending this one at home with Dolores and the children," I said. "I was away last Christmas, remember?"

"Why not bring them along?"

Before I could answer, I heard yelps of "Say yes, Daddy." My two oldest kids, Tony and Linda, were eavesdropping on an extension.

"Bring Dolores and your Tony and Linda with you," Stu said.

"Wait a second," I said. By that time Dolores was on another extension, saying, "I'd be thrilled to come."

My hand was forced. "You've got yourself a bet," I said.

A short time before Stu's call, Dolores and I had gone to the premiere of that great film about World War II, *Twelve O'Clock High*. Gregory Peck was the star, but his role was based on the real-life story of General Frank Armstrong, Jr., who had headed one of our Eighth Air Force groups in England during World War II. I'd met him in London during the war, and I'll say this: Frank's real story was a lot more exciting than the film version of his wartime efforts. He'd taken over a disorganized group and had lifted it by the seat of its pants.

That Christmas Frank lifted the seat of my pants right out of Hollywood. He was in Los Angeles and was flying north that afternoon. On the phone Stu said, "Frank will fly you to Seattle. I'll pick you up there in my plane."

Stu's call had come through at ten o'clock in the morning. The next thing I knew, Armstrong himself was on the phone. He said, "I'll meet you at four o'clock at my B-17 on the Hughes Aircraft runway."

It was panic time. I had about five hours to get together an entire entertainment unit.

I called the cowboy singer Jimmy Wakely, and asked, "How'd you like to go to Alaska this afternoon?"

He took it in his stride. "Sure," he said.

"Pack your guitar and meet me in two hours," I told him.

Next I called Geoff Clarkson, Les Brown's piano player. And, of course, old Brush Head himself, Jerry Colonna. Then I buzzed Patty Thomas, who had been my dancing partner on tours of the South Pacific during the war. Without a moment's hesitation, all of them signed up for the quickest quick freeze in history.

I had to let my writers know I'd be gone for a while. I called Norman Sullivan, one of the best. "You figure out the radio show for next week," I said. "I'm going to Alaska."

"You're doing *what?*" he asked.

"I'm going to Alaska, Norman."

"When?"

"This afternoon."

There was a moment's silence, then he came back with a great line. "Very well," he said calmly. "We'll move your pin on the map."

We all went up to Seattle together, met Stu, and took off in his plane the next day. Stu had brought an extra star for Brigadier General Frank Armstrong. He had been promoted to major general but didn't know it till then.

It was good flying weather from Seattle until we neared Anchorage. Then the area socked in. You know me, old Steel Nerves Hope. It takes more than a little bad weather to scare me. But my voice cracked like a boy soprano's when I asked Frank and Stu, "We'll be able to land okay, won't we?"

"Yes," they said. "But we'll have to go in on ground-control approach."

Because of the brass we had on board, our pilot was a lieutenant colonel. Symington picked up the intercom and said, "Colonel, switch the instructions from the ground back here into the cabin. We want to hear them."

As we squished through the soup, we heard instructions coming through from the tower in Anchorage: "You're 1,000 feet from touchdown . . . Let down to 800 . . . A little more to the left . . . You're now 500 feet from touchdown . . . Let down to 300 . . . Steer it just a little right rudder . . . You're now 100 feet from touchdown . . . You're on your own . . . You should be there now . . . Good luck!"

We couldn't see a thing. It was twenty-eight below outside. The ground fog was putting up a dense curtain. It was even hard to see anything after we'd touched down. If anything had gone wrong with our ground-to-plane communications, we would have been in a mess. Under those circumstances I can understand why a planeload of civilians sometimes takes up a collection and buys a pilot a watch.

Naval Air Station, Kodiak, Alaska, 1949. (U. S. Navy)

When we landed somebody asked me if I wanted a cold drink or a hot cup of coffee. I said, "Just give me a minute to change my shorts and I'll be right with you."

Believe me, below zero is coooold! But they had a band out there playing for us just the same. All we could see of those poor guys were their lips sticking out. They had hoods over their faces.

Within half an hour Dolores and I were on our way to our first show at the hospital. Tony and Linda divided their time between riding sleds and building snowmen.

Patty Thomas, Linda Hope, Tony Hope, Jimmy Wakely, Geoff Clarkson, Secretary of Air Force Stuart Symington at Eielson Air Force Base, Alaska, 1949. (U. S. Air Force)

Up there they gave us the full treatment, a Christmas with all the trimmings—dinner, stuffed stockings, the lot. On Christmas Eve we took in church with the children.

Then we flew inland to do a show in Fairbanks. The Air Force had built a base nearby at Eielson for our long-range B-36 bombers. They were trying to keep that fact a secret from everybody, so there had never been an entertainer at that base.

When we deplaned at Eielson it was forty-eight degrees below zero. That's

The last Christmas show

really cold, especially to the blood streams of us California characters. Even inside a so-called warm room, icicles formed around the keyholes. Everybody wore hats indoors. I tried to give the guys at Eielson a few funnies in the biggest Quonset hut I ever saw. After all these years I can still remember a line from that monologue. I said, "I'm delighted to be up here in the Palm Springs of Alaska along with God's frozen people."

After the show at Eielson, we went to another big Quonset hut with hundreds and hundreds of GIs inside. It was so cold breath vapors steamed all across the place, as big as it was. There we had lunch. I asked, "Who are all those people in uniform standing around staring at us?"

The colonel said, "They drew lots. The winners saw your show. The losers got to come in here and watch you eat your Christmas dinner."

I couldn't stand it. I said, "Do you have a good electrician on the base?"

"None better," the colonel said.

When the electrician came, I asked him how long it would take him to make a public address amplifier out of a telephone I saw nearby. "About thirty minutes," he told me.

I said okay. So in half an hour we did our show all over again for the losers. We did another show that night, so by the time we finished, we'd done three Christmas shows during one Christmas Day. In all, we did twelve shows in two days. Running between shows I worked up a sweat and caught a heavy cold. That knocked out my voice. From then on I had to stand so close to the mike I got the feeling we were going steady.

By the end of the trip I had a cold and sore throat that were meant for Hitler. So Stu stayed on to inspect some bases and dispatched us back to Burbank by Constellation. In seven hours we went from six below zero in Anchorage to a beautiful, clear, warm seventy-five degrees in Burbank. It seemed like a miracle. The same trip today would take only three and a half hours. That's if you only want "warm"—if you want "and clear" it still takes seven hours.

Tailor Maids, Judy Kelly, Gloria DeHaven, Les Brown, Jimmy Wakely, Corporal Royce W. DeVaughn of Dorsey, Mississippi, at Tripler Army Hospital, Hawaii, 1950. (U. S. Air Force)

56   *The last Christmas show*

CHAPTER 7

Buttons and Bows and some White Christmas shows

The first trip we made with Les Brown and His Band of Renown was in 1950. Les was one of the hottest bands in the country and they had a lot of records at the top of the charts. We booked them first on the radio show and when we finally got enough plane space to carry a full band, we took them with us on all our Christmas shows, knowing it would give the show a tremendous charge. I'm not knocking Tony Romano on guitar, he's beautiful, but when a big show band sits up there it really does lift an audience right off the benches.

During the course of the last twenty-five years I must have done 100,000 band jokes. "The tuba has three valves on it—scotch, bourbon, and vodka." "The band loves flying. Sometimes they even come inside the plane." "We had to bring the band back to Tokyo. It was time for their annual bath." "We had to stop here in Guam to refuel the band." "We had a little trouble with the band. While the medics were giving us shots for the trip, they kept going back for seconds."

I'm afraid these are pretty typical musician jokes. But the Les Brown Band is not a typical band. They can play anything—Christmas carols to rock. They can play anywhere—from the Top of the Mark to a hangar deck on an aircraft carrier. I've seen 'em play when there was snow forming on drummer Jack Sperling's head and in heat that made side men Bobby Gibbons, Lou Ciotti, Bobby Clark, and Ralph La Polla look like lobsters on the way to a steam bath. Butch Stone, our librarian and band mother, took care to see that the band was first in war and first in peace—and first in the PX. And Les probably made the grandest sacrifice of any. He gave up his bridge game in order to do last-minute orchestrations on the plane. And of course Stumpy, Les's brother, and Butch Stone used to break all the guys up with their novelty dance act.

That was quite a group we had on that trip. Gloria DeHaven made it to Hawaii, our first stop. And Marilyn Maxwell picked things up for the rest of the tour, joining us in Okinawa. Also we had the great country-western singer Jimmy Wakely; Judy Kelly, an acrobatic dancer whose specialty was bouncing —I don't have to tell you she was a hit; three beautiful young gals called the Tailor Maids; and the High Hatters—two great tap artists who used to dance with me. I use the words "dance with me" rather loosely. Actually in the South Pacific heat it was more of a survival contest. Whoever was still standing at the end of the number got to take the bow.

At Okinawa we were met by my old friend General Rosy O'Donnell, who came out from Japan to meet us. We stayed in the American compound with Major General Ralph F. Stearley. I was shown to my quarters—the Okinawan guard aimed his gun at us and didn't put it back on his shoulder until we gave him the password. I said, "Why is this? What's going on here? Isn't the island secure?"

And Rosy said, "Oh yes . . . There's been some looting in the compound and some of the guards are a little trigger-happy. That one took a shot at the chauffeur last night."

That night we did a big show at a baseball stadium. The field was so muddy, the girls in the troupe had to be carried from the jeep to the stage. By the time we got the guys to put the gals down the show was an hour late.

That was for the Army. That night we had a dinner at an Army club. And Rosy and I, who were rooming together, sat up and yakked half the night. The next day we did a show for the Air Force and they had a big party for us that night. Rosy left to go back to Japan and I went back to the room in the compound alone. I'd had a little too much to eat and a little too much to drink and about four o'clock in the morning I got up to relieve myself. I remembered about the guard so I turned on the light so he could see it wasn't some stranger wandering around the area. I went to the bathroom, came back to the room, and looked out the window. And there was this trigger-happy guard looking at me. I didn't want to offend the guard so I smiled. He smiled back at me—he was very friendly. I sort of waved to him and he sort of waved back at me. I pointed to my nose in a joshing manner to establish my identity. He pointed to his nose. I didn't think that was too funny. I stared at him—he stared back. He was right. He did look like me. He *was* me. He was my reflection. I turned off the light and he disappeared. Two of me is an impossible redundancy.

When we took off to fly into Tokyo, Colonel Lionel Leyden, a Special Services officer, stood in the aisle of our plane and made a speech. "Ladies and gentlemen," he said, "you're now in General MacArthur's command. It's the best damn command in the world. From now on, you're going to be treated as VIPs. Your rooms will have the smallest rats."

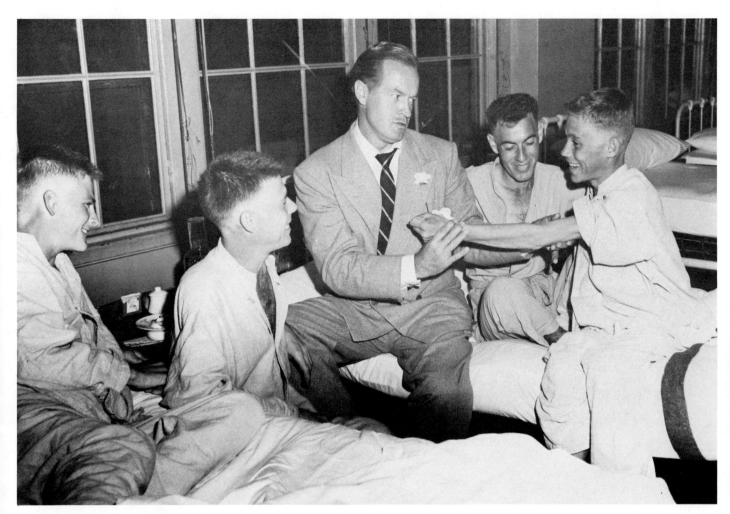

U.S. soldiers who escaped after the march from Taegu to Pyongyang at U.S. 118th Station Hospital, Fukuoka, Japan, 1950. (U. S. Army)

In Tokyo we were invited to lunch by General and Mrs. MacArthur. What with Les Brown's band and the cast we had about fifty people with us.

I couldn't take my whole troupe because there was only room for twenty at the luncheon table. But everybody wanted to go to the American Embassy for lunch, so we drew lots to see who'd go.

I had four writers with me, Fred Williams, Charles Lee, Larry Gelbart, and Chet Castleoff, and Fred and Larry won the lottery. The other two were left out. Chet wanted to go in the worst way and was very, very disappointed.

When he asked me if there was any way in which I could work him in, I said, "Chet, you can take my place and I'll stay home if you want to."

"No," he said, "I wouldn't do that. But I did want to see the general."

"It's tough," I said, "but only twenty people can go and we don't want to

Buttons and Bows and some White Christmas shows   59

7th Division in the swimming pool, Pusan, Korea, 1950.

embarrass them. They only have seating arrangements for twenty of us, you know."

The lucky twenty went over to the Embassy and met Mrs. MacArthur and young Arthur MacArthur. Finally the general showed and we had a talk with him too. Presently luncheon was announced, and we sat down, but to my astonishment one fellow was left standing up minus a seat. Obviously somebody had come who wasn't supposed to be there and I was pretty embarrassed. I looked at the general to see how he was taking it, and next to him—on his right—was Chet Castleoff.

The MacArthurs were nice about it. They had another chair brought in, tightened the circle, and made room for the fellow who was still standing.

When the general made a speech and thanked us all for coming, nobody applauded louder than old Chet. When I spoke to him sternly about it later he grinned and said, "Well, anyhow, I'll have something to tell the folks."

After lunch we went over to the Ernie Pyle Theater. Mrs. MacArthur and

The last Christmas show

young Arthur were among the celebrities who joined the huge GI audience. But I'm afraid the general missed such diamonds as:

Well, here we are in occupied Japan . . . and let me tell you it's really occupied . . . I know every girl I've called has been.

But I love it here in Tokyo. You know what I love about this place? The whole country looks like it was made in Japan.

Errol Flynn is expected here soon. He has a brand-new yen.

At first I thought the Japanese people knew me when we arrived, but then someone explained that hissing is a national custom.

When everyone hisses here on a quiet night you think the whole nation has developed a slow leak.

And the Japanese people are so polite. I'm not used to all this bow-ing. I've been here five days and I haven't seen anyone's face yet.

Everybody here rides a bicycle. No one buys a bicycle, though. You just wait till a guy gets hit by a car and then grab his.

And the traffic cops here in Tokyo stand up on boxes like old-time bookmakers. And they act like them too. They'll bet you eight to five you can't get across the Ginza.

Ginza. That's a barefoot Broadway. What a place. They sell every-thing there. I opened my mouth to yawn and before I could close it somebody sold my teeth.

But buying things here is real simple. First you take a ten-dollar bill and change it to military script, then you change the military script to yen, then you change the yen into chit books, and in no time at all you're out twelve dollars.

★

After the show in Tokyo I dropped in at the big Army post exchange. A song was blaring from the loudspeakers in the music department. It seemed to me that in some queer, oriental way there was something familiar about the tune. Then, ah so! I recognized it. It was "Buttons and Bows" sukiyaki style, with Japanese musicians. My movie *The Paleface* had just played in Japan and that song had become a smash hit. Everywhere I went the Japa-nese grinned at me, bowed, and said "buttons and bows," as if it were my name.

We did our show in Osaka in a huge swimming pool equipped with seats for forty thousand people. Swimming meets are the national sport of Japan and this thing was built like one of our football stadiums. Only ten thousand

President and Mrs. Syngman Rhee at Seoul, Korea, 1950. (U. S. Army)

of our troops were on hand, so we only used one end of the pool, but two or three hundred Japanese sat along the sides. I sang "Buttons and Bows," and every time I came to the title words, the Japanese applauded. Those three words were the only ones they recognized. Our boys got a boot out of that, and every time I came to those three words they applauded too. Before long we were all laughing so hard I couldn't go on.

On the way to Korea, I flew from Itazuke, Japan, in a T-39 jet. I'd been wanting to fly in a jet ever since I'd seen those beautiful P-38s over Africa. I'd always wondered what it would be like. But I didn't learn much that trip—I blacked out instantly.

When we arrived at Seoul, Korea, there were about ten thousand guys standing around when I stepped out in my G suit with the big jet helmet on —trying to pretend this was really my bag. Actually, I was looking for a bag.

The last Christmas show

Korea was a constantly changing campaign. Towns changed back and forth every night; the battle lines were changing all the time—it nearly drove them crazy on the eleven o'clock news. And we worked the whole area from as far south as the 7th Division at Pusan and Taegu, all the way as far north of the 38th parallel as Pyongyang, the capital of North Korea, where we talked about exactly what was happening:

★

I really didn't intend to perform so far north but the 1st Cavalry went through and the suction pulled me with them.

And some of these towns are changing hands so fast one soldier bought a lamp with three thousand won and got his change in rubles.

Seoul has changed hands so many times the towels in the hotel are marked "His," "Hers," and "Who's Sorry Now?"

But the way the war's going doesn't bother the Russians. They just run the newsreels backward and it looks like the North Koreans are advancing.

★

And then I introduced Marilyn Maxwell, and let me tell you, that little round eye really got a welcome.

MAX: Thank you . . . thank you.
BOB: What have you been doing here in Seoul?
MAX: Shopping, Bob . . . I was out looking for some old brass.
BOB: That's funny—they've been out looking for you.
MAX: Bob, have you had a chance to do any shopping here?
BOB: Yeah, I stopped into the five-and-ten for a while.
MAX: The five-and-ten . . .
BOB: Sure, you saw the familiar building with the red in front of it, didn't you?
MAX: Bob, that was no five-and-ten . . . that's the former North Korean Communist headquarters.
BOB: I wondered why the complaint desk was a T-34 tank.
MAX: Bob, isn't this country interesting? I've never seen so many children.
BOB: I know, one father here in Seoul has fifty-one kids.
MAX: Fifty-one children?
BOB: Yeah, I passed his home today and the birds and bees were lined up listening to him.
MAX: Of course, the women marry very young here, don't they?

Buttons and Bows and some White Christmas shows   63

Vice-Admiral Arthur D. Struble aboard USS Missouri, *Wonsan, Korea, 1950.*

Marilyn Maxwell, Pyongyang, Korea, 1950.

Dead North Korean, Pyongyang, Korea, 1950.

BOB: I'll say. It's not uncommon for a seven-year-old boy to marry a five-year-old girl.

MAX: That's what I've heard.

BOB: Matter of fact, I passed this house today and the mother was changing the baby and the father was changing the mother.

MAX: Well, I think the fellows have done a great job, Bob, and I really—

(*sound: door knock*)

BOB: Come in.

(*sound: door open*)

GI: Are you Mister Hope?

BOB: Yes, I am.

GI: I'd like to talk to you, sir.

BOB: Then what're you staring at Marilyn Maxwell for?

GI: You we can see any time.

BOB: What's on your mind?

GI: I have a message for you from the men of the 1st Cavalry.

BOB: Oh, that's nice. Let's hear it.

GI: Okay . . .

(*sings*)

Mr. Hope, by coming to Korea
You have shown you have no fear.
And for paying us this visit
We will always hold you dear.
When you leave us our whole outfit
Will shed one great big tear.
So do us just one favor . . .
Leave Marilyn Maxwell here!

(*he exits*)

MAX: Well now, why do you suppose they said that?

BOB: What? . . . either you're kidding or you've gone rock-happy.

(*applause*)

I had heard that the 1st Marine Division was supposed to be somewhere around in that area. I've always been very sentimental about the 1st Marine Division and so I asked our project officer if there was some way we could work for them. We got word back that they would be in Wonsan the following day.

As we flew into Wonsan we saw a lot of shipping in the harbor and small boats headed toward shore.

"That's nice," I thought. "They're coming in to see our show."

But when we arrived at the Wonsan airport, there wasn't a soul in sight. We wondered where everybody was. We just went over to the hangar and

Les Brown at Seoul, Korea, 1950.

stood there. Finally the brass—Major General Edward M. Almond, Vice-Admiral Arthur D. Struble, and the rest—showed up.

"When did you get here?" they asked.

"We've been here for twenty minutes," I told them.

"Twenty minutes!" they said. "You beat us to the beach."

"How do you mean, we beat you to the beach?" I asked.

"We've just landed," they said.

They had just made the landing, but fortunately it turned out to be a bloodless invasion. When we landed at the airport there were guerrillas all around us, but we didn't know it, and the fact that we beat the Marines to the beach made the AP wire.

After the show we had a cocktail party, with General Almond and the

The last Christmas show

High Hatters and Country Cousin, Tokyo, 1950.

Marine Corps general and Admiral Struble and a lot of brass, in a little tent. The party was complete with K rations and beer and such items.

"Why don't you come out and stay with me tonight?" Admiral Struble asked.

"What do you mean, with you?" I inquired.

"Well, I have my flagship, the *Big Mo*," he said. "I'm in charge of the Seventh Fleet."

"I'm with you," I said.

We flew out to the *Missouri* by helicopter. Halfway to the *Big Mo*, I looked out at that beautiful sunset and I said, "If I only had one more drink of scotch it'd be the best day of my life."

And Admiral Struble said, "I'm sorry, Bob, but we're on a battleship and that's one thing about our ships—we're not allowed to have liquor aboard."

"Well," I said, "I'll just have to fake it."

Somehow the pilot of the helicopter overheard our conversation and passed the word.

What a kick when we landed on the *Missouri*. I walked along that deck with Admiral Struble and the sailors yelled, "Hiya, Ski Snoot"; "Hey, Bob"; "How are ya—landlubber!"

The admiral said, "You'll probably want a bath and a change of linen, so Captain Ott will show you to your quarters."

When I arrived at my digs—it was the suite the Trumans used then they visited the *Missouri*—the officer who showed me around said, "If you feel like anything to wet your whistle just look in that medicine cabinet."

I opened the cabinet and surprise! In it was a bottle of scotch. I had a small belt, followed by dinner, then did a show on the fantail to the crew of two thousand sailors. No spotlight, just by moonlight. I did every joke I knew, and after the scotch, a few I didn't.

The next morning the *Big Mo* radioed the shore. Marilyn Maxwell, Judy Kelly, and the Tailor Maids were flown out to us by helicopter, and we did another show. Then we took a helicopter to the *Valley Forge* and did a show on her flight deck for Admiral Hoskins and two thousand more guys. We helicoptered back to Wonsan, got into our C-54, whipped over to Pyongyang, and did a show in the yard of the former Communist headquarters for a lot of troops who'd just been pulled out of the front lines.

On the way to the Commie headquarters we saw a dead horse, dead people with straw all over them, and a kid twelve years old who had just been shot. Not a very good warm-up for the show we did for the 1st Cavalry Division, Marines from the 1st Marine Division, men from the Air Wing, and remnants of the 11th Division, who were all defending us on the Yalu River.

It was a very dramatic show, and for some, their last. Because as it turned out we lost over fifteen thousand men when the Chinese crossed over the Yalu.

That was our last show in North Korea, and as we were closing the door of the plane to go to Tokyo, one of the soldiers on the ground yelled up to me, "How about your parka!"

I said, "Okay," and threw mine out.

And then somebody yelled up to Les Brown, "How about yours!" And before they closed the door we threw out fifty parkas because a lot of the guys didn't have one.

Back in Tokyo, Mrs. MacArthur invited us over for tea and I was talking to one colonel and he asked me what I thought about the situation. And I told him that I'd never seen a war like this. The dead lying all around, the confusion . . . and the colonel said to me, "Don't worry about it, Bob. We've

North Korean prisoners, Pyongyang, 1950.

Communist headquarters, Pyongyang, Korea, 1950. (U. S. Air Force)

Arriving Elmendorf Field, Anchorage, Alaska, 1950. (U. S. Air Force)

got it all in hand. We should have North Korea secured and be home by Christmas."

As it turned out, that colonel was a flop at handicapping wars. The Red Chinese troops crossed the Yalu River, they took back Pyongyang, they took back Seoul. Before it was over we were lucky we weren't run into the East China Sea. And that was just a minor battle. The big fight was between General MacArthur and President Truman in *Time* magazine.

It ended up with General MacArthur retiring from the service, whereupon he was hired by Remington Rand, the typewriter people, for obvious reasons —he had more ribbons than they did.

In 1951, 1952, 1953 I stayed close to home, if traveling up and down the length of California can be called close to home. In 1951 Constance Moore, the Nicholas Brothers, and I did a gig for our flying sailors aboard the aircraft

The last Christmas show

carrier USS *Boxer*, temporarily in San Diego after some hard knock off the coast of Korea. In 1952 I dropped in at Long Beach Naval Hospital, and in 1953 I traveled up to Letterman Hospital at San Francisco and to the Oakdale Naval Station, meeting guys we had met before on the front lines.

For obvious reasons I have never dreamed about a white Christmas. Why should I dream while *he's* getting all the royalties? And I certainly never dreamed of spending Christmas in Thule, Greenland, even though it is about as white as Christmas can get.

When I called the writers to tell them that Thule was our next destination they were ecstatic. Johnny Rapp said, "Beautiful, Bob, beautiful. Where the hell is it? And what the hell is it?"

What it was was an early warning radar station and an SAC base—a vital link in our defense against atomic attack.

Where it was was in the Arctic Circle, several hundred miles from the North Pole—a small dot on the coast of Greenland. We had five or six thousand men stationed there. It was classified as a "hardship base," the understatement of the year. A year there isn't a tour of duty, it's a sentence to darkness, to loneliness, to a desperate fight against a penetrating cold and relentless wind.

We not only had quite a few icebound shows ahead of us, but a new and chilling experience as well: for the first time our Christmas show was televised. Not only was it shown in America, but thirty-five copies of the show were made thereafter and distributed to armed forces bases around the world. There was no way they could escape us.

Until that time television had stuck close to the studios. The idea of going out to film where the temperature is sub-zero and where it's dark twenty-four hours a day, as it is in Thule during the yule season, concerned everybody. But the boys in Thule had it all figured out. They were used to the Birds Eye way of life. They thought that if we could take a picture back home it would save them a fortune in postcards.

After Air Secretary Harold E. Talbott proposed the Thule show, I phoned Bill Holden, then a hot favorite in the Oscar derby for his performance as the conniving GI in *Stalag 17*. Bill hesitated and then said, "I'll call you back in a few minutes and let you know."

I had the icy feeling that I was getting the chilliest brush-off of all—the Beverly Hills brush. I should have known better. Ten minutes later my phone rang. "I'll go—on one condition," he said. "My wife wants to come too."

"No problem," I said. With Bill's lovely wife Brenda Marshall along, I'd be getting two stars instead of one.

Secretary Talbott phoned me to say that the boys at Thule suggested that maybe Marilyn Monroe might come with us. In fact, if she didn't come they saw no reason for anybody else to come. I agreed with that kind of reasoning.

I put in a call to Marilyn (that's Hollywood talk for I had my agent call her agent) and as it happened Marilyn really wanted to come, but couldn't because of studio commitments (that's Hollywood talk for we'll never know if she wanted to or not).

Each day Secretary Talbott would call to see if we'd gotten Marilyn. And each day he'd put on a little more pressure. One day he mentioned that the Defense Department wanted to know if we'd gotten Marilyn because the guys in Thule had to be kept happy. The next day he mentioned that Marilyn was the subject of a Cabinet meeting and had we been able to get her? A day later he called to say that President Ike on the way to the golf course stopped in to see how Project Marilyn was going.

I hated to break the news to them that Marilyn wasn't coming until I had someone to fill Marilyn's . . . uh . . . shoes. We called several of the biggest stars but none of them could make it. And to be honest, none of them really had that kind of excitement.

I had just about given up when, a few nights before we were set to leave for Greenland, I emceed a Big Ten Conference football banquet at the Biltmore Bowl in Los Angeles. Among the guests was a beauty contest winner, Miss University of California at Los Angeles. She was wearing a sweater with UCLA on it and the U and the L were outstanding. Although she was a virtual unknown at the time, this doll was strikingly beautiful and unbelievably stacked. Obeying an impulse, I invited her to come along to Thule. Her name was Anita Ekberg.

I asked her what she was doing over the holidays. And she said she was going to do a show with Ty Power in Cincinnati. And I said that I had a better idea and that I thought she ought to come with us to Greenland. She looked at me as if I might be just slightly strange.

So the next day I called Ty Power and he said, "Sure, why not. I think it would be good for her."

TV studios used to produce things called "spectaculars." Well, to put it mildly, Anita was a one-girl spectacular. On the tour I introduced her by saying, "Her father and mother should get the Nobel prize for architecture. She's the greatest thing to come out of Sweden since smorgasbord!" A TV commercial has stolen that line now and has substituted the word "blondes" for "smorgasbord."

The next day when Talbott called I admitted I had no chance of getting Marilyn. His libido was sputtering and losing altitude, but I told him not to bail out yet, but to wait until he saw what I was bringing in her place.

When we landed in New York, Talbott was waiting on the runway. I stepped off, he looked right past me . . . and past Bill Holden . . . and past Brenda Marshall. But when Anita Ekberg hit the top of those stairs, you never saw so many teeth in your life. Talbott completely forgot us, took Anita's arm, and led her to the Air Force plane that was to take us to Thule.

Kelly and Nora Hope at North Hollywood, California, 1950.

I whispered to Anita, "Listen, if you play your cards right, by the time you get back there'll be an Anita Ekberg Field."

In addition to Bill Holden, his wife Brenda, and Anita, I also corralled the Hollywood columnist Hedda ("the Hat") Hopper. The rest of our GI bait was Margaret Whiting, Patty Thomas, Professor Brush Lip Jerry Colonna, plus actors Peter Leeds and Charlie Cooley. For music we had two bands, Les Brown's and the United States Air Force Band from Bolling Field Air Force Base near Washington, D.C.

If I haven't told you—and I already have—Greenland is anything but green in the middle of winter. Thule looked to me like the land God forgot until the Air Force came along and built a $300-million outpost there. When we landed it was thirty-six below zero. Once on the ground (or ice), we were asked to stay in our seats inside the plane. After a short delay, we taxied into a heated hangar. I said to our project officer, Major Joseph Lynch, "It's mighty thoughtful of you, having us disembark in a nice warm hangar like this!" He replied, "We have to be careful, Bob. If we're not, the plane will freeze up! Lubrication and all."

That was the actual truth. In those Arctic temperatures everything freezes very solid, very fast. Not only will the water in a jeep's pump freeze in a few minutes, the oil will too. Some of the newer cars at the base had heaters built right into the engine block. When they parked one of those cars, they plugged it in like an electric toaster. Cars without heaters were left running the year round. Their engines weren't even stopped for repairs; the mechanics worked on them while they were running. We were told that one jeep at the base hadn't been shut down for six years.

On the base were miles and miles of what amounted to aluminum iceboxes. I'm not kidding. The structures the men lived in were so well insulated they could have been used as cold storage plants—except they were rigged to keep heat in and cold out instead of vice versa.

Ever since I was a kid I'd heard how the nights at the North Pole were six months long. I can verify that. Greenland, home of the midnight sun, was only the home of midnight to us. We were at Thule for three days and the sun never did show. That kind of visibility made me homesick for the smog in Los Angeles.

With the approach of spring, everybody would get out his sunglasses and wait for the sun to put in its first appearance. When it finally peeked over the horizon like a bashful flashlight, a big cheer would go up. The rest of the so-called day was spent celebrating. As the months went by, the local ice worms would get more and more sun until it got to be too much of a good thing. I heard that one guy opened a drive-in movie there. He went broke waiting for the sun to go down. One GI said to me, "I feel silly coming home with a happy little skinful from a party at five in the morning and it's broad daylight. You get the feeling you missed a day."

74   *The last Christmas show*

TV show, Thule, Greenland, 1954.

We put on our shows in the gym. If you wonder how a gym can be used as a theater, it's easy. All you need is the help of two hundred GIs who work from morning till night erecting a temporary stage, laying cables, setting up lights, connecting microphones, and filling the floor space with chairs.

We gave two shows in Thule. The men began lining up for our 2:30 matinee at 10:30 A.M. At our evening performance, some of the three thousand brave souls who showed up were repeaters! For any hitchhikers who wanted to try for it, we offered a New Year's Day performance in Goose Bay.

I always start things off kidding about the base and its surroundings.

Buttons and Bows and some White Christmas shows   75

I'm very happy to be here at Thule. The temperature is thirty-six below. Only we don't know below what. The thermometer just went AWOL.

But it's really cold here. One guy jumped out of his bunk at six this morning, ran in, turned on the shower, and got stoned.

Up here, a nudie pin-up calendar isn't a luxury, it's a necessity.

We certainly got a wonderful reception when we landed. All those soldiers standing so stiffly at attention! I understand they've been that way for four months.

When I walked into General O'Donnell's quarters, the first thing I noticed was the tail of a reindeer sticking out of the wall over the fireplace. I said, "How come you didn't mount the antlers?" He said, "Don't be silly, it's not mounted. That's a live one trying to get warm!"

★

The weather wasn't the only hardship our GIs had to put up with at Thule. Another gripe was the lack of female companionship. When we played the base, there were six thousand guys stationed there and only three women, female nurses at the base hospital. You get better odds than six thousand to three at Las Vegas, so I threw in a few gags about the woman shortage:

★

The guys get pretty lonesome up here. When a wolf howls, he starts a community sing.

It's so lonely here, one guy is going steady with his tattoo. And his friends keep asking him if she's got a sister.

You're not even allowed to think about girls up here. At night a sergeant walks through the barracks and wakes up anybody with a smile on his face.

After the monologue, we went into a skit in which a couple of GIs write back to the States for a mail-order bride. Anita Ekberg played the girl. And believe me when I tell you she was right for the part. She entered in a fur coat and three thousand men stood up, applauded, cheered, and whistled. Then she took off the coat and stood there in a low-cut gown which showed cleavage that made the Grand Canyon look trivial. It was bedlam. We were afraid the screaming would start an avalanche so we had to ask her to retire

The last Christmas show

Secretary of Air Harold E. Talbott, Maggie Whiting, Peter Leeds, Jerry Colonna, Robert Strauss, Brenda Marshall, and Bill Holden en route to Thule Air Force Base, Greenland, 1954. (U. S. Air Force)

Bill Holden and Anita Ekberg, Thule, Greenland, 1954. (U. S. Air Force)

Secretary of Air Harold E. Talbott, Mrs. Talbott, and Lieutenant General Emmett O'Donnell, Jr., Labrador, 1955. (U. S. Air Force)

Anita Ekberg, Hedda Hopper, Jerry Colonna, and Bob Strauss, Goose Bay, Labrador, 1954. (U. S. Air Force)

to her dressing room and change into something more restful. Ridiculous . . . Anita is so richly endowed, she'd get whistles wearing a laundry bag.

Hedda Hopper covered the whole thing in her syndicated column. She wrote a lot about Anita and when we got back Anita was in tremendous demand. John Wayne and Bob Fellows, through their production company Batjac, signed Anita to a long-term contract. The next time I wanted to hire Anita for a movie, her price jumped from scale to $75,000. And in an unbelievably short time she was a film star and an international celebrity. I don't know what's the matter with me. I should have been the one that signed her. I guess it's because when I looked at Anita the grubby world of business escaped me and in its place were waves pounding on the shore, rockets and Roman candles, and the *1812 Overture*.

The finale of the show is one of those moments I'll never forget. It was exactly midnight of New Year's Eve when the cast all gathered onstage and we sang "Auld Lang Syne." There wasn't a dry eye in the house. And at the last note somebody screamed, "Happy New Year!!" Then another . . . then madness. As if by signal five thousand people in that tightly packed gym were yelling and screaming, laughing and crying. People were blowing horns, throwing confetti. The stage was overrun. The orchestra was blasting. Everybody was hugging everybody. The din was overwhelming. It was a moment of sheer animal hysteria that I can still see and hear vividly. And everybody in the cast felt the sheer enjoyment of participating. And people say we gave up Christmas.

Ginger Rogers at Anchorage, Alaska, 1956. (U. S. Air Force)

The last Christmas show

1955–56

CHAPTER 8

School of hard knocks

As Christmas approached in 1955 I was in England, making a picture called *The Iron Petticoat* with Katie Hepburn. The USO caught up with me just the same, and asked if I would fly over to Iceland to do a Christmas show.

Cold weather doesn't scare me: I've spent more time on ice than a bottle of Dom Pérignon. So I said, "Sure. That'll be easy."

And it would have been, if I hadn't signed up a girl named Joan Rhodes to go with me. Joan was very attractive and very feminine, but she was also very strong. That was her business—doing a strong-girl act. Her agent told me she could tear a telephone book in half. If I didn't believe him then, believe me, I believe him now.

Joan and I worked up a great routine. While I sang "Embraceable You," she picked me up and held me in her arms. It played so big the first time we tried it, I decided that for the finish of my Iceland show I'd put my foot in her hand and have her lift me up.

When the big moment came, she hoisted me up and I stood on her hands. There I was, high over Iceland. Then she began to totter backward. I thought she was ad-libbing that totter. Well, she wasn't. I went over her head onto the floor. The floor was cement. The audience roared when I hit; they thought it was part of the act. The TV cameras that were filming the show were still going, and while I was flat on the floor, I yelled, "Cut!"

I put my hand up, felt around, and found that my nose was bleeding. I stood up and said, "I'll be right back." I rushed into the dressing room, felt my head once more—it was still there—wiped my face, and went back to finish the show.

For my encore, I went to the hospital. The doctor on base examined me and said, "I haven't got the right X-ray equipment. You'd better go back to London and have proper X rays." Back I flew, right into the clinic. I was so nervous I went to X ray without make-up. Fortunately, they couldn't find anything wrong.

School of hard knocks   81

Purdue Glee Club, Al Stewart, director, at Anchorage, Alaska, 1956.

82   *The last Christmas show*

Mickey Mantle at Anchorage, Alaska, 1956.

I learned one lesson from that fall: I don't work with strong ladies any more. I've had my head reblocked once too often. When I see a Women's Lib headquarters, I cross the street.

My 1956 trip was just as hard on my head—and hard on the nerves as well. You remember the '49 landing in Anchorage? Well, the '56 version in Alaska was a rerun, with no residuals. The weather was the kind that makes you want to turn around and head for home, but there were five thousand men down there in a hangar at Ladd Air Force Base in Fairbanks waiting to see Ginger Rogers, Mickey Mantle, Peggy King, Jerry Colonna—and me.

The field was socked in with what's called ice fog. That means more ice particles than fog moisture. After a lot of jibber-jabber with the tower, we got permission to come in on instruments. So we fastened our seat belts and

School of hard knocks   83

*Ginger Rogers, Irv Kupcinet (r.), arriving
Ladd Field, Fairbanks, Alaska, 1956.*

*Ginger Rogers at Ladd Field, Fairbanks,
Alaska, 1956. (U. S. Air Force)*

prepared for the approach. We were okay on our cross-wind leg and making
the turn into our final approach.

Suddenly it was very quiet on the plane. Outside there was just black gunk.
We let down for what seemed an hour. At last we saw a light below. The
trouble was, it wasn't an airport light; we had overshot the runway. The pilot
jammed on the power. There was a sickening lurch until we regained air
speed and started up again. I don't know how low we came, but I do know
this. After we passed over the officers' club, I found a drink in my hand.

84   *The last Christmas show*

We finally set down at Eielson Air Force Base, the roost for our B-36 birds that I'd played in '49. We made it back to Ladd Field by bus, and while the cast gnawed some dry turkey sandwiches backstage, Les Brown and his band went out on the podium in the hangar to try to get some movement into their fingers and lips.

In that show I did a scene with Ginger Rogers in which Ginger played Klondike Lil and I played the boob. I don't know how I always get that part; maybe I've got natural talent. In the skit Ginger was supposed to belt me over the head with a bottle. Naturally it was a prop breakaway bottle, which had worked fine during rehearsals in Hollywood. It was a lot colder in that hangar in Fairbanks. The bottle froze and when Ginger conked me, I stood there with my eyes crossed. I would have moved, but I was unconscious. To wake me up, she hit me again. I hit the floor fast.

Ginger ad-libbed her way around my limp form until I came out of it and was back on my feet. The show must go on and all that, and besides those GIs wanted to get a look at Mickey Mantle.

I can't say I blamed them; I'm full of hero worship for star athletes myself. I've had a lot of them on the show at one time or another—Ben Hogan, Jack Nicklaus, O. J. Simpson, Mark Spitz, Bobby Fischer, Cary Middlecoff, Arnold Palmer, Sandy Koufax, Rafer Johnson, all the athletes on the Gillette Cavalcade of Champions. And of course every year we do the Associated Press All-America football team. They all have that confidence that comes from having been under pressure in front of the public. The only thing that bugs me is that they all get big laughs. That probably has something to do with the fact that they are big men in every sense of the word.

The Alaska audience really flipped for Mickey Mantle. We did a sketch about the pampered modern Army and used Mickey as a draftee dressed in Doctor Dentons—those pajamas with feet on them. The Mick enjoyed the bit. He never shanked a line onstage.

That's one of the special pleasures you get working with pros. They adapt to any situation; they work under any conditions. Ginger Rogers, for instance, could rehearse all day, work two shows, visit the service clubs in the evening, and dance all night with the GIs—and very few of them were Fred Astaires.

The same is true of Jill St. John and Ann-Margret and Raquel Welch. They'll drive you crazy about hair dryers and make-up men and how much bosom they can show without getting arrested and who gets to sit next to whom on the plane and who is billed as "special guest star" and who is billed as "extra special guest star," but when it comes to show time that's where the flaky stuff ends. They're there, they're ready, and they've got it all together. They're like postmen—neither rain, nor sleet, nor hail will stay these chicks from their appointed rounds.

Jayne Mansfield at Tachikawa Air Base, Japan, 1957.

CHAPTER 9

A funny thing happened on the way to the geisha house

By 1957, Christmas tours had become a habit. This year the Air Force called me to say they were routing us through the Far East.

I don't know how word gets around—maybe my phone is tapped—but before I have a chance to mention the trip to anybody on my staff, they are all off and running.

My writers split into two working teams. Those who will go skiing while I am gone and those who will go golfing while I am gone. Sil Caranchini, our associate producer, and Johnny Pawlek, our sound man, take off on Thanksgiving Day to plan the trip. I've never understood that. Why does it take a month to plan a fifteen-day trip? And where did they go for a month this year—we didn't even make a trip!

And Les Brown is at his busiest. He not only has to go down to Woolworth's to buy band arrangements for all the service marches at $2.50 apiece, but he has to sell them to me at $300 apiece. It was only last year I said to Les, "Maestro, I don't mean to be a complainer, but couldn't you do these march arrangements yourself while we're on the plane?"

With a pained look, he took his thumb out of his mouth and said to me, "What? And break up the bridge game!"

There's no fighting real logic.

The departure from Burbank was delayed an hour and a half. The weather was fine, but somebody had forgotten the club soda. Finally we were settled into a couple of Boeing Stratocruisers and were given clearance from the tower. We thundered down the runway for what seemed to be forever. Suddenly it struck me: "They forgot to weigh Hedda Hopper's hats." But Jayne Mansfield's scanty costumes must have made up for that, and we finally got off the ground.

Approaching Hawaii, we were treated to a rare sight: Mickey Hargitay, the weight lifter and wrestler, was kneeling in the aisle giving his wife, Jayne Mansfield, a pedicure. I know Jayne had sexy toes, but for Mickey to stay loose enough to slap on the old nail polish before everyone's staring eyes took a lot of *savoir-faire*. I couldn't help admiring what someone called "the superb detachment of our Cuticura da Vinci."

There are no sour grapes hanging on that last paragraph. La Mansfield was a trouper and a half. She never griped about anything, and there were times when she had plenty to gripe about. Before each stop she had to change into a new costume, quite a chore in the tiny lavatories on the plane—particularly with Mickey wedged in there helping her. I finally understood what togetherness meant.

The military made our arrival in Hawaii a big deal. Lined up at the foot of the ramp was a platoon of pretty WAVES. As each member of the troupe deplaned, he was greeted with a smooch and a lei thrown about his neck. I had leis piled so high I couldn't get my hat on. After that many kisses my head was so big my hat wouldn't have fit me anyhow.

We were four hours late getting to Hickam Field, and our audience of 6,600 at the Block Arena had been sitting on their rear ends for each of those hours for fear of losing their seats. With that kind of enthusiasm, we skipped dinner. Who wants dinner anyhow? An audience like that is solid caviar.

Not to keep them starving too long, I brought Jayne out immediately. A roar went up that had me looking over my shoulder for the lions. I knew how the Christians felt in the Colosseum. When she stepped out on the stage, so many flashbulbs went off I thought Pearl Harbor was exploding all over again. For five solid minutes they popped away with their Brownies while I stood there feeling sorry I hadn't bought Eastman Kodak stock. I went into one routine with Jayne, but I knew I didn't have their undivided attention. From then on *I* opened the show; Jayne's a hard act to follow.

It was nearly midnight when we finished at the Block Arena and were whisked to Don the Beachcomber's restaurant for a late snack and sip. Don is a great host, but he's rum-happy. He serves rum in scooped-out pineapples. Thirty pineapples later (or about 3:30 A.M.) we were wheeled back to the Stratocruisers for the takeoff to Wake Island. Since the Stratocruiser was a double-decker, it had one big advantage on long hops: while the rest of the troupe curled up for the night in reclining seats, there was a little room on the deck below where the crew threw a couple of cushions and put up a sign "Children & Comedian First."

A few hours before we reached Wake, we crossed the international date line. The crew had a ceremony for people making it the first time. After you were blindfolded they explained that anybody crossing the date line had to be dunked into the Pacific. They helped you into a Mae West life jacket and told you not to worry. They said that the plane's altitude was only fifty feet above the water and that a destroyer had been assigned to pick up the initiated.

I couldn't help worrying a little when they led me down the aisle. I heard a door open and felt a rush of wind come at me. I had no way of knowing they'd only opened the door to the rear luggage compartment and that I was standing on a suitcase. Nevertheless, some sort of insane bravado prompted me to jump when they told me to. That six inches back to the floor was the longest trip I'd ever taken.

During our refueling stop at Wake Jayne shook up our finny friends when she went for a dip in a pink angora bikini studded with rhinestones and pearls. That was also the day most of the male population of Wake took up skin diving. The rest of us battled the heat under warm salt-water showers. This wouldn't have been worth mentioning except that the Wake Island laundry had broken down a couple of days before and towels were non-existent. My coeducational cast used the honor system (at least one eye closed) as we took turns romping around under the tropical sun to get ourselves dry.

Les Brown's band handled the laundry problem with their usual aplomb. They ignored it. One NBC executive who went with us on the tour still wears the Purple Heart we awarded him for being aboard the band's plane the day its air conditioning conked out.

From Wake we droned on to Kadena Air Base in Okinawa. The island is only three hundred miles from Communist China, but once we got there, we lived like capitalists. For the first time in three nights we bedded down on genuine innersprings. The Air Force put us up in lush quarters that cost us only one buck a night. If that doesn't lick communism, nothing will.

We rehearsed a spy sketch our first night on Okinawa. The cast was drawn from the ranks of reporters who were covering the trip. Mike Connolly, then a columnist for the *Hollywood Reporter*, barely managed to look like a butler who was supposed to be a Chinese spy. Getting him to perform like one was a job for Henry Higgins. Irv Kupcinet, the Chicago talk man, played every scene like a man going into business for himself. But I shouldn't beef. Without those newspaper people doubling as actors, that scene would have been just me and Jayne Mansfield. Come to think of it, that's not bad casting, but I always seemed to be a minority of one when it came to making those decisions.

Early the next morning a bus took us to White Beach, where we were doing a show on the heavy cruiser USS *Los Angeles* docked in Buckner Bay. The *Los Angeles* had a complement of one thousand men. The seaplane tender *Kenneth Whiting*, tied up on the other side of the dock, carried another 750, so we played to two audiences.

I opened by telling the sailors, "I've just come from Hawaii. It's the most difficult spot in the world to leave. Everywhere else they wave good-by with their hands.

A funny thing happened on the way to the geisha house   89

"My grandfather was a naval hero. He once shouted, 'I have not yet begun to fight.' And you know, he never did. You probably remember him, Admiral Tuna, the Chicken of the Sea.

"The food on this ship must be terrific. I've never seen such fat seagulls."

When I introduced Jayne I said I had also "just introduced her to two pilots. It's the first time I ever saw pilots leave vapor trails without their planes."

After a skit that included Jayne, Jerry Colonna and I did one of our routines. Jerry pretended to be one of the sailors on the *Los Angeles*. "What's your job?" I asked him. "I polish the brass," he said. "I've got the shiniest captain in the fleet. I like being in the Navy—great spirit—everybody is 'Mr.'"

My line was, "There might be even more spirit if a few of them were Mrs."

At this point I denied a rumor that Hedda Hopper had asked the captain to turn the ship around so that the sunlight would create a flattering halo effect on her hair. I said, "What Hedda actually asked was if the *island* could be turned around."

After Hedda we brought on Erin O'Brien. Jayne was meat and drink to the boys, but Erin was milk and honey, a lot like the girl next door—if you happened to be very lucky with neighbors. As Erin sang, we got some of the most memorable film footage of the trip—closeups of the faces and eyes of the sailors who were watching her. If you saw our Christmas TV show in mid-January 1958, you might remember the looks on those faces. When I saw the film it convinced me all over again that those Christmas tours were worth everything they took.

Following the shipboard shows, we went to Sukiran to do an outdoor performance for the Marines at Okinawa's Camp Courtney. The guys there trained under actual combat conditions.

"Pretty rugged out here," I said. "I hear one Marine rolled out of his lean-to this morning and shaved three times before he realized he was staring into a bear, not a mirror.

"You think you've got it tough here? We all had to take shots before leaving home. In fact, Les Brown and his band got seconds."

That night we did another show in a giant gym at Stilwell Field. And, if you collect firsts, later in the evening Jayne became the first American movie star to make a personal appearance in an Okinawan movie theater. A thousand jostling fans jammed the Kokuei Theater in downtown Naha where one of her pictures was playing. Kotara Kokuba, reputedly the richest man in Okinawa, was so grateful for Jayne's appearance that he threw a lavish feast at one of his teahouses. The entertainment included dancing girls doing things Fred Astaire never taught.

The next morning seven thousand Marines marched out to the local baseball field to watch our show. We not only entertained those gyrenes, they entertained us. Nobody has really got all the feeling out of the lyrics in the song

7th Infantry Division, Bayonet Bowl, Korea, 1957.

A funny thing happened on the way to the geisha house   91

"There Is Nothing Like a Dame" until he's heard seven thousand Marines singing it in a lonely outpost on Okinawa.

A chain link fence enclosed the ball park. Plastered against it were hundreds of Okinawan children. They looked like kids outside a candy store watching a taffy machine. I was flattered that my humor meant so much to them until I noticed they weren't watching me at all. Their eyes were glued to the box lunches being devoured by the cast members. As dessert for the knothole set, I introduced a seventeen-year-old Okinawan beauty named Sumiko Yosayama. She sang rock-'n'-roll tunes she'd learned phonetically from jukeboxes. She had no idea what she was singing about, but just listening to her killed our side. There's no doubt about it: a rock-'n'-roll beat must be a universal language.

A routine the servicemen everywhere loved went over particularly well there. I brought out Alan Gifford, a fine actor who's worked with me all over the world. He was made up as an Air Force general, and his job was to welcome me to the base. He offered me all kinds of hospitality until I introduced him to Jayne. Gifford was a head shorter than she, and from the moment he first met her, his West Point training was apparent: he kept his eyes dead ahead. He forgot I was alive, and whenever I broke in he shut me up curtly. The sight of this military martinet hypnotized by a breastwork really flipped the GIs.

We celebrated the end of the flight from Okinawa to Japan in true Air Force tradition. A pair of interceptor jets met us at twenty thousand feet and made with the aerobatics—barrel rolls, Immelmanns, and dives. They came so close they almost scratched our paint. They're wasting their talent. They'd really be stars in a supermarket parking lot.

We made our first stop in Japan at Itazuke Air Base in Kyushu. There 2,500 servicemen and their families roared hello to the accompaniment of screaming F-100 jets overhead. I stepped up on the stage to roll them in the aisles—only to stand there stunned. Barney McNulty, our ace cue-card man, had printed my first card entirely in Japanese. All I could say was something like, "A funny thing happened to me on the way to the geisha house." That didn't bother the audience. They laughed as if they were in on the gag with McNulty, and they probably were.

The troupe was billeted at the Imperial Hotel in Tokyo, so I mined a few nuggets from the superservice we were getting. "There's a button next to my bed marked Room Service," I said, "and a maid to press it for me. You order scotch and soda and four bellhops come to your room. One carries scotch, the second carries soda, the third carries ice, and the fourth arrives empty-handed. He's there for the tip.

"The accommodations are very lush and comfortable. The bath in my suite is big enough to float a Buick. It even comes equipped with a special back scrubber. I had a heck of a job trying to talk her out of it.

"The Japanese regard the bath as a kind of community activity, like a PTA meeting. Feeling around for the soap, you're likely to come up with two people you didn't even know were in there with you. But it does eliminate the line outside the bathroom door.

"And keyhole peepers are unheard of. After all, who's gonna settle for a little television-screen-eye view when the real thing is available?"

We were in a hurry to finish dinner because we had a show to do in Yokohama, so we took cabs back to the hotel. Tokyo cab drivers are all ex-kamikaze pilots. You haven't really lived till you've ridden with them, and sometimes you stop living shortly thereafter.

Since most of them speak no English, you have to act out where you want to go. One night I stepped into a cab at the Imperial and was driven to four different places I didn't want to be before I found the one magic word the cabby understood: "Imperial." He drove me back to the hotel, and I stepped into another cab hoping for better luck.

In Yokohama we did a show at the Fryar Gymnasium for a few thousand of our Far Eastern personnel. Carol Jarvis, the popular young rock-'n'-roll singer, was a sensation. I accused her of having relatives in the audience. The fact was those guys had already heard Carol's latest platter. It's amazing how fast hit records made it to the jukeboxes at our bases.

That night we relaxed for an hour in Benibashi's, one of Tokyo's larger nightclubs. That oversized boîte featured an American-type floor show and hundreds of hostesses of various nationalities. Some of the mixed racial strains on view were quite interesting. I saw one pretty Chinese-Hungarian, sort of an oriental Zsa Zsa Gabor type, eating goulash with chopsticks.

Bright and early the next morning we were hustled to Tachikawa Air Base, twenty-three miles east of Tokyo. Come to think of it, we weren't bright, but it *was* early. Tachikawa had been a Japanese airfield during the Second World War, but when the Americans took over after the 1945 surrender, there were only three blackened buildings left. Very thorough, those Nipponese.

Back home Congress had just slashed the annual budget for all of our armed services. I told the airmen how drastically the Air Force would be hit. "We're going to have to let all our generals go who are over twenty-five," I said, "and you'll have to cut down many essential services. From now on, a bomber will carry only one stewardess.

"And that reminds me, nobody's allowed to send telegrams any more. Commanding officers are cautioned to check through their Christmas cards carefully. War may have been declared. But if you think the budget cuts are serious here," I went on, "you should have seen the Army-Navy game this year. The Army mule was missing. So was the Navy goat. The hot dogs had a farmyard taste."

That afternoon we moved to Johnson Air Base to do an outdoor show at

A funny thing happened on the way to the geisha house   93

Walker-Schade Stadium. One of the bits we did was a spy sketch in which I was a GI about to take off on a six-hour pass. The sketch opened with the commanding officer warning that we were in a dangerous area full of spies. We were to be on our guard at all times. No drinking. No women. I demanded to see the chaplain. When he showed up I told him, "If I'm going to be dead for six hours, I want a military funeral."

Thirty seconds later, I was surrounded on three sides by Jayne Mansfield. She was a luscious Mata Hari and I was an overeager security risk. It was a part every man in front of us could identify with and enjoy. I liked it myself.

> MUSIC: *Oriental*
> (*dissolve to living room and Jayne Mansfield*)
> (*Bob enters*)

BOB: Baby!

JAYNE: Sweetheart!

> (*they kiss*)

BOB: Tell me, what's a doll like you doing in a place like this? You belong in New York, or Paris . . .

JAYNE: No, I like the plain, ordinary, simple things.

BOB: You do?

JAYNE: Yes . . . sit down.

BOB: You may go home by bus. I've only got eight hours, baby, let's make the most of it.

> (*they sit on couch*)

JAYNE: Here we are.

BOB: Yes, here we are.

JAYNE: Well.

BOB: Care to shoot a game of pool?

JAYNE: Come on, get with it, Clyde . . . take me in your arms.

BOB: Well, uh, this is the first time we've . . .

> (*she grabs him, bends him back on couch*)

JAYNE: You're awfully shy. Are you sure you're with the Air Force?

BOB: We have to be careful, baby. We can't get too friendly . . . they told us to watch out for spies.

JAYNE: What spies?

BOB: People who get a GI drunk and try to get information out of him.

JAYNE: You don't have to worry. You're perfectly safe here.

BOB: I know it, baby.

> (*she snaps fingers*)
> (*mike is lowered*)

JAYNE: Special Spy Number 52 calling Agent 35. Bring in the whiskey. That is all.

Miss Japan and Jayne Mansfield at Block Arena, Honolulu, 1957. (Photo by Gerald Smith, NBC)

A funny thing happened on the way to the geisha house   95

(mike flies up)
(Bob sits up)
BOB: What was that?
JAYNE: I just ordered some drinks.
    (oriental servant wheels in cart covered with towel)
Would you like a little drink?
BOB: I better not have any. I'm on guard duty tonight and it might keep me awake.
JAYNE: Oh, come on, Clyde . . . just a little sip.
BOB: Okay. Maybe just a little one.
    (she removes towel from tray)
    (gives large glass to Bob)
Why so stingy? What is this, Jackie Gleason's finger bowl?
    (Jayne turns away)
    (Bob switches glasses)
She'll never know.
JAYNE *(reaches over and takes small glass)*: Drink up.
BOB: I hope my Blue Cross covers this.
JAYNE: L'chayim. That means "good luck."
BOB: Sayonara . . . that means "good-by"!
    (they drink)
    (Bob holds it in his mouth . . . leaps up . . . rushes to window)
    (flashpot)
Where do they age that stuff, Yucca Flat?
JAYNE *(pulls Bob down)*: Oh, you're so cute and witty . . . I want to know all about you—your hopes, your dreams, your ambitions, the number of men in your outfit, where you're storing your new long-range weapons . . .
BOB: There's 3,500 men in my outfit, not counting the fifty engineers who're building a missile-launching pad which will command the whole harbor area.
    (man stands up behind couch)
JAYNE: Isn't that interesting. Fifty engineers building a launching pad near the harbor area.
    (man behind couch semaphores out of window)
BOB: It's gonna be terrific. It shoots anything from an atomic shell to hot matzoh balls.
    (Jayne raps on TV set)
    (it lights up, revealing man inside sending Morse code)
    SOUND: *Amplified Morse code*
    (Bob rises)
What's that?

JAYNE (*rises*): Nothing . . . just a mouse.

BOB: Some mouse . . . he must've studied under Marconi.

JAYNE: Darling, we have so little time. Let's make every moment count. Tell me that you love me—tell me I'm the only one . . . tell me what kind of rocket they're sending up at your base to-morrow morning.

BOB: It may be me! Please. You're bending my good conduct medal.

(*she pats Bob's jacket*)

JAYNE: What's that bulge in your pocket?

BOB: Oh, nothing that would interest you. It's only the top-secret plans for the new long-range missile with the improved atomic det-onator.

JAYNE: Honey, why don't you take your coat off? It's kind of warm in here.

BOB: Are you warm? I'm cold.

(*she kisses him*)

Mind if I take off my coat?

JAYNE: Of course, darling, let me help you.

(*she helps him out of his jacket*)

BOB: I'm feeling chilly again.

JAYNE: I'll take care of that. Kiss me, darling.

(*she locks Bob in embrace and holds jacket over back of couch*)

(*man takes jacket*)

(*takes out plans*)

(*photographers take pictures*)

BOB (*reacts to flash*): Did you leave the gas on in the kitchen?

(*another flash*)

Must be the monsoon season.

JAYNE: It's just your imagination, dear.

(*she kisses him again*)

(*men rip jacket*)

(*return it to Jayne*)

(*the men exit*)

You'd better put your coat back on. You're out of uniform.

(*she hands him coat*)

BOB: I better. If they caught me like this . . .

(*jacket is in shreds*)

. . . I see you had it cleaned and pressed.

(*tries to put jacket on*)

That's swell. I like a vent in the back. Here, wait a minute, where's my plans?

JAYNE: I have them.

(*he reaches for them*)   (*she pulls them away*)

A funny thing happened on the way to the geisha house

What are you interested in—the plans—or me?

BOB: The plans.

    (*to audience*)

And you didn't think I could act! I get it—underneath that gaudy exterior beats the heart of a spy!

JAYNE: You catch on fast. The party's over, Clyde.

    (*she claps her hands*)

    (*spies appear with guns*)

You may as well know, I'm Tokyo Jayne, the most wanted spy in the Far East. Every Man in the Army is looking for me.

BOB: I'll buy that. Look, honey, I—

    (SOUND: *MPs' whistles offstage*)

JAYNE: The MPs! Quick!

    (*the spies grab Bob, hustle him out*)

    (*all exit*)

    (*colonel enters with MP*)

COLONEL: Looks like they've flown the coop.

    (*they search apartment*)

This is a bad situation. This woman is very beautiful . . . Private Hope will be putty in her hands!

MP: You don't have to worry about Private Hope, sir. No woman's gonna twist him around her finger.

COLONEL: You're right. It was silly of me ever to doubt him. Nobody but a complete idiot would give up his career and everything he has just for a pretty face!

    MUSIC: *Oriental*

    (*Jayne enters in rickshaw pulled by native coolie*)

JAYNE: Get along, get a move on! Quickly! Chop-chop!

COLONEL (*to coolie*): Hold it—you look familiar! Aren't you Private Hope?

BOB: So solly, no spikkee Englis'. Goo'bye!

    (*rickshaw continues offstage*)

    MUSIC: *Playoff*

    (*blackout*)

Back on the plane for the flight to Korea, we were delighted to find that the crew had brought aboard mistletoe and a small Christmas tree. Suddenly I felt at home. For years, just about the only home I've had at Christmastime has been a Military Air Transport Service plane.

We were approaching the climax of the tour and everybody was keyed up. Korea, however, was a bleak country saddled with grinding poverty and the ruin of war. Although the shaky truce just signed had ended the fighting, it hadn't helped conditions in Korea. The armistice divided the industrial north from the agricultural south, where people lived in caves and mud hooches, gathering scraps of wood to get through the night. Cold winds were plentiful and trees were a rarity, so men trudged along the roads lugging stacks of branches on their heads.

We actually arrived on one of Korea's milder days. Only a few days before, it had been seven below. But since practically the whole of Kimpo Air Base had turned out to say hello to us in spite of the deep freeze, it didn't seem fair to say good-by without doing some kind of a show for them. So the troupe climbed aboard a flatbed truck and we did forty minutes of loud yelling, with no microphones to help us pipe up. This no-mike situation put most of us at a disadvantage—except Professor Colonna. His high note at the end of his usual rendition of "Ebb Tide" had the boys running for the air raid shelters with their mittens over their ears.

As usual, I'd worked up some special material to suit the surroundings:

"I've figured out why the Koreans wear the weird-looking double-decker hats they do. The upper deck has a rock in it to keep the man under it from blowing away.

"Jayne Mansfield drew quite a crowd when she got off the plane. That surprised me. I didn't think a couple of extra hills would be a novelty to the Koreans.

"We were all set to jeep into Seoul when I discovered Jerry Colonna was missing. It turned out he wasn't really missing. I just didn't recognize him. He had tucked the ends of his mustache into his mouth to keep it from freezing."

We were a pretty chilly group after that show as our little caravan tailed along behind the "Follow Me" jeep assigned to lead us into Seoul. We thawed out a bit when we discovered that almost half the population had turned out to greet us. It was very touching to see some of the younger Korean citizens run up to our slow-moving jeeps, shake our hands, swipe one of the gas cans or steal a spare tire. Even the pen I was all set to write my autograph with was swiped.

That was my first experience with the "slickey boys" of Seoul. The slickeys are the most accomplished sneak thieves in the world. They made *West Side Story* look like an Our Gang comedy. General George H. Decker, then commander in chief of the United Nations Command in Korea, told me that the average wage in South Korea was $92 a year. No wonder they stole.

In Seoul they tell a story about a GI who ignored his pals' warnings and ventured into the off-limits section of the city. An hour later he returned triumphantly, his hand in a vise-like grip on the button-down pocket of his jacket. "I've still got my wallet," he boasted. When he looked down, though, his pants were missing.

The guidebooks all tell you that Seoul is an ancient city, and many of its buildings date back to the fifth century. That must include the hotel where

A funny thing happened on the way to the geisha house   99

we stopped, which shall be nameless in this book. Actually, in terms of Korean culture, the Nameless was a modern hotel. Every john was a Genghis Khan and the whole thing was probably designed by a rising young architect named Sheraton the Conqueror.

We spent Christmas Eve doing a show in Seoul's modern International Theater for General Decker's UN forces. Its only concession to old Korean tradition was the dressing room chairs: they were nailed to the floor. I gave those servicemen a little Seoul food when I led off with, "You fellows certainly came a long way to avoid the draft.

"What with the sputniks and the intercontinental missiles flipping around in space, the people back home are so nervous it's a pleasure to be here in this rest area."

That day most of the cast had ransacked the town for Christmas presents. They picked up beautiful hand-hammered ash trays and intricately carved opium pipes for next to nothing. The crusher came when they tried to buy Christmas wrapping paper, which was in such short supply and long demand that it cost more than the presents they were supposed to wrap. Hedda Hopper wound up with the prize package. Some clown gave her a knitted shawl wrapped around four sheets of Christmas paper.

One of the biggest thrills of that tour was meeting Cardinal Spellman in Seoul. I had never actually met the cardinal before, though I'd worked in several of his New York Catholic Charities shows. I breakfasted with His Eminence at Major General Thomas J. Sands's headquarters on Christmas morning. The retinue accompanying the cardinal got quite a bang out of our ad-lib session.

When we shook hands I said, "Cardinal, it's amazing how far we've had to travel before we finally met."

"Yes," he said, "I'm glad we're not competing for audiences over here, although I understand we're playing some of the same spots."

I said, "Yes, I play them first. Then you come along after me and give the troops absolution." I couldn't let His Eminence have all the lines.

I introduced Al Scharper to the cardinal and explained that Al was editor of the show business bible, the *Daily Variety*. The cardinal didn't miss a beat: "I'm very pleased to meet you. I work for the other Bible."

After breakfast the troupe climbed aboard a fleet of twenty-passenger twin-rotor helicopters to fly from Seoul to Bayonet Bowl near the 38th parallel. The pilot made the trip memorable by pointing out the 38th parallel —almost directly below us and much too close—and told us that if we strayed to the north of it, we'd probably be shot at. We survived the flight okay, but the colonel who supervised the landing did nothing to ease our tension by remarking casually about the show site, "We've never had so many men congregate in one spot. It would be just like those bastards to fly over and bomb us today." Ho, ho, ho.

Seven thousand GIs of the 7th Infantry Division were perched on a hillside crouched in the snow, waiting for us to perform. There was a potbellied stove pumping out a little heat in our dressing room tent and we really huddled close to it. Three feet away was freezing. The engineering crew had rigged a hot blower to keep the band warm. They were red in back and blue in front. But those kids sitting in the snow, thousands of miles from home, didn't need any potbellied stoves and didn't need any blowers—they were a red-hot audience.

★

Here we are in Korea, the Miami Beach of the Far East.

How about this weather? All day long my undies have been creeping up on me looking for a place to hide. If they find one, I'm gonna crawl in myself.

I don't want to start any rumors, but I think there's a spy here. I saw one fellow with a tan.

They don't bother with roll call here. No sense counting noses. Nobody's got one.

In a climate like this you don't need a marriage ceremony. You just wet your lips, kiss the girl, and freeze till death do you part!

★

They laughed even harder when Erin O'Brien's act was interrupted by a voice with just a touch of brogue that yelled from the audience, "My name is Tom Coughlin." Erin replied, "A fine Irish boy like you deserves a kiss." And he got one on his cheek. In no time at all the place sounded like a mob scene of Pat O'Briens.

Hedda Hopper's specialty was delivering impertinent answers to questions about Hollywood. Despite the cold, she went through her routine in a thin lace shawl. We were congratulating her on her inner warmth when she confessed that she was wearing four or five dresses underneath. When Erin closed the show with "White Christmas," she had the real backdrop to go with it.

Two hours later, we choppered over to 1st Cavalry Division headquarters to entertain in another chilly setting, Wallenstein Bowl. It was five below zero as I introduced the members of the cast. They reluctantly broke away from their shivering huddle around the coffee urn to do their acts. Nobody cut his act despite the cold and a warning by our pilots that the fog tended to roll in thick and fast when the winter afternoon shadows begin to fall. Every time I'd come to a line I thought might let us get out of there before the weather hit, I was held back by the eyes of the men out front following the members of the cast as one by one they were hustled off to the waiting

A funny thing happened on the way to the geisha house   101

choppers. It was like the look on the faces of people at airports seeing other people off, or on the faces of your kids when you tell them you'll be going out for the evening. I'd start another routine, then another.

I couldn't help it. The shadows were getting longer and darker. The crew of the last chopper felt their way through the dim cabin counting noses. One that should have been easy to find was missing—mine. They figured it was the ham in me that wouldn't let me get offstage, so finally they came up and grabbed me firmly, leading me away shouting a last punch line.

I asked the pilot, "Which way is Seoul?"

"Who knows now?" he said. Then, seeing the shocked look on my puss, he quickly reassured me: "Don't worry. We've got the best natural compass in the world going for us. We take off and fly for three minutes and if anybody starts shooting at us, we'll know we've drifted over the 38th parallel."

As we lifted off into the gloom and looked down below, we could see the kids, thousands of them, forming into squads and squads into lines—marching against the snow to their barracks. And as far as the eye could see there were the trucks taking the troops back into the hills—a vast, lonely panorama. And as I turned away from the window I felt like a deserter.

A mighty weary group of us gathered at Yokota Air Base outside Tokyo to take off on the last leg of our journey home. I was ready to climb on board the Stratocruiser and sleep the whole way, but the Colonel Sanders chicken in me took over. I asked the pilot if the plane didn't seem a little tail-heavy to him. He nodded and said, "Your cast's been Christmas shopping. Unless we unload a few knickknacks, we may have to jettison the co-pilot."

I felt guilty about the stone Buddha I had latched onto in Tokyo for practically twice what it was worth. I had also brought along a few other trinkets in a large packing case. I was about to confess when I was saved by a timely tap on the shoulder. It was General C. G. Lessig, commander of Gilkerson Field SAC Base, asking me if I would mind stretching our itinerary to include a few lonely soldiers on Guam. "It's not far out of the way," he said, "and you'll have a chance to ride one of our SAC B-47 jets."

That decided me. I'd get a fast ride and my Buddha wouldn't get bumped. You should have seen the balding squire of Burbank sitting up there in the observer's seat of that big silver bird complete with oxygen mask, crash helmet, and chute. The pilot of the B-47, Captain James Stillson of Berkeley, took one look at me and suggested that I bed down in the narrow catwalk and knock off a couple hours of shut-eye. When I opened my eyes, the captain was shaking me, saying, "Crawl up in the co-pilot's seat and you'll see why I'm still in this business."

The co-pilot's seat is directly behind the pilot's perch. I pulled myself into it and took a look at the sun glinting on beautiful cloud formations; it looked like mounds of whipped cream with a splash of grenadine. As we moseyed along at six hundred miles per hour, the captain told me, "If you

102   *The last Christmas show*

want to see a little better, just pull the lever on the right-hand side. It'll raise your seat."

"You mean this lever with the red knob?" I asked.

"You and your death wish!" he yelled. "Get your hands off that!" Then he explained: "It's the ejector knob."

Dizzily I looked under the seat for a barf bag. It's a good thing they have a protective device on that knob or this would have been the last chapter of this book.

We made Guam in a little more than three and a half hours, and I spent most of the time wrapped around my St. Christopher medal. After we touched down I thought I must be showing signs of strain when the liaison officer suggested that I visit the naval hospital. It turned out that what he had in mind was a little give and take with the patients. I toured the wards for a couple of hours; I would have stayed longer, but they told me they needed all their beds.

After a quick stop at my bunk room, I joined the rest of the cast at the show site. Johnny Pawlek, the sound engineer, set up the equipment, checked the mikes, and restarched my spine. Gilkerson Field on Guam was used as a football stadium between USO shows. The general's "few lonesome men" turned out to be twelve thousand, the largest audience we played to on the whole tour. It was sunny, and the frostbite I'd collected in Korea did a sudden shift to the pink beginning of a nice even tan.

I told those airmen, "The Defense Department insisted that I play here. It's been a long time since you fellows have seen any action. They wanted to see if you could still take it.

"They were going to send Jack Benny, but Jack's sick. He had a horrible mishap. His electric blanket short-circuited and the four thousand bucks he had stashed in it went up in smoke.

"Jack has the only mattress in the world with a burglar alarm."

We took the scenic route home, heading for Kwajalein, a tiny speck in the Pacific, to refuel. I had planned on doing a quickie show there, so we had a whole hour to kill while the stage was being set up. I spent my time strolling barefoot along the coral-strewn beach collecting specimens for my son Kelly's shell collection. In no time at all I really hit the jackpot. I collected a sack of assorted shells, a two-inch cut on my big toe, and an angry red dose of sunburn.

After lugging my trophies back to my quarters, I dumped them on the bed, stripped to my shorts, and went to work on my wounds with mercurochrome and Unguentine. Hedda Hopper chose that moment to enter and greeted me with a quiet scream of horror. "Come on now, Hedda," I said. "Jayne's husband Mickey shows more skin than this by just unbuttoning his collar."

"It isn't that, Bob," she said, pointing a trembling finger at my bed. I glanced at my collection of beach debris and couldn't believe my eyes. Four of my "sea shells" were standing up on long hairy legs and were walking across my pillow!

I'm glad the door was as wide as it was, because Hedda and I both made it in a dead heat. My clothing would still be moldering in that quiet little cottage on Kwajalein if somebody hadn't explained to me about hermit crabs and their quaint habit of starting a new housing project every time a sea snail moves out of its old house.

Back at Hickam Field sometime after midnight, my travel-worn gypsies disembarked looking unhappily forward to a dreary inspection of our bags by customs officials. It could have taken hours if it hadn't been for my brother Jack, who happened to be leading the way.

As the customs man opened Jack's suitcase and prepared to make a microscopic inventory of its contents, Jack cautioned him, "Be careful. Don't cut your hand on the coral in there." The inspector jerked his hand out as if Jack had a sack of cobras. Hurriedly scratching a chalk mark on Jack's bag, he called nervously, "Next!" Jack's words went down the line like a brush fire. From that point on, everybody's bag was full of coral.

And so thanks to the Air Force and a small lie we had safely traversed two of life's major hazards—the Pacific Ocean and the United States customs. I wonder if Kissinger has to wait in line!

CHAPTER 10

She sins as well as she acts

In 1958 we ended up with a schedule that covered sixteen thousand miles in twelve days, doing shows for forty thousand servicemen and their families in seven countries. As I ran my eye down the list—the Azores, North Africa, Spain, Italy, Germany, Scotland, Iceland—it looked easy. The only way I could cover all that territory in such a short time would have been by rocket from Cape Canaveral.

I faced up to our military liaison man and asked in a mean voice, "Who dreamed up this crazy schedule? I've got a few rude words I'd like to say to that lame-brain." (I used a stronger noun than lame-brain.)

He looked me straight in the eye and said, "You can take it up with him any morning when you're shaving. That's him you'll see in your mirror."

I have to admit it. I was the guilty lame-brain (stronger word). We had received requests from friends and families of GIs stationed at various spots along our route asking us to do a show for them. After you write a few of these requests into your schedule, you find yourself making more stops than a suntan-lotion salesman in a nudist colony.

With travel time as tight as that it's no wonder things happened during the trip that I'd never bargained for. Somewhere along those sixteen thousand miles my blood pressure climbed out of sight, my pulse began to cha-cha, and I starred in a couple of blackouts that weren't in my script. When I was finally forced to take things easy, I could only thank God I'd signed up some performers who could carry a show all by themselves. Hedda Hopper, for one, had established herself as a regular on my Christmas safaris, God rest her gay, bubbling soul. After a long flight that left the rest of us limp, Hedda would skip off the plane looking as bright, fresh, and crisp as if she'd just stepped out of a fashion magazine.

Professor Jerry Colonna was as familiar to GIs round the globe as Spam and powdered eggs, but a lot more welcome. The professor didn't just sing a song, he lambasted it like a butcher pounding a slice of veal. His high

Jerry Colonna, Elaine Dunn, and Molly Bee, USS Forrestal *sick bay, Bay of Naples,
1958.*

note was terrifying; it sounded like the mating call of a pair of corduroy
pants. And what a traveler! You've heard of people falling asleep the minute they get on a plane? Colonna had to be carried on board. He was
such a sound sleeper he was listed on the manifest as baggage.

Among our newcomers were Randy Sparks, a folk singer I'd first seen at
the Village Vanguard in New York, and Elaine Dunn, a lovely young
dancer from my home town, Cleveland. I also signed on Molly Bee, a pert
and pretty young lady who could have stepped right out of a Norman
Rockwell *Saturday Evening Post* cover. Although she was still in her teens,

Molly was already a seasoned performer featured on the Tennessee Ernie Ford show. When she took over a stage, she socked a song with all the authority of Hank Aaron belting a home run.

We couldn't very well play eight countries in twelve days traveling Greyhound, so the Military Air Transport Service (MATS) came to the rescue with a pair of C-118s. Since almost every guy in the armed services has been flown by MATS at one time or another, I had a ball kidding my audiences all along the way about the planes:

"We flew up here in a C-118. That's not the model number. That's the year it was built. The No Smoking sign was in Latin. We thought they were kidding until the pilot came on wearing a toga and sandals. I don't know how old the plane was, but Lindbergh's lunch was still on the seat. And the plumbing was outdoors."

But I kidded with crossed fingers. MATS guys and gals have given up a lot of time they might have had off to ferry us safely all over the globe. That year, as our planes took off from Burbank and started their climb over the Sierras, I noticed Molly, Randy, and the other youngsters looking down at the San Francisco valley dropping rapidly behind us. They were already experiencing the strange sense of excitement that would go halfway round the world with them before they'd see that valley again. I understood how they felt. I've never started one of those trips without that same feeling.

Our first stop was McGuire Air Force Base at Fort Dix, New Jersey. We were scheduled to have dinner and take off immediately for the Azores, but our second plane had developed engine trouble back in California and had been forced to land at Edwards Air Force Base. We stayed at McGuire until it caught up with us, then took off the next morning after three hours' sleep.

We landed in the Azores in a near hurricane. When we got off the plane, the wind was blowing so hard it was raining sideways. We struggled over to a hangar as leaky as an old sieve to do a show for the island personnel. Inside there must have been seven hundred guys packed together like Norwegian brislings. The weather gave me the perfect lead-in for my monologue:

"They tell me that you get your share of mist here. Is it true that your dress uniform is a blotter? You gotta be a fast man on a weekend pass here; if you sit around just gabbing too long your date rusts. I know a lieutenant who got married, then spent the first three weeks of his honeymoon wringing out his bride."

It may have been a hangover from those jokes, but during the show, a strange feeling came over me. I actually felt tired. Afterward, we ate a quick dinner and clambered back into the two planes to take off for Port Lyautey, Morocco. As I sagged into my seat, I had to admit to myself that the old bones could really do with a little rest. Usually I'm a great one for racking up cat naps and snoozes, but on that flight there was no shut-eye for any of us. As soon as we left the Azores we banged into a thunderhead, and the plane tossed around like a soap bubble in a high breeze.

After doubling for table-tennis balls we landed at seven in the morning at Port Lyautey. When I wobbled off the plane and headed for my quarters, every nerve in my body yelped for sleep. But no luck. Captain Jack Counihan had scheduled a charity golf match, and I couldn't disappoint him no matter how groggy I felt. The jeeps were waiting and away we shot, scattering gravel.

A golf course under the relentless Moroccan sun is a hard par. The fairways were all sand, and every now and then there were little patches of grass. They were the traps. After that match I was so beat I could barely climb out of my divots. I hurried back to my quarters with the idea of grabbing an afternoon nap. Again, no dice. The cast was climbing into a convoy of command cars.

"What's up?" I asked sleepily.

Hedda Hopper told me they were going to Rabat to meet the Sultan, King Mohammed. That did it. I told myself I can always take a nap, a Sultan I didn't meet every day. I piled in and we were off.

As it turned out, I didn't meet a Sultan that day either. King Mohammed hadn't been told we were coming—or maybe he had. Anyhow, he wasn't at his palace. But his Cabinet chief, Abderahamane Naggai (now that's a name for you), took us in hand and guided us around the joint. Every door we went through had an armed guard of tough Moroccan soldiers in front of it. I asked, "Why all the guards?" It turned out there was temporary dissension among the tribes, and occasionally some of them swooped down from the hills and tried to make shish kebab of their enemies.

On our way back to Port Lyautey, we stopped in to take tea at the home of the Pasha of Kénitra, Abdel Hamid El Alaoui. Abdel was a stocky, round-faced, jovial type. I remember thinking, "Now here's a guy who really has a sense of humor." He laughed at each and every one of my jokes. I found out later he didn't understand a word of English.

Be that as it may, when I walked out on the stage at Port Lyautey that night, there was the Pasha in the front row flanked by an entourage of at least six aides. He laughed like crazy all through the show. Naturally when he laughed his aides laughed too.

Next day Charles W. Yost, then the ambassador to Morocco, took us on a fast tour of Rabat, which was a fascinating city, half French, half Moroccan. It was a crazy mixture of Paris and Casablanca. We wound up in the local medina, a native quarter not recommended for tourists. So instead of taking a quiet nap as I should have done, I spent the afternoon in an anthill of cutthroats, pickpockets, and shady characters. I was told

Berber band, Port Lyautey, Morocco, 1958.

they'd committed every crime in the book. And they were still at it. To me they were just snooty. Not one of them even asked for my autograph.

That evening we got back to Port Lyautey, and for the first time since I'd left Fort Dix, I undressed, got into a real bed, and slept. I was allowed to do that for a blissful ninety minutes. Then somebody shook me, and I was on my way to a hangar to do the show.

All that time a little voice had been whispering inside my head, "Slow down, stupid. Don't be a fool. You're overdoing it for a man of forty-two!" I should have listened. I really should have. That little voice knew my *real* age. After the show there was a big party; naturally I was there. I got

She sins as well as she acts   109

Les Brown at Port Lyautey, Morocco, 1958.

to bed at 3:30 A.M. and hopped up at 8 A.M. bleary-eyed, scraggly-tailed, and punchy.

There I was, after four and a half hours' sack time, standing on the Port Lyautey airstrip in the dawn's early light, saying good-by to our hosts, then stumbling aboard the plane. I had promised to do a show that afternoon for the Air Force at Morón in Spain. We'd been on African soil twenty-four hours.

After we were airborne a few minutes, we flew into our second in-flight thunderstorm, and lightning struck the plane. The blinding flash of white light and the crackling noise as that bolt streaked through the fuselage had many of us thinking that some ground-to-air missile had homed in on us. We made it through—somehow—and finally touched down at Morón on an airstrip glistening with rain. We squelched through puddles to the mess hall to lap up hot coffee.

Seventy-six hours had whizzed by since I'd left Burbank, and I'd slept seven of them. As I shook hands with the commanding officer, Colonel Ernest Nance, something inside my head went out of whack. I saw his welcoming smile through a haze. The walls of the room closed in on me. I shook my head to clear away the mental fog, but it was still there. I thought for a minute that some of the L.A. smog had tracked me down.

I was supposed to put on a show at Morón for several thousand Air Force men and their families. Instead, I ended up in the base hospital, stretched out on an examining table. My face had turned a ghastly white, and two young Air Force doctors were counting my pores or something. They were very thorough, and the more they were, the more worried I was. They listened to my chest, poked, prodded, then ran up and down my ribs a few times as if they were playing scales on a xylophone. "Look, fellas," I said, "just tell me what's haywire and let me out of here. I've got a show to do, you know."

But they took advantage of me while my mouth was open and popped a knockout pill into it. While I was dead to the world in the hospital, Hedda Hopper, Professor Colonna, Molly, Randy, Elaine, and Les Brown and his band started the show. I woke up a couple of hours later greatly refreshed. In fact, I felt so much improved that I went over to the hangar where the performance was going on and walked out on the stage for the last part of the show. The audience didn't know anything was wrong with me. I did, though. That Mother Nature you see on the TV margarine commercials had given me a warning bell—a red stop light.

That afternoon we flew to Madrid, one of the high points of the tour. We were in a real city for a change, billeted in a real hotel, the elegant Castellana Hilton. One of the reasons we had included Madrid was to get together with Gina Lollobrigida, who was making a film there. I had met her briefly a few years before. Since then she had become world-famous, one of the handful of cinema stars who booted Italy onto the map. My idea was to film a musical number with her for my NBC-TV show. First I had cabled our agents in Spain the following instructions: FIND OUT IF SHE CAN SING.

The reply had arrived next morning: SHE SINS AS WELL AS SHE ACTS. I stared at those seven words, wondering how to take them. I needn't have worried. I should have known her notes would be well rounded too. We were filming at Torrejón, a base near Madrid, and Gina sang "Non Dimenticar" ("Don't Forget"). Although not many of our boys understood the Italian lyrics, as Gina stood there in the spotlight shimmering in a gold lamé sheath, they got her message just the same.

Gazing at her sultry loveliness, I realized why pizza had become Italy's second most popular dish. Even her name is unusual. Gina Lollobrigida! It sounds like a stick being run along a picket fence. Believe me, the resemblance ends there.

She sins as well as she acts   111

Like all actresses whose beauty is their letter of credit at the bank, Gina was worried about how she'd look on TV. In a studio every shot is elaborately lighted, the angle is carefully considered, every shadow is perfection. And there we were shooting her in an aircraft hangar with crude field equipment, hoping the cameraman could see through the crowds to find the stage with his lens.

Gina was so worried that I decided to have a talk with Allan Stensvold, our genius cameraman. "Don't worry, Bob," Allan said, "she's a beautiful woman. We'll get all her beauty on film. All we need is a little light." He fiddled around with two lamps and a Zippo lighter, and when we looked at the finished film, it was tremendous. Gina has sent him Valentine cards with love and kisses from then to this day.

I've seen our sound man, Dave Forrest, do the same sort of thing. People would be hitting the mikes accidentally and I'd look at Dave to see how things were going. He'd give me the three-ring sign that meant fine. It had to be; when we got back to the States, those little rolls of tape were all we had to show for our efforts.

Back in Madrid, I ran into an old friend, our ambassador to Spain, John Davis Lodge. A member of an aristocratic Massachusetts family, John didn't let his lineage limit his activities. The last time I'd seen him was twenty years before at the Paramount studio, where he'd been Marlene Dietrich's leading man in *The Scarlet Empress*.

Bad flying weather scrubbed a show we were supposed to do for a contingent of U.S. airmen at Zaragoza, Spain, so the next scheduled stop was Naples. It was only a four-hour flight, but after two days of Spanish cooking we were all a little tail-heavy.

So was the plane. We were supposed to spend Christmas in Naples, so our band of traveling locusts had practically stripped the PX at the Madrid airport. The plane's hold was so loaded with Christmas goodies, we didn't know until we landed that we had accidentally shanghaied the sergeant in charge of loading. Somehow he had got wedged in between a case of castanets and a pearl-handled garlic press and couldn't get out.

When we got to the Vesuvio Hotel in Naples, I thought I'd impress one of my writers by telling him that Caruso had died in this hotel. I should have known better. Nothing is sacred in show business. He snapped back, "I didn't even know he sang here."

That night I was in my pajamas brushing my teeth when I looked out at the Bay of Naples and saw a sight I'll never forget. Half a dozen ships from the Sixth Fleet had pulled into port for the holidays. They were anchored in a row across the bay, hung with strings of twinkling Christmas lights all the way from crow's-nest to water line. Those ships blazing with necklaces of colored Christmas lights top every visual memory I've got.

Gina Lollobrigida and Allan Stensvold at Torrejón Air Base, Madrid, Spain, 1958.

Part of that armada was the aircraft carrier *Forrestal,* and we were going to do an open-air show on her deck for six thousand sailors. But the next morning the clouds were dark again. The skies opened up and dumped a steady, drenching downpour all day. We decided to postpone the show.

The next day the skies cleared and we climbed on board the *Forrestal.* The commanding officer, Captain Allen Shinn, thoughtfully volunteered to take me on a tour. I didn't realize what I was letting myself in for. The *Forrestal* is a sleeper jump from bow to stern. She's so enormous the captain himself hasn't seen all of her. After hiking the length of the deck, Les Brown quipped, "Now I know why they call it a poop deck!"

We finally came to rest and began setting up for the show. As we worked, dark clouds started gathering overhead once more. The wind was blowing in gusts, and there were whitecaps all around us on the bay. But hoping for the best, we kept on stringing cables and setting up lights. The bay was so choppy that even the huge *Forrestal* rocked a little.

The skies grew darker, but we started the show anyway. The wind made so much whistling noise in the microphones that our engineers had to borrow some woolen socks and pull them over the mikes. Soon it became obvious that we might not be able to finish before another storm zapped us. What to do?

The eager faces surrounding us made the decision for me: on with the show. Despite the wind blasts and an occasional shower of spray flung at us, things were going along fine. Just when I began to think I might thumb my ski nose at the weatherman after all, the last of my luck gurgled down the drain. Rain hit the deck with a roar. In a second or two all of us, players and audience alike, were soaked. There was no way to continue the show in those falling sheets of water.

We were willing to call it quits, but not the Navy. Two or three hundred sailors grabbed the stage, cameras, equipment, everything portable, and lugged it all to the huge plane elevator. The elevator slowly sank, carrying the stage and our whole show to the deck below, where it was sheltered from the rain. The sailors reassembled everything exactly as it had been on the deck above. An hour later it was "on with the show."

On Christmas Eve our little band gathered in the dining room of our hotel in Naples to have dinner together. There's something about Christmas Eve that makes people emotional, and we were all pretty subdued. But after a glass or three of vino we perked up enough to chirp "Deck the Halls with Boughs of Holly" and "Silent Night." As was our Christmas Eve custom, later on many of us went to midnight Mass at the beautiful cathedral, one of the most awe-inspiring in all Europe.

The next day we hopped to Vicenza to put on our Christmas show for the men stationed at the rocket base the United States had leased there. You begin to take flying for granted when you're making a long tour with a lot of stops and you climb in and out of a plane every day. But after the show in Vicenza we had a close call, much too close. By the time we got to the airfield, our planes were refueled and ready. The musicians and several members of the cast were already boarding the first plane when the pilot arrived. He sniffed the air, which was still laden with the fumes of the fuel that had been pumped into the planes' tanks. An alarm bell went

Jerry Colonna on USS Forrestal, *Bay of Naples, 1958.*

Hedda Hopper at Morón, Spain, 1958.

bong in his mind. He quickly had the plane cleared of all human beings. Every drop of fuel was immediately pumped out.

By mistake, the planes had been loaded with the kerosene-like fuel used by jet fighters stationed on that base. If our piston-engined bird had taken off, it would have died in mid-air.

And that's not my gig. I know what goes up must come down.

But I'm in no hurry about it.

Once we had the right kind of fuel in the tanks, we flew northward to Rhine-Main Air Base at Frankfurt, Germany. A big bash had been laid on for us there at the home of Lieutenant General F. W. Farrell, chief of the Berlin command. The general had leased an attractive dwelling in Frankfurt. When we walked in we found not only the general and his wife waiting for us, but also an elegant gourmet buffet dinner in a large room bathed by candlelight.

Madrid, 1958.

After our fuel fright and struggles with bad weather in Italy, the gracious and civilized surroundings, the good food and super drinks, and the hospitality of our hosts got to me. I hadn't known it, but ever since my physical letdown in Spain, I'd been revving my motor on nerve alone. One minute I was chatting away with a small group of people, and the next someone was grabbing my arm and saying, "What's up, Bob? You don't look so good."

I tottered over to a chair, sprawled in it, and watched the room and the people whirl by like horses on a carousel. Noticing my plight, several people helped me upstairs to the general's bed. I couldn't believe it: one minute I was great and the next I was laid out like a smoked salmon in the window of New York's Stage Delicatessen.

My previous illness in Morón hadn't kicked up much of a stir. For one thing, only a few people had known about it. This time was different. I'd

She sins as well as she acts   117

picked a fairly public place for my swan dive, and it's hard to zonk out in a roomful of people without attracting attention. I could hear one of my press outriders, Ursula Halloran, saying, "Don't get excited, folks. It's really nothing."

Ursula hadn't counted on the reporters who'd been waiting throughout the tour for some kind of news break. As is usual with them, news meant bad news; good news wasn't worth cable tolls. Within minutes, the press commandeered every phone in the vicinity. The next morning, I was reading the papers to find out how I felt.

The doctor wanted to move me to a hospital for a few days' relaxation, but I argued my case well and joined the troupe for our afternoon show at Hanau. What an ovation they gave me as I walked out on the stage. Talk about medicine, after that, everything looked beautiful to me. It was just another workday. When we finished at Hanau, we piled aboard DC-6s for the flight into Berlin.

Flying into Berlin's Tempelhof airfield is quite a trick. It's located in the middle of a heavily populated suburb, and is hemmed in on all sides by apartment buildings. As we circled over these man-made cliffs, I asked our pilot how he finds his way in. "It's a cinch, Bob," he said. "I follow the clotheslines right down the runway."

Looking like bums on the make for handouts, we drove to the brand-new Berlin Hilton. West Germany was in the midst of a bursting-out-at-the-seams business boom, which was one of the reasons the Russians have always wanted the Americans out of Berlin. The contrast between the good living possible in the democratic sector of Germany and the poverty in the eastern zone was a handicap to those giving Marxism the old hard sell.

When we checked into the hotel, what bugged out our eyes most was the crowds of people staring into the shop windows in the lobby. It was like Saturday night outside the nurses' shower tent. All day long people four and five deep were trying to peer in the windows.

When I got to my room the phone was ringing: Dolores calling from North Hollywood. Her first words were, "Are you all right, Bob?" I told her I was just great, that my seizure had been only temporary. When I finished she commanded, "Now stop lying and put your doctor on the phone!" That's one of the things I love about Dolores, she's one third Irish, one third Italian, and one third lie detector.

We gave our Berlin show that evening in the Fluegelhorst gym. At that time Russia was putting on extra-heavy pressure to try to push the Americans out of West Berlin, but the West Berliners were standing firm. A banner across the stage read, WEST BERLIN, THE OUTPOST OF DEMOCRACY!

That sign summed up how the audience felt. The monologue jokes about the Russians fetched roars!

Fieldhouse, Berlin, 1958.

★

Thank you very much. Here we are in West Berlin—that's a PX surrounded by Russians.

Flying here is really dangerous. This is the only place in the world where the pigeons travel by bus.

Sometimes the Russian fighter planes come alongside to look you over . . . and you hope they're just window-shopping.

She sins as well as she acts   119

Really, what a contrast, going from West Berlin to East Berlin . . . It's like giving up Rhonda Fleming for Ma Kettle.

You know there's quite a tense situation here. The Russians want to take over West Berlin. Of course, that was before I arrived!

I know one thing. The Russians will never take over the Berlin Hilton . . . Not at those prices!

Yes sir, this is a hot spot right now. And you know, the people over here really know me. Whenever I walk down the streets of Berlin, everybody follows me yelling and cheering. Anybody know what a Schweinehund *means?*

★

After almost every show several GIs come up and say hello, or shake hands, or talk about having seen me at some other base or camp. At Fluegelhorst one youthful GI pulled a new one on me. As he shook my hand, he said, "My father told me if I ever met you, to say hello for him."

"That's great," I replied. "Who's your father?"

"You don't know him," he told me, "but he saw you in 1944 on Guadalcanal."

That aged me plenty. I could barely croak out, "I hope your grandfather caught me at Appomattox. I knocked 'em dead there!"

We played a three-day stand in West Berlin, and during our stay several members of the group went sight-seeing in East Berlin, the Russian sector. My press agent, Frank Liberman, tried to strike up a conversation with a soldier who stood guard at the Russian War Memorial. When Frank walked up to him and said, "Hello, Ivan," the Russian soldier at first stared impassively, then he gave a grudging nod. Frank knew how to break the ice. He held out a $5 bill and pointed at the hammer-and-sickle insignia on the collar of the Russian's tunic. Using sign language, Frank indicated he'd like to make a deal. The Russian looked around cautiously, took Frank's money, then removed the emblem from his uniform and forked it over.

It was so dismal in East Berlin that I was almost glad our trip was on its last leg. The way I'd been feeling, that made the trip and me even. I was looking forward to the short fuel stop at Prestwick, Scotland. I knew that while the planes were being refueled I'd have almost two hours to browse among the kilts and sporrans in the local PX. I should have known better. The moment we touched down, the commanding officer told us that some Air Force families were watching a movie nearby, so we trotted over. The projectionist hit the stop button on the film when we trooped in. I ran through a few routines onstage, then I made a mistake. I asked for questions from the audience.

Unless you happen to be Art Linkletter, asking for questions is always a mistake if there are children in the crowd. A little kid in the front row had one all cocked and aimed at me. He fired it: "When are they gonna start the movie again?"

A long hour later we were airborne again, this time headed for Iceland. I learned afterward that our second plane had had to turn back to Prestwick to pick up a drummer who had dallied too long in the snack bar. After the plane was in the air once again, the drummer remembered the saxophone player, who'd gone to the men's room. A check of the plane revealed the sax player wasn't on board, so the plane had to turn back and make a second landing. The pilot insisted that another nose count be made before the plane took off again. "That won't be necessary," Les Brown said. "Get out your instruments, fellows, and strike a chord. I'll know then if anyone's missing!"

Despite the dark and freezing cold when we landed at Keflavik, an Air Force band was standing beside the runway playing "Thanks for the Memory." When I asked an officer to please get these guys out of the cold, he said, "Shhh! It would be bad for their morale and hurt their pride. They've been practicing that thing all week!"

Those GIs at Keflavik were really homesick, and when we did our show it wasn't hard to tell what they were most homesick for. Two of our chicks, Molly Bee and Elaine Dunn, drove them wild. The rotation system was their biggest gripe, so I hit them with, "At night it's very quiet here. All you can hear are two things: the wind blowing and the sobbing of a sergeant who doesn't have enough points to go home!"

The show went over so big it was 3 A.M. before we got back in the planes. A few minutes later we were headed over the North Atlantic toward our last stop before home, Goose Bay, Labrador. I immediately fell fast asleep in my seat. I was having a terrific dream—lining up a putt at the Lakeside Country Club—when I felt someone shaking me. It was the pilot, Captain Ray Coddington. "Excuse me, Bob," he said, "but we're flying over some weather stations. I thought you'd like to say hello to the men down there."

The plane was like a flying mattress. Everyone lay sprawled over seats and floor snoozing away. I climbed over a carpet of bodies to the captain's cabin. Someone handed me a microphone. Standing behind the captain's seat, I talked by radio to those weather-station boys somewhere down there below us in the dark.

The first voice I heard identified himself as an officer at Ocean Station Bravo. "How're you doing up there, Bob?" he asked me. "Sorry we didn't get to see any of your shows."

"You guys stationed out here away from all the traffic and urban sprawl have got it made," I said. "How'd you get the job—political pull?"

His voice crackled back, "They *had* to give us this job. We own the thermometer!"

Butch Stone and Stumpy Brown at Keflavik, Iceland, 1958.

The last Christmas show

Imagine being in an ad-lib session at four in the morning twenty thousand feet over the North Atlantic!

"I'll write to Washington," I said, "and have your option picked up for another four years' stay out here. I don't need your kind of competition, brother."

I woke up Jerry Colonna, Molly Bee, and Randy Sparks so they could get into the act too. Colonna sang his fog-dispelling version of "Mandalay," Randy did a few numbers, and Molly sang and talked with a couple of southern boys in the weather ship's crew. That night our radio was the busiest party line in the North Atlantic.

As Ocean Station Bravo faded out of range, the Coast Guard weather ship *McCullough* came in. So we stayed on with them. When they faded we worked a station on the Pinetree early-warning radar line.

Molly talked to one boy from a place called Belt Buckle, Tennessee. After singing a song for him, she asked him what else he'd like to hear. His lonely voice came back, "Don't fret about songs, ma'am. I like it when you clear your throat."

We landed in Goose Bay, Labrador, at dawn just long enough to freshen up, eat breakfast, and say good-by to our MATS crew, who had piloted our planes safely for more than fourteen thousand miles. As they boarded another plane to fly back to their base near Washington, D.C., we gave them a round of applause. As I shook hands with Captain Coddington, who had seen us through all those hairy moments, I said, "I wish I could steal you from the Air Force. Have you ever thought of going into show business?" He looked me in the eyes, and said, "No thanks. It's too risky!"

Mort Lachman, Jack Hope, Steve McQueen (seated), and John Chambers, Johnny Pawlek (standing) en route to Alaska, 1959.

The last Christmas show

CHAPTER 11

To Naknek and back

In 1959 we headed north to Alaska once more with a bagful of stars for our Christmas show. With us on his first tour was a good-looking young actor, Steve McQueen, who brought along the actress he was married to then, Neile Adams. Neile made a welcome addition to the group. Her singing and dancing turned out to be among the highlights of the show. We talked Frances Langford out of retirement. She joined us with her husband Ralph Evinrude—who came by outboard motor. And for a touch of nostalgia we had Skinnay Ennis, one of the greatest band leaders who ever hid under an airline seat.

We were going to see a lot of wildlife and unexplored regions, but we took along our own natural wonder as well. After a year off Jayne Mansfield had signed on with us again. Jayne loved publicity, and after a few hours in the air she got restless with only the plane's motors going for her.

When we landed at McChord Air Force Base, Jayne went to the telephone. At the time we didn't know whom she was calling or why. We left a few minutes later and it was late evening by the time we landed at Elmendorf Air Force Base in Anchorage. Snow was falling heavily, and it was bitter cold. The plane taxied in and the white stuff was so deep we were afraid we'd never be seen again. What a way to go . . . a funny snow man.

By the time they dug me out I looked around at Jayne and somebody had slipped a lion cub in her arms. Every photographer in the fiftieth state was taking her picture. The light went on in my head—that was what the phone call from McChord Field was about.

When they were finished with the pictures she dropped the lion cub and had nothing more to do with it. If you ever want to have your cool tested, try shaking hands with a general and his staff while a lion is nibbling at your bobby socks. But Jayne got the pictures she wanted and they were going out over the wire services even before the cub buried his teeth in my ankle bone.

At most of the bases I visit, the cast and crew get transported from the

Tony Romano, Patty Thomas, Jerry Colonna, Frances Langford, Jayne Mansfield, Steve McQueen, Neile Adams, Peter Leeds at Ladd Air Force Base, Alaska, 1959.

airport to the show site by jeep or staff cars. There were none at Elmendorf, just a few dogsleds equipped with natural air conditioning. Fortunately, the hangar where the show was going to be held was only a few hundred yards away. So we all decided to mush that far—that is, all of us except Steve McQueen. His hobby was racing sports cars, so he took over a sled and set out to discover how much dog power his team of huskies could generate. He soon found out. His team did nothing but fight with the dogs pulling the other sleds. Steve gave up and decided to stick with horsepower.

By this time my old *Twelve O'Clock High* buddy, Frank Armstrong, Jr., was in charge of the Alaskan command. He made a warm welcoming speech at Elmendorf. It was the only warmth in the hangar. I tried to follow him with:

★

It's hard to believe that since I was last up here this great territory has become a state of the Union. Just think, all this slush is now government property.

Yes sir, Alaska is officially a state. Now they can send you here even when you haven't been court-martialed.

★

126   *The last Christmas show*

Steve McQueen, Anchorage, Alaska, 1959.

The GI audience cheered that one right into the introduction of Frances Langford's opening song.

There were no dull moments in the show, especially with La Mansfield along. She could start an avalanche just by bowing. I asked the audience, "Would you like to hear Jayne sing?" A GI shouted, "We just like to see her breathe." That kid should have been given a field commission on the spot.

We were assigned quarters at the "Chateau," a French Provincial Quonset hut where I'd stayed before. In all fairness, its rooms were fairly comfortable and not bad-looking. We had nothing to complain about except the heating problem—and that wasn't what you'd think. To keep everything from freezing solid (including us), the Chateau was kept hotter than where Bing is going to go. Outside, of course, it was still below zero, but that was a hard fact to remember inside that steam room. Jerry Colonna opened the window once, took a deep breath, and the water on his brain froze over.

The Chateau was the only really warm place for miles around. We returned to defrost after each of our excursions to outlying bases. The food was more than okay, with a menu ranging from king crab to caribou steak and back again.

After doing a couple of shows a day, we spent our R-and-R time in the Chateau rumpus room. I don't know whether it was out of habit or boredom but the troupe members whiled away the time entertaining each other. Tony Romano would strum his guitar, Colonna would unleash his trombone, and Frances Langford was always good for a couple of songs. But it was Ralph Evinrude who wound up getting the most laughs.

Big-hearted Ralph was always ready to grab the tab when one actually found its way into our midst, which naturally had something to do with his popularity rating. He made Perry Como look like a flash act. One night he really surpassed himself. He snored right through Colonna's impression of an air raid siren. During this battle of noise pollution the waiter appeared with the check. Colonna took the check, put a pen in Ralph's hand, guided him through his signature, added a tip, and Ralph never missed a "zzzzz."

Whenever the temperature rose above zero, we'd sneak in a little shopping. Souvenir shops in Anchorage went in big for primitive desk sets and ornaments carved out of ivory.

Fur was another big thing with the local craftsmen. They tried their hand at working it into bow ties and lapel or blouse decorations that were supposed to look like baby seals. It gave me quite a start the first time I saw one pinned on La Mansfield's blouseful of goodies. It looked like a muskrat on the moon.

Some of the outlying bases we played had names that must have been dreamed up by the poet of the Yukon, Robert W. Service. One scarcely habited ice flow near Naknek was called King Salmon. General Nick Nicrasson, the Air Force's head man in those parts, flew out there with us.

When we landed at King Salmon all you could see were ice and snow. There were no trees, no rocks, and none of those black skid marks left by previous planes. The landing field was so smooth the plane couldn't skid— it just "slud" to a stop. I didn't have to worry, though. The pilot set the plane down so deftly that it came to a stop easily—20 short feet from the side of a sheer outcrop of big rock mountain.

King Salmon was then—and probably still is—a pretty important radar base. Because of its isolation, the chilled souls stationed there were relieved every three months so they wouldn't suffer from snow blindness or become a bunch of shivering crazies.

The natives up around Naknek think it's spring when the temperature jumps up to thirty below. Since everything was frozen solid, there wasn't much action for the men stationed at King Salmon. As a result they'd become extraordinarily weather-conscious and were always watching the thermometer. You couldn't blame them—it was the only thing up there with a figure.

Nobody walked around outside at King Salmon unless his brains had congealed and he didn't know what he was doing. Everything was connected by long, nightmarish tunnels. If moles wore mukluks, you could call it a mole-like existence. We emerged from one of the tunnels into a huge mess hall big enough to hold more than a thousand starving servicemen.

I always tried to do my eating before a performance. It wasn't so much that I wanted to feed the butterflies, but why challenge a mess sergeant after he's seen your act. This particular mess sergeant, however, had gone all out. The main course was an enormous ham sculpted to resemble a suckling pig, complete with an apple stuffed into a carved-out mouth. It tasted as good as it looked, but I couldn't help wondering if that GI disciple of Escoffier was trying to tell me something.

After that hammy lunch we gave our show in a hangar. The planes had just been moved out, and there were enough gas fumes left to make a cigarette a dangerous weapon. Smokers were ordered to do their inhaling outside, at thirty-five below. I could tell by the color of those GI faces how much of my audience was entertained enough to keep from slipping out for a cigarette break. I felt like Picasso during his blue period. It may have had something to do with my patter:

Well, here I am in Alaska. So much for your early-warning system!

But I'm happy to be here with you gentlemen, walruses, seals, and caribou at King Salmon. Alaska's a state now and everybody has equal rights.

I was anxious to get here. When I saw the Air Force recruiting poster for King Salmon, and it showed golf, water skiing, and outdoor barbecues, I thought they were kidding. Then not long ago I saw a second lieutenant turning crisp, brown, and succulent on a charcoal spit outside.

I'll never forget those four hundred lost souls manning an installation in that white desolation. There wasn't even an Eskimo igloo for hundred of miles. Still, they loved me in King Salmon; I must have been a welcome change from the usual spectator sport of walrus mating.

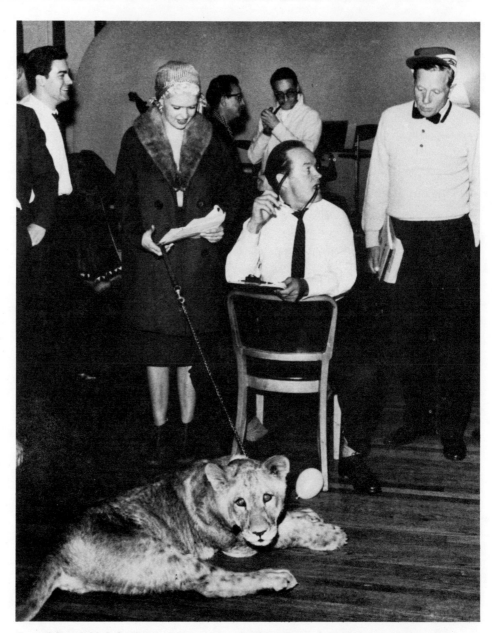

Jayne Mansfield, John Rapp, Mort Lachman, Jack Hope at Anchorage, Alaska, 1959.

Three hours and fifteen minutes after we arrived in King Salmon we were off the stage and one plane was swimming back upstream to Elmendorf and Christmas Eve dinner. The flight was pretty festive since everybody, including ground control, was in a yuletime mood. Coming into Elmendorf, I was in the cockpit talking on the radio to the tower. I asked the tower man, "When are you going to clear us for landing? We're late for Christmas dinner."

"You can land as soon as we get this big red-faced guy with the reindeer out of the flight pattern," he replied.

The last Christmas show

Christmas Eve at Elmendorf looked as if it was copyrighted by Hallmark. We were surrounded by tall pines, their branches heavy with snow. The sunlight bouncing off the snow-clad mountains blinded us with its brilliance. The blanket of snow was disturbed by hoof prints where wandering moose had passed. The only man-made thing around was the deep ruts left by the tires of a jet bomber.

General Armstrong gave us a Christmas Eve party that was really something else. At each seat were silver cigarette lighters engraved with our names and the symbol of the Alaskan command. By then just about everything that moved in Alaska had seen our show, so we had to come up with something different by way of entertainment. We did some special lyrics to the tune of my standby, "Thanks for the Memory." We incorporated into the lyrics the names of all the officers and men who had made us feel so royally welcome. Everybody in the cast came up with something unexpected. Jayne Mansfield, of all people, sang "White Christmas" . . . and beautifully. Somewhere beneath that blond hair and that plastic make-up was a lovely young woman singing softly and meaning every word of it.

She made three Christmas trips with us altogether and appeared on many of our shows, and each visit was a delight. The audience loved her, the crew adored her, even the other girls in the cast liked her. She had joy. She had bounce. She was an upper all the way. She had fantastic style. I could never figure it out. One moment she was the most naïve little girl in the world and the next minute you had the feeling she was putting the whole world on.

She had a pool that was pink and heart-shaped . . . and that was Jayne, pink and heart-shaped. I really miss her.

Janis Paige, Anita Bryant, Jerry Colonna, Andy Williams, Zsa Zsa Gabor, Delores Gay at Guantánamo Bay, Cuba, 1960. (U. S. Navy)

CHAPTER 12

When you're hot you're hot and when you're not you're not

In 1960 we were booked on the Bikini Circuit: the Panama Canal zone, Puerto Rico, Antigua, Eleuthera, and Guantánamo, in Cuba. In 1961, just as we had accustomed ourselves to Don Juan and señoritas our extremist in the Pentagon mapped out a tour of dismal. Argentia, a soggy naval base on the tip of Newfoundland; Harmon Air Force Base, a vital SAC link, also in Newfie; Goose Bay, a nice little ice plant on the overpopulated shores of Labrador; and of course my two home towns, Sondre Strom and Thule, Greenland, where it's always dark and it's just as well. I've got to be honest. There's nothing worse than a frosted sun tan.

We had a fantastic cast for the Caribbean tour. We had a young recording star by the name of Anita Bryant who was married to a young ex-disc jockey called Bob Green. Then we really got lucky. We captured Andy Williams, who had not long been a single. It's wonderful how they discovered Andy. He always sang great, but one day they took Kay Thompson from in front of him and there he was. He borrowed a sweater from Perry Como and it was instant stardom. And we had Janis Paige, who stole one of our early television shows when she came to us from *Pajama Game*. And of course we had Stash Colonna and Les Brown. To make sure it was a quiet, peaceful, pleasant trip we hired an inconspicuous little waif who had emigrated from Hungary, who called herself Zsa Zsa Gabor.

I remember when I called Zsa Zsa on the phone to invite her, she said, "Dear, dear what's your name. I'd be delighted to come but it's impossible. However, darling, in case I could, would it be all right if I sent a few gowns out to wardrobe at NBC for alteration?" But I knew Zsa Zsa had decided to go. An hour later, a Bekins van pulled up outside of NBC with her entire wardrobe.

Zsa Zsa joined the troupe at Ramey Air Force Base in Puerto Rico and

Anita Bryant, Zsa Zsa Gabor, Janis Paige, Delores Gay at San Juan, Puerto Rico, 1960.

The last Christmas show

Marine fighter detachment, Guantánamo Bay, Cuba, 1960.

immediately took over the entire base. She came off the plane with an entourage of seven carrying her luggage. None less than a full bird colonel. She sent a general out to find a hair dryer. When he came back with a hair curler instead of a hair dryer she demoted him.

We usually carry one make-up man and one hairdresser for the whole troupe, and that's usually enough—unless you have Zsa Zsa. I don't know how she does it. I don't know whether she bribes people or whether it's a superb sell she does with that Hungarian accent you could cut with a strudel knife; whatever her method she stole the make-up man and the hairdresser for herself. The rest of the girls in the troupe had to fake it.

The next day was Christmas Eve, time for our annual party for the troupe. The crew was all there and all the male members of the cast. But none of the girls showed up except Zsa Zsa. We loitered over our drinks, held dinner as

When you're hot you're hot and when you're not you're not   135

long as possible—the girls still didn't show up. Finally a note was hand-delivered to me. The girls were on strike and would remain on strike until such time as the make-up man and the hairdresser were returned. You talk about delicate negotiations, eye-level détentes, I never argued so persuasively in my life. Zsa Zsa finally agreed to release the hostages. Peace was restored till show time on Christmas Day, when, of course, the hairdresser and the make-up man were missing again and the general's staff was again carrying luggage for Zsa Zsa. We did have a funny spot with Zsa Zsa. I can't remember all of it but some of the jokes were:

(*Zsa Zsa enters*)
(*applause*)
ZSA ZSA: Thank you, Bob . . . (*to audience*) . . . and thank you, darlings.
(*blows kisses at audience*)
BOB: I'm over here whenever you're ready.
ZSA ZSA: You'll have to forgive me, Bob . . . I've never seen this many men before.
BOB: She means at one time.
ZSA ZSA: Are these boys all Air Force?
BOB: We got everything here, Zsa Zsa . . . (*pointing*) . . . that's Army . . . they're Coast Guard . . . and those sailors are off the battleship *Utah*.
ZSA ZSA: Why are their uniforms wet?
BOB: It docks tomorrow.
ZSA ZSA: What a wonderful country America is . . . Imagine sending all these fellows down here on vacation. Maybe I'll become a WAC.
BOB: You're closer than you think. I'm only kidding, honey. You don't mind a little ad-libbing, do you?
ZSA ZSA (*laughs*): Of course not, I like it. And I liked it at rehearsal too.
BOB: I hope you like it on the way home on the banana boat. You're looking very glamorous today. Is that a new set of fatigues?
ZSA ZSA: Bob, this is not fatigues . . . this is my combat suit.
BOB (*to audience*): Battle stations?
(*to Zsa Zsa*) Zsa Zsa, I don't know how you do it, but you seem to get more beautiful every year.
ZSA ZSA: I'm glad to hear you say that . . . I was afraid I was losing my touch.
BOB: What gave you that idea?
ZSA ZSA: Well, I walked back to my quarters last night and I had the strangest feeling that I wasn't being followed.

BOB: Just for the record, are you married or single now?

ZSA ZSA: Single . . . I think.

BOB: Tell me, Zsa Zsa, as one of the true scholars in the field, how do you feel about American men?

ZSA ZSA: Well, it's hard to say, they're all so different. Cary Grant, well, he's a man of the world. Jack Kennedy . . . he's the boyish type. And Marlon Brando . . . he has animal attraction.

BOB: What about me? Have you left the dessert for last?

ZSA ZSA: Well, Bob, you're partly man of the world, partly boyish, and partly that wonderful animal attraction.

BOB: Yeah, but how would you describe me?

ZSA ZSA: I don't know the American word, but in Hungary we call it goulash.

Poor Zsa Zsa . . . her parents were so poor she had to use the same first name twice.

Flashlight show, Antigua, British Antilles, 1960.

When you're hot you're hot and when you're not you're not 137

Peter Leeds, Jerry Colonna, Andy Williams, Zsa Zsa Gabor, Anita Bryant, Janis Paige, Delores Gay, Les Brown in the finale, Guantánamo Bay, Cuba, 1960.

Christmas Eve at Gitmo I went to midnight Mass with the crew and I noticed the chaplain really worked very dramatically. He delivered his sermon walking up and down in the aisle. I turned to our director, Jack Shea, and whispered, "Do you get the feeling the chaplain's a little show biz? Do you think it's because of us?"

And Jack whispered back, "I know it's because of us. He's got to work that way so the people can hear him. We borrowed the church's public address system for the show tomorrow."

Somehow we got along without Zsa Zsa the next year. In 1961, when the

Ramey Air Force Base, Puerto Rico, 1960.

Defense Department dared me to go back to Greenland, I called Jayne Mansfield and asked her to "come along to Thule with me."

"It sounds so wonderful, Bob," she breathed. "I've never been to South America before."

We were also lucky enough to bag that blond and beautiful femme unique, Dorothy Provine. And Anita Bryant was back and she brought her husband again. I'm the kind of man who can make the same mistake twice. As the icing on my baked Alaska, I also signed up Miss World, Rosemarie Frankland from England.

One of our first stops was the Riviera of the North Atlantic, a base called Frobisher on Baffin Island. It's so far out in the Atlantic that even then it cost a dollar to send a postcard to it. But with a population of five counting caribou and ice worms, there wasn't much of anybody to send postcards to anyway.

Professor Jerry Colonna and Les Brown and his band joined me and my toothsome foursome and we were off to nature's icebox. When I asked the pilot where Frobisher was on the map, he said, "It's not on the map."

When you're hot you're hot and when you're not you're not   139

Jerry Colonna, Dorothy Provine, Anita Bryant, Jayne Mansfield, Miss World (Rosemarie Frankland) in Newfoundland, 1961.

"How do we get in there?"

"With the weather they usually have, by boat. It's the only SAC base in the world that uses kayaks for transportation."

But we were lucky. We came in on one of the three crystal-clear days they had that year. We played to an audience of men from the American Air Force, Canadian Air Force, Canadian Royal Navy, and Royal Canadian Mounted Police. Jayne pulled a good one. She looked out at the Royal Canadian Mounted Police in their bright red blouses and said, "I didn't know you were real. I thought you were just in the funny papers." The Mounties just smiled warm, fatherly smiles—sex appeal sure can make up for a lot of diplomatic boo-boos.

The last Christmas show

Mounties and Jerry Colonna at Goose Bay, Labrador, 1961. (U. S. Army)

Air Force Secretary Zuckert at Thule, Greenland, 1961.

The last Christmas show

Jerry Colonna, Les Brown, Onnie Morrow, Jayne Mansfield, Dorothy Provine, Rose-marie Frankland, Anita Bryant at Frobisher Bay, Arctic Circle, 1961.

The weather was as good as our audiences. It held up through our arrival in Thule, where it was clear and quite warm, somewhere barely below zero. For those parts that was practically a heat wave.

Secretary of Air Eugene Zuckert, who had come along with us, and I put on all the long johns we could find before going out on an official jaunt to open an ice road between the base and a nearby Danish village. Later I found out that the road had been officially opened three times that week. I guess they opened it after every blizzard.

We were scheduled to do two shows because the gym couldn't begin to hold all the GIs on base. The afternoon show went off okay. The place was packed—maybe five thousand guys squeezed in and roaring away. But just as we were winding it up, a voice came over the PA system announcing that a Phase One had been declared. That meant that winds up to 40 m.p.h. had suddenly come up. Actually it was pretty normal for the area—just a hurricane. By the time we left the gym, Phase Two was announced. Every-one said it only meant things were a little rougher and tougher, with winds

When you're hot you're hot and when you're not you're not   143

up to 60 m.p.h. It didn't sound like much, but when I stepped outside the door, I was blown sixty feet off the course to my car before I beat my way back. It was impossible to move outside alone. In fact, there was a rule against going outside without a group. The only way to make it was to lock arms with three or four people and stagger through blinding snow, feeling your way in the pitch black.

Within thirty minutes we had advanced to Phase Three, and all the so-called roads were blocked with cars that had been abandoned in snowdrifts. Everyone was supposed to take cover. We barely made it back to our quarters, where we sat waiting for the weather to do a little ladder climbing. Instead the PA system announced that a Phase Four was expected. That was the ultimate: winds over 100 m.p.h. Everyone was confined to quarters, emergency rations were issued, and sandbags were piled around the commanding general.

Then the general announced that the evening show would be canceled. I begged him to hold off for a while, telling him that if it was at all possible, the cast wanted to do the show. He said, "Wonderful, Bob. But I can't guarantee you much of an audience on a night like this." So we sat back to wait, crossing our fingers, hoping.

Mort Lachman remembers us all sitting there in the officers' club when they announced that the storm had risen to Phase Four—that's Army talk for grab the stove, there goes the roof. Mort was sitting next to Anita Bryant and her husband.

Anita asked him, "What do you think's going to happen?"

Mort said, "Oh, we'll do the show, don't worry about it."

"How can we do a show? They just announced a Phase Four."

Mort, who loves to put Anita on, said, "Because Bob is talking to the Man."

Anita said, "What man?"

"There's only one—the Man," and Mort pointed skyward.

"How dare you say a thing like that!" Anita is very religious.

"Would *I* tell you a thing like that if it wasn't true? I don't take these things lightly either, you know. It's happened before. Typhoons, plagues, floods. Then Bob talks to the Man and the show goes on. You'll see, in thirty minutes it'll clear and the show'll go on."

Anita moved across the room to another chair, a safe distance away. She didn't want to be struck by the bolt of lightning.

Sure enough, ten minutes later the wind was still howling, but the buildings weren't leaning quite so much. About fifteen minutes before show time it went down to Phase Three and by show time we were in Phase Two and the show could go on. We played to a jam-packed house. There was standing room only—on the rafters. As midnight neared the guys were so emotional

The last Christmas show

Les White, Mort Lachman, Johnny Rapp, Bill Larkin at Sondre Strom, Greenland, 1961.

When you're hot you're hot and when you're not you're not   145

Jayne Mansfield at Argentia, Newfoundland, 1961. (U. S. Air Force)

they started to scream. It came out of their guts and it went on and on. It was an almost agonizing scream of loneliness.

We closed the show with everybody singing "Silent Night," and it was so moving, it was unbelievable. In fact, it was almost unbearable. The show was perfect.

I made it back to my quarters and stretched out in my bunk pooped, but feeling pretty happy. We had wrapped up another trip without a mishap.

Then the phone rang.

It was Jayne, and she was hysterical. When I finally simmered her down I discovered she had lost a diamond earring.

"Jayne," I said, "look around the floor. On second thought, have your husband, Mickey, do it. I know it's hard for you to look down."

"Bob, you don't understand," she said. "I lost it out in the snow."

"Go back to bed," I said. "It's pitch dark outside. It's twenty below and

146   *The last Christmas show*

Goose Bay, Labrador, 1961.

there's a gale blowing. No sane man is going to search fifty thousand acres of snow for a diamond earring."

There sure was a lot of insanity there. A few minutes later I noticed lights going by my window. I looked out and there were at least a thousand GIs with flashlights searching for Jayne's diamond.

They never found it, but Jayne did. By mistake, she'd put both of them on one ear.

Bayonet Bowl, Korea, 1962. (U. S. Army)

The last Christmas show

1962

CHAPTER 13

Filet of Seoul

Just before Christmas 1962, the Perry Como show headed for Guantánamo, in Cuba, for a double-barreled TV attack against Castroites and Como's other competition, the "Beverly Hillbillies." In a second pre-Christmas wave, Ed Sullivan's commandos waded ashore. Not to be outdone, the Hope troupe boarded a MATS cargo jet and headed west to Japan, Korea, Vietnam, Formosa, Okinawa, Guam, and the Philippines. We had a great cast on board. In addition to such regulars and semi-regulars as Colonna, Anita Bryant, and Les Brown, I'd signed up Lana Turner, Janis Paige and the reigning Miss U.S.A., Amedee Chabot.

We were just three hours out over the Pacific when the Defense Department canceled our shows in Nam. They felt that a group our size—and with our talent—would probably draw tremendous audiences. In a combat area like Vietnam that might shape up as an unnecessary risk to both us and the troops. There's no arguing with the Defense Department so we settled for a reduced schedule: ten days to fly twenty thousand miles and do seventeen shows. For our crew that was like only playing the front nine.

I had settled in for a long winter's nap expecting to wake up in Tokyo, but as soon as we landed and I stepped off the plane somebody threw a lei around my neck. Either we had a very confused navigator or somebody had transformed Tokyo into Honolulu. The way the men with the solid-gold yen have been buying up Hawaii these days, that wouldn't have been so surprising.

The explanation was an even simpler one. While I was snoozing away, the plane had been bucking 110-m.p.h. head winds, so it was running pretty low on kerosene. Using his noggin, the pilot had turned the wick down and headed for Honolulu.

Not being one to waste a golden opportunity, I called my good friend General Emmett "Rosy" O'Donnell, who was head of our Air Force in the Pacific, to say hi. Always hospitable, Rosy invited me for lunch. I asked him if I could bring a few friends. He blithely agreed, so I hijacked a bus, and ten minutes later I was knocking at his front door with the plane crew, technical crew, cast, and band in tow. We polished off everything that didn't move—the turkey, the ham, the potato salad, the scotch, the bourbon, the cornflakes, and two candy canes. For dessert the still-hungry band ate a bowl of wax fruit.

Leaving Rosy with little more than the stars on his shoulders, we zipped back to the plane and started out once more for Tokyo. The flight was less eventful than the drive from Tokyo International Airport to our hotel. I was delighted to find that the Japanese had finally found an ingenious solution to their traffic problem. Instead of blowing a lot of money on freeways they were driving on top of each other. There really wasn't a lot of room to drive anyplace else. All the main roads were being rebuilt for the 1964 Olympic Games, which were still two years away.

Keeping face is a big thing in the Far East, and Tokyo certainly went all out to keep its share. It may be the Land of the Rising Sun, but before long nobody was going to be able to see either the land or the sun through all the new Nipponese skyscrapers.

There was some good to be got out of all the urban renewal, though. We stayed at the Okura Hotel, just one of scores of new luxury hotels. I had a beautiful suite. I just hope I can get back to see it sometime. We spent the first two days in Japan in helicopters hurrying to be on time for shows at Tachikawa Air Base, the Iwakuni Marine Base, and the Atsugi Naval Base. Those aren't sneezes; they're real places.

The schedule was so frantic we had only a half hour to ourselves the whole time we were there. The cast headed madly off on shopping expeditions for radios, tape recorders, and watches. I bought Dolores a stunning string of genuine pearls for only $7. At least I think they were genuine. The oysters they had irritated to grow them had honest faces.

For the hop to Korea we switched over to a prop plane. From then on the runways we were going to land on couldn't handle our big jet, and I'm a guy who likes plenty of parking space for planes. One thing I hate is an airplane with bent curb-feelers.

As soon as we landed at Seoul we were hustled to the Hartell House in the Yongsan compound. We were going to do what the USO laughingly called "sleeping there" for the next three nights. Later we were given a lengthy briefing by Navy Lieutenant Frank Poyet. He explained the complex Korean money system, warned us not to drink water or eat any fresh vegetables while we were off the base, and told us to be sure to keep our luggage locked at all times. By the time he warned us about the luggage, it was too late. There was nothing to do but file a claim against my insurance company for a $1,000 pearl necklace.

Lana Turner, Peter Leeds, Amedee Chabot, Anita Bryant, Janis Paige, Les Brown, Jerry Colonna, and controversial Christmas tree at Panmunjom, 38th parallel, Korea, 1962.

The following morning I was abruptly awakened by two MPs. I spent five long minutes trying to recall what rule I had broken before I realized they were just picking me up for a golf foursome with the commanding general, Guy S. Meloy, and two other staff generals, Palmer and Thatcher. That was what you could really call all-star golf.

We played on a pleasant straw pasture maintained for the servicemen who were rotated back and forth from the 38th parallel. Golf is healthy recreation for the guys on those lonely bases. It gives them something to do instead of thinking about what they really want to do. It helps that they have girl caddies in Korea, just as in Japan. They understand the game and I like the way they keep score. They were very good at subtracting figures from other figures. I did extraordinarily well that day. I shot my age for eighteen holes. Pretty good for a man of 114.

The 6th Transport Company coptered us all over Korea. They took us to the Ascom area, where we played in a baseball field for six thousand GIs and Air Force and Marine personnel. The next morning we sweated out fog for three hours, hoping it would clear enough for the copters to find their way to the Schoonover Bowl and the 7th Infantry Division. We were about to get on buses when the sun came through.

This part of the trip was like homecoming day. When I'd played Schoonover in 1957 it was called Bayonet Bowl. All I had to do was close my eyes to recall the guys sitting there in the snow. Thanks to my memories I'd come prepared for the same type of weather with a few crunchers like: "It gets so cold here they use brass monkeys as hand warmers," and "I sneezed last night and my nose shattered . . . Don't stare. I had to put it back together in the dark."

This time when I stepped out of the copter I almost disappeared, nose and all, into the mud. So much for memories. There wasn't any snow on the ground, the sun was out, the sky was clear, and the temperature was a balmy sixty-five. Racing backstage, I yelled for Barney McNulty, to get him to change my idiot cards. But no answer. Barney was late and he didn't turn up until two minutes before show time. When he finally staggered into my dressing tent I was about to chew him out. He stopped me cold. "Sorry I'm late, Bob," he said. "I had to buy my idiot cards back from the natives. They were using them to build houses." I knew it was a lie, but it was such a good lie I gave him back his passport.

We were playing mostly to Air Force and some Army people who came from Pusan, Junsen, and Taegu, which was three hundred miles away. I walked out onto the stage wearing a papa-san hat and carrying a long, thin pipe. I ad-libbed back and forth with the guys out front until they got too fast for me. After all, I'm the one who's supposed to be getting the laughs. We were filming the show, and they were such a responsive audience, we used that dialogue to open the television show when we edited it back in Burbank three weeks later.

We also used a stand-up shot we filmed that day with Lana Turner. It was some time since Lana had appeared before a live audience, and she was pretty nervous. Believe me, when those guys saw Lana they were really live. Lana needn't have worried at all. I got in three bows while the guys were applauding her.

North Korean soldiers, demilitarized zone, 38th parallel, Panmunjom, Korea, 1962.

HOPE: Here's the glamour doll of them all . . . Miss Lana Turner. Right here.

> MUSIC: *"You Are Too Beautiful"*
> (*Lana enters*)

LANA: Thank you. Thank you, fellows.

BOB: All right, everybody back in their seats . . . down, down, down, you bearcats!

LANA: Thank you, thank you so very much, fellows. (*to Bob*) And thank you, *sir!*

BOB (*to audience*): I run a tight ship. (*to Lana*) At ease . . . adore me if you like.

LANA: Bob . . .

BOB: Sir!

LANA: Sir, may I ask you a question?

BOB: No sweat. What's on your mind?

LANA: Well, if you're an officer like you told me and I have to polish your shoes every night . . . why don't you wear a uniform?

BOB: Well, I don't want this to get around, but I'm with Central Intelligence.

LANA: Oh . . . What are you investigating?

BOB: You!

LANA: Well, you know—I'm flattered that you asked me on this trip. After all, I don't sing or dance . . . I'm just an ordinary girl.

BOB: If you're an ordinary girl . . . I've been going out with soldiers! How do you like the trip so far, pretty rugged?

LANA: I thought it would be, Bob, but the fellows in the band have been so helpful, so nice, so polite, so gentlemanly.

HOPE (*reacts*): What plane are you flying in? Which one of these Philharmonic 4Fs are we talking about?

LANA: The cute orchestra leader . . . What's his name again?

HOPE: What difference does it make? You'll never hear it again. (*calls*) Oh, Lester, would you come over here a minute . . . Lester, boy . . .

> (*Les stumbles onstage, carrying baton*)

Les, have you been . . . making overtures to Miss Turner?

LES: Bob, I wouldn't do anything to jeopardize my career.

HOPE: You wouldn't, huh? Have you been making goo-goo eyes at Miss Turner?

LES: Bob, I wouldn't do anything to jeopardize my career.

HOPE: Was that you in the hall at the hotel last night singing "Fly Me to the Moon" through her keyhole?

LES: Bob, I told you . . . I wouldn't do anything to jeopardize my career.

LANA: Les, why don't you meet me after the show and we'll have a nice long talk? Hmmmm?

> (*Les looks at Lana, then at Bob. Breaks his baton in two, hands the pieces to Bob, exits with Lana.*)
> MUSIC: *Playoff*

That night we played a second show, this time for the combined services at Collier Fieldhouse. The show went over big so it wasn't until 11 P.M. that the hungry cast and crew sat down to tuck away our annual Christmas Eve dinner. We usually exchanged gifts at these dinners. It was no big production; we just drew names out of a hat and bought something that might get a laugh.

This year was different. Our production gal, Onnie Morrow, had heard that a Salvation Army warehouse in Seoul had burned down, destroying an immense amount of clothing intended for Korean orphans. So instead of exchanging gifts, Onnie passed the hat and we all tossed in a few won. It was a small gesture on our part, a spur-of-the-moment thing, but three weeks after we'd returned to the States we received a magnificent letter of thanks for our ton of won.

On Christmas morning Santa Claus dropped in with special passes and badges for us to visit the demilitarized zone in Panmunjom. From the look of the map, it should have been a simple, straight flight. But we zigged and zagged around for so long that I thought our copter pilot was an ex-taxi driver. He not only followed every curve on the road below us, he never even crossed the white line. When I asked him why he was doing all that fancy flying, his explanation was a good one: "We follow the road below in case we have to make an emergency landing. The area on both sides of the road is heavily mined." I not only tightened my safety belt, I crossed two more fingers.

We landed safely at the helipad in the joint security area, where we were greeted by various members of the United Nations force, including American, Swiss, Swedish, and South Korean officials. Though the North Koreans and their Czech and Polish representatives were not on hand to meet us, the Commie sentries watched us closely from their boxes on the hill.

The escort officers assigned to us showed us the conference hut where the weekly truce talks were being held. He explained that everything was supposed to be identical, not only on either side of the table, but also on the table itself. We were shown one fascinating thing we hadn't heard about before: the North Korea flagpole was a quarter of an inch taller than the United Nations flagpole. The North Koreans had insisted on it.

With nonchalance that is hard to believe now, we walked freely back and forth across the demarcation line that ran through the exact center

Jerry Colonna at Clark Field, Philippines, 1962.

The last Christmas show

of the zone. As we strolled along the road, two Red sentries came down the hill toward us. I brazenly turned and walked toward them. They retreated. Then a Czechoslovak general came down the hill toward us, walked over, and shook hands. The United Nations party was amazed at this new high in sociability in the security area.

The general and I had some minor language difficulties, but everything was very cordial until I asked him if I could take a look at their sentry box. The general stiffened and replied, "It is not my matter. I have heard about your visit and I am pleased to meet you. That is all." Then he turned and walked away.

It was here we saw the Christmas tree that caused an international incident. The UN troops had found a straggly pine tree and in a sentimental moment had put it up, decorated it, and lit it. The Reds demanded it be removed from the demilitarized zone. They claimed it was a capitalistic weapon. But that Christmas Day the tree was still there—a small strategic victory in the war of the inane.

At noon we flew a few miles south of the zone and had lunch at the enlisted men's mess at Camp Casey. There was quite a stir when Lana, Janis, Anita, and Miss U.S.A. stood in the chow line with the guys. The metal trays were piled high with a delicious turkey dinner, which the gals ate heartily with their usual equipment—teeth. The guys ate with their eyes. Meanwhile, Jerry, Les, and I sat in the corner eating humble pie. There are very few male celebrities who are worthy of that kind of attention in an Army camp.

After lunch we did a big show for the men of the 1st Cavalry Division at a football field near Yonjiko. I had trouble with the name, but the audience was a pushover. In addition to eight thousand servicemen, we had fifty Korean orphans as special guests. These kids were being fed, clothed, and educated with money donated by the men of the 1st Cavalry. One solemn little boy in the audience wore the NBC emblem on his sweater. He was the ward of the engineering and technical crews back at the NBC studio in Burbank; they used the profits from their coffee canteen to support him.

It turned out to be impossible to reach as many guys in Korea as we had hoped to in the short time we spent there. Since it was so lonely for them and there was practically no entertainment, we tried something new. Christmas night we did our regular show for the Eighth Army at Collier Fieldhouse near Yongsan. At the same time the entire show was telecast over a special closed-circuit hookup to remote outposts all over Korea. Once I'm in a country, there's no place to hide from me.

I spouted a lot of material that brought the guys up to date on happenings back home. Jokes about television, about Zsa Zsa's latest marriage, about China and India, about the newspaper strike in New York, and about their commander in chief:

★

It's been a slow year back home. Only one Kennedy got elected.

The Kennedys had a nice Christmas. Jackie got a new pair of water skis, the President got a pair of hair clippers, and Ted got a nice present—Massachusetts.

I'm only kidding. There was a wonderful Christmas spirit in Washington this year. The Kennedys held a drive to raise money to buy toys for needy Republicans.

And the Teamsters Union pickets the reindeer for carrying freight without a Teamsters card.

★

From then on, the troupe hopped around pretty fast. In Taiwan we did a frantic show at the City Hall Theater for the U.S. military assistance and advisory group. Lana lost her voice and had to whisper her act, but the miracle of electronic amplification took care of most of the problem. Colonna drove me onstage in a Taiwan pedicab, a kind of mixed-up bicycle turned rickshaw. The next thing I knew we almost zoomed out over the footlights. Luckily Colonna had good brakes.

We went on to Taipei, where the cast was mobbed everywhere they went by frenzied people. Some of them even followed me into the washroom. Fortunately, Barney was in the next booth cuing me with my idiot cards.

At Subic Bay in the Philippines we did a show on the flight deck of the carrier *Kitty Hawk*. Just a few hours later we were at Clark Field, where we played to twelve thousand men in the Bamboo Bowl. There hadn't been time to load the equipment on and off the plane, so it was trucked to Clark over ninety miles of rough terrain. Somewhere along the way the sound equipment flipped off the truck and was damaged. The technicians were still patching the PA system back together again when we started the show. I don't know what that bump did to the amplifier, but during the first three minutes of the show I sounded like a boy soprano.

Before taking off for Guam we paid a quick visit to the Negrito village near Manila, where we were greeted by the Negrito chief, or general, as he was called. He invited me to inspect his troops, who stood there in loincloths, holding spears and blowguns. It was my first experience with a sensitivity group.

The Negritos lived in simple straw huts perched on poles. They wore castoff clothing from the base and made a meager living selling feather-

Clark Field, Philippines, 1962.

trimmed spears to the tourists who happened by. Yet these primitive pygmy head-hunters were savage, loyal fighters and experts at psychological warfare. The Negritos slipped behind the Japanese lines at night and slit the throats of every other man they found. I don't know why they were wasting time in the Philippine jungle. They could have made a fortune working as Hollywood agents.

Our last stop was at what was left of Guam. I was their second big wind of the year. The first one had been pretty destructive, and only a few

Filet of Seoul 159

heavy planes were left. But our audience filled the big hangar at Agana Naval Air Station all the way out to the runway.

The show went okay, but as we were about to board the C-135 jet for home, the project officer, Major Ed Swinney, whispered to me, "Bob, the starter on engine number four is broken. We'll start engine number one, then transfer the starter to engine number four and get it started. Please don't tell the others." I didn't. I tried to, but I couldn't make my mouth move.

We hit thunderstorms all the way home. It was rough, but a bigger bump came when we hit customs in Los Angeles. They were pretty easy on me, but some of the cast and crew were two and a half hours getting through. I was plenty aggravated and a little tired. Anyway, I popped off to the press about it. Then, as I was riding home, it hit me. What was I so mad about? Just forty-eight hours before in Okinawa I'd been onstage in front of an audience filled with litter patients, guys just off the ambulance planes from the fighting in Nam. When I looked down at the time I'd noticed that one of the guys who was laughing at some joke I was telling was getting a plasma transfusion at the same time.

That sight alone was enough to make it up to everybody in our show for our time and trouble. It was a good and sufficient reason for anybody's making a trip like ours. How could anyone fly twenty thousand miles on the same plane with Lana Turner, Janis Paige, and Anita Bryant and complain? All I want is to catch the sneak who locked me in the washroom.

CHAPTER 14

The Mediterranean and eye

One afternoon while we were planning a Mediterranean tour for Christmas 1963, I sneaked over to Lakeside Golf Club for a fast nine. I hacked my way out of the second green in regulation, took out my putter, looked toward the hole, and staggered to see there were two flags there. My first thought was that two flags were a hell of an improvement. With my putting stroke I can use an option, but then I stumbled over my feet. I knew I was in a little trouble. My eye doctor in Beverly Hills, Dr. Maurice Biegelman, sent me to New York to see Dr. Algernon Reese at Columbia Presbyterian. Dr. Reese took a quick look at me and told me to grab the next plane to San Francisco to see Dr. Dohrmann Pischel, the great eye man who was head of ophthalmology at Stanford University. He was not a man to waste a minute. He put on that serious expression doctors use on television and said, "Mr. Hope, you check in at Children's Hospital this afternoon and lie down. Tomorrow we're going to give you a couple of touches with the new shrecker beam."

The operation is not physically rough but it's emotionally hairy. They lock your head in a vise and clamp your eyes open and aim the electronic gun at you. And for the first time in your life you know what it's like to be in front of a firing squad.

Then you sweat it out while they figure out if they had pointed in the right direction. Dr. Pischel looked again and said, "We've got to take another little flash at you," so he took me back in again and they opened my eyes with these clamps and he gave me a couple more blasts with that beam.

Then they sent me back to my room. I lay there in bed with blinders on while the troupe took off for Turkey without me. And we had put together a fine troupe—Tuesday Weld, Anita Bryant, the Earl Twins, Michele Metrinko (Miss U.S.A. of that year), Peter Leeds, a fine dancer and comic named John Bubbles—and, naturally, Professor Colonna and Les Brown's band.

Well, I gotta tell you I had the lows, but if there was anything that was going to pick me up it was the letters I received when I was having eye troubles. If ever you've had a doubt about man's humanity to man, read these letters.

All in all I received thousands of cards, letters, and telegrams wishing me well, but these letters offering eye transplants are still something I can't get over—still something I am unable to handle emotionally. They were overwhelming.

A couple of endless days later Dr. Pischel said, "If you take it easy now for the next couple of weeks you're gonna be all right."

I said, "That's fine, Doc, but come back tomorrow and see how I look because I gotta get to Turkey." He came back the next day and I begged, "What about it, Doc? Is it possible?"

He said, "If it were up to me I'd tell you to stay in bed for a month. Unfortunately it's up to you, so keep your head from any sudden moves and send me a postcard from Incirli."

I flew commercial from the States to Frankfurt, Germany, where I was supposed to hop a twin-engined military jet for a fast flip to Turkey. The only trouble was, we had to fly over the Communist-controlled Balkan countries, and we had to get permission. The only way we could get it was to agree to have a pilot with the rank of colonel or higher. I guess if there was a little accident and our plane got shot down, they wanted to be sure it was worth it.

In Ankara, Sil Caranchini, our associate producer, got word that I was on the way. The Air Force got the same word, so they went to Sil and asked him whether it would be all right to move the show from two to six o'clock that evening, in hopes that I would put in an appearance.

Sil was waiting in the hotel in Ankara when I showed up. He and Johnny Pawlek, our audio expert, looked at each other. If I was going to make the rest of the tour, it would have to be some kind of luck.

I sacked out for a couple of hours. They went ahead with plans for the six o'clock show—with me or without.

The show started with Jerry Colonna taking my place. The gang was about twenty minutes into the performance when I walked out onstage. It was in a tremendous building that had been used originally for trolley cars, then converted into a bus barn.

There were about six thousand people in there. I was very happy to see them. And I must say they were happy to see me. I went into my monologue—a little shaky at first.

★

I've been doing a little sight-seeing today. I visited twelve mosques.
Not that I'm so religious; I was just trying to get my shoes back.

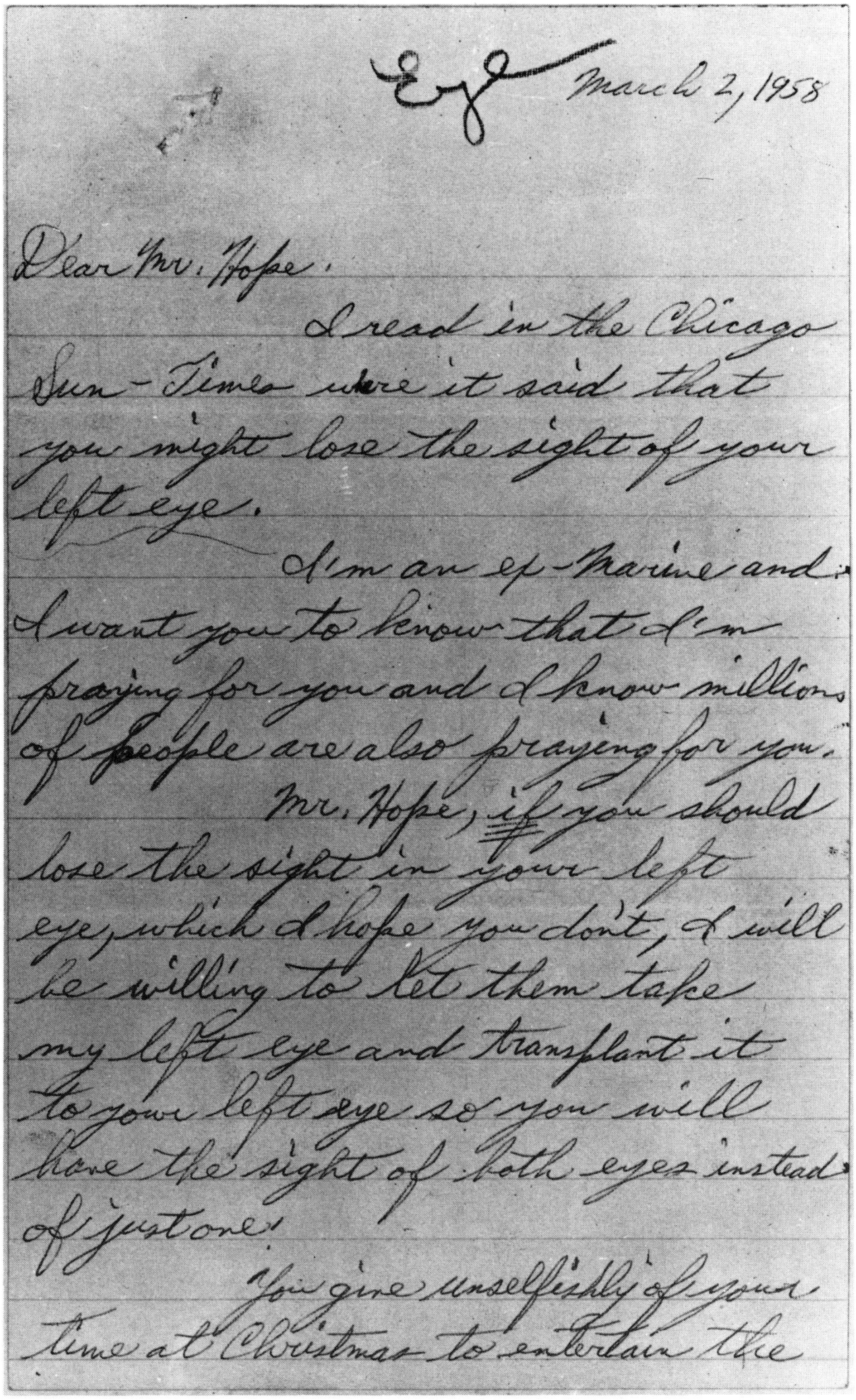

March 2, 1958

Dear Mr. Hope:

I read in the Chicago
Sun-Times where it said that
you might lose the sight of your
left eye.

I'm an ex-marine and
I want you to know that I'm
praying for you and I know millions
of people are also praying for you.

Mr. Hope, if you should
lose the sight in your left
eye, which I hope you don't, I will
be willing to let them take
my left eye and transplant it
to your left eye so you will
have the sight of both eyes instead
of just one.

You give unselfishly of your
time at Christmas to entertain the

Eye letter, 1963.

men and women of the Armed Forces who are overseas and also many times through out the years you have put on shows for the Armed Forces.

By donating my eye to you (if you should need it) is only a very small token compared to the joy and happieness that you have brought given to the men and women in the Armed Forces during World War II and the Korean War and all so for the joy & happieness you have given us even in peace time —

Please do not let anyone know who wrote this letter to you because I am not looking for publicity or anything what so ever, I only want to

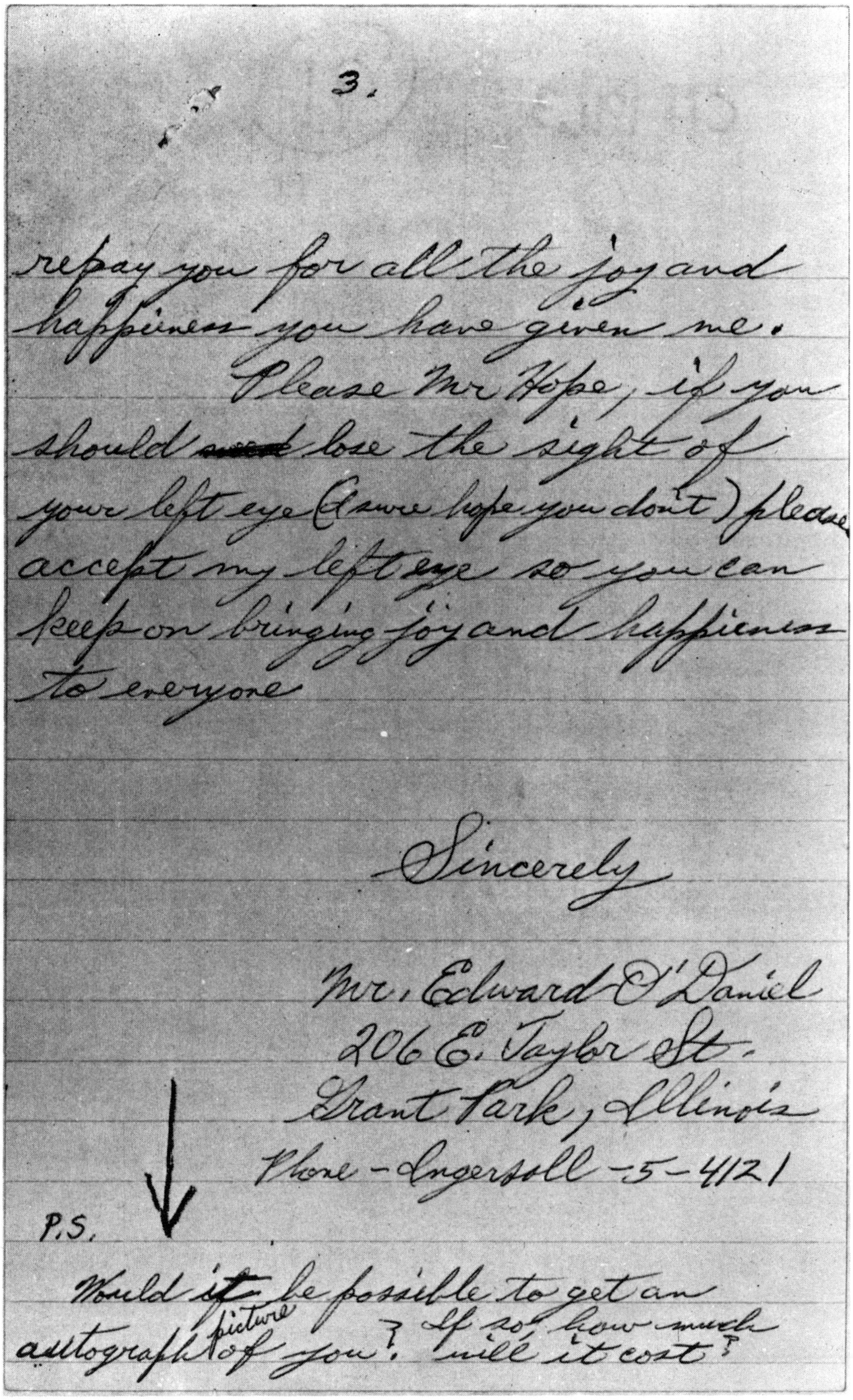

3.

repay you for all the joy and
happiness you have given me.
        Please Mr Hope, if you
should ~~seek~~ lose the sight of
your left eye (as we hope you don't) please
accept my left eye so you can
keep on bringing joy and happiness
to everyone

        Sincerely

        Mr. Edward O'Daniel
        206 E. Taylor St.
        Grant Park, Illinois
        Phone – Ingersoll – 5 – 4121

P.S. ↓

Would it be possible to get an
autograph picture of you? If so how much will it cost?

WESTERN UNION TELEGRAM

CLASS OF SERVICE

This is a fast message unless its deferred character is indicated by the proper symbol.

1201

SYMBOLS

DL=Day Letter
NL=Night Letter
LT=Internation. Letter Telegra

The filing time shown in the date line on domestic telegrams is STANDARD TIME at point of origin. Time of receipt is STANDARD TIME at point of d...

KNAOO4 45 PD INTL VIA NCU (NFU)=N HONOLULU VIA RCA MAR

LT BOB HOPE=CARE DOCTOR ALGERNON   3 1103=

REESE=COLUMBIA UNIVERSITY NYK

(DLR 635 W 165 ST)=

DEAR BOB SORRY TO HEAR OF YOUR EYE DIFFICULTY IF YOU

MUST LOSE YOUR EYE AND MINE COULD BE OF HELP TO YOU

PLEASE CONTACT ME

=DONALD ROBINS 280 LEWERS ST OFFICE NO 8 WAIKIKI=

:280 8=

THE COMPANY WILL APPRECIATE SUGGESTIONS FROM ITS PATRONS CONCERNING ITS SERVICE

Eye telegram, 1963.

And I love the taxis here. I must love them. I bought one. And it was such a short ride too. They told me not to argue with the driver, and now I know why. He got excited, sneezed twice, and nearly flogged me to death with his mustache.

★

I thought that all I'd do was come on and tell a few jokes, then get off and go back to bed. But the electric current that sparked between me and the crowd had to be the world's greatest therapy. It sure was for me, anyway. I stood there, feeling stronger and stronger with every laugh. In the end we put on a tremendous show that ran almost two hours.

From Ankara we moved on to an air base we shared with the Turks at Incirli. Remember the Gary Powers incident where he was shot down in a high-altitude photo reconnaissance plane over Russian territory . . . and the Russians accused us of spying on them . . . and we denied spying . . .

166   *The last Christmas show*

Colonel Woody Mark, Wheelus Air Force Base, Tripoli, Libya, 1963.

and denied knowing who Gary Powers was. Well, Incirli was the base he didn't take off from. I know it's the base he used because there are a lot more of those planes he didn't use. I still felt a bit woozy, but at least this time there was no question about whether I'd go on or not. I pranced out there, greeted our boys, and welcomed the Turkish troops to the show.

★

I'm very thrilled that you could make it. I'm very proud to be here —I just thought you might like to see a new kind of Turkey.

It's wonderful working at bases with exotic names like Karamursel, Eskisehir, Incirli, and Diyarbakir. In case of war, I hope we don't have a phone operator that stutters.

I can't tell you what I've seen here today, but this is part of our NATO defense. Personally, I think they're going to an awful lot of trouble just to keep Khrushchev out of Disneyland.

★

I wasn't kidding about those names; our next stop actually was Diyarbakir.

★

I smoked my first Turkish cigarette last night. It's part of basic training here, I understand. I took one puff and my lungs went over the hill.

Talk about stunting your growth—I took one drag and had to reach up for the ash tray.

And for lunch today we had some of the famous shish kebab. That's a meat popsicle.

It's an ingenious dish. When the meat's tough, you have a stick to poke it down with.

★

From Turkey we flew west to the Mediterranean island of Crete. By this time a doctor was traveling with us—a gynecologist. I refrain from comment. Along the way, Anita Bryant had collapsed right onstage, and we discovered that she was pregnant. The military assigned a physician to ride along with her for the rest of the trip. He not only did a beautiful job with Anita—the baby was born back in the States in fine shape—but he also took good care of my six-and-a-half-pound bouncing baby eyeball as well.

Crete is magnificent—everything the tourist ads claim. Don't let these monologue jokes deter you:

★

I want to thank you for the wonderful reception we got at the airport today. When we arrived the men cheered for fifteen minutes. They thought we were . . . replacements.

And it was a thrill coming in from the airport over those curvy mountain roads. I felt like I was riding in Dean Martin's caddie cart, and Phil Harris was driving.

The commander took me on a wonderful tour of some ruins. Then I found out it was the air base.

Crete has the largest oranges in the world. I'll delete that line when we get to Los Angeles. No, you've never seen these kind of oranges. It's the only place where you can go bowling and make a screwdriver at the same time.

★

Next stop: Athens. It's one of the most colorful cities in the world, and our project officers *generously* gave us an hour off for shopping, sight-

USS Shangri-La, Bay of Naples, 1963.

John Bubbles, Michele Metrinko, Phil Crosby, Tuesday Weld, Anita Bryant, Jerry Colonna, the Earl Twins, Peter Leeds at Villa Barra, Naples, 1963. (U. S. Navy)

seeing—and shaving. We gave the show in an immense hangar at the Athens airport, where we were honored by a visit from the Crown Prince and Princess of Greece, Constantine and Helen. Since then, Constantine has not only reigned in Greece, he's been deposed and exiled to Italy. He's not very happy about it and he'd love to go back—but that's just a lot of damns over the water nowadays.

Besides the Greek Prince and Princess, there was a lot of U.S. royalty in the audience—five thousand GIs! It was Sunday, so I started the monologue with:

The last Christmas show

★

I'm delighted to be here in Never on Sunday *land. We're leaving tonight, so I'll never know.*

Everywhere you look in town you see Greek ruins. I saw a sergeant with one last night.

Greece is a tiny country. A jet can fly from border to border in twenty minutes. My taxi driver made it in ten.

And Greece won its independence in 1829 after four centuries of domination, without firing a single shot. They did it on their cooking alone.

I owe so much to the Greeks. Just think, if it hadn't been for Hippocrates, the Father of Medicine, today Ben Casey would be a bellhop.

I know, because I've been studying up on Greek mythology. Now, there's Mercury; he was the first Western Union boy. Then there's Pan, the god of woods and fields, with the legs of a goat. I don't know what he's become, but I've seen him on Hollywood Boulevard. And then there's Zeus, ruler of the universe and hurler of thunderbolts. He's number one draft choice with the Los Angeles Rams. Then there was Aphrodite, or Venus, as the Romans called her. She was the first woman to shave her arms.

★

Our girls hardly had time to do the same before we were whisked off, south across the Mediterranean to Wheelus Air Force Base in Tripoli, Libya. It seemed quiet enough when we arrived, but by the time we went on for the men of the Seventeenth Air Force a giant wind was blowing across the desert.

Jerry Colonna and I did one of our typical service sketches at Wheelus. The camera panned over the audience while I said, "These men of the Seventeenth Air Force are all sturdy, well-tanned types." Then the camera passed Colonna dressed as a Bedouin tribesman, did a double take, and swung back. "Wait a minute," I said. "What's that? You, sir. Are you with the Air Force?"

"No," said Colonna. "I've been against it from the start."

"That's a very interesting costume you're wearing. Are you an Arab?"

"No, I'm a Chinese laundryman. I'm just delivering these sheets."

"Do you take me for a fool?"

"I will if nobody else will."

The servicemen loved Jerry. They also loved an ad-lib routine that John Bubbles sprang on me during one show. John had been a song-and-dance

The Mediterranean and eye 171

Tuesday Weld at Diyarbakir, Turkey, 1963.

man for fifty-five years, and for thirty of those years had been half of the famous vaudeville set of Buck and Bubbles. He'd played the Palace, done a command performance for George VI of England, and created the role of Sportin' Life, which was written into *Porgy and Bess* for him by George Gershwin. He was the first black performer who'd ever gone along on one of our trips. In our act, I played a dance director and he was the student—a

The last Christmas show

little soft-shoe routine. When he finished and went offstage, I called him back to take a bow. Once, when he came back, he walked over to me and said, "Bob, I want to ask you a question."

"What is it?" I asked.

"Do you believe in integration?"

"Why, sure."

"Well then," John said, "kiss me."

It was probably one of the first integration jokes, and it brought the house down. We did it everywhere. Once we got it backward. It still played.

Tuesday Weld, surprisingly, turned out to be one of the show's biggest fans. Up till then she'd been one of the top rebels of all time. At first she didn't seem to be able to relate to any of us. All she wanted to do was perform, run her lines, give that little prop smile to a lot of people, and then go back and read *Mad* magazine.

When we left Tripoli, she was late for the plane, and we were all standing there tapping our feet. After fifteen minutes she came driving up in a car and she said, "I'm sorry, but I was at the hospital."

"What's wrong?" I asked, not believing one damn word.

"Nothing," she said. "I was just visiting the kids at the hospital."

That was a new kind of Tuesday Weld, a Tuesday Weld who finally got involved. She said later that she never knew she could care about other people that much.

By the time we reached the aircraft carrier *Shangri-La*, anchored off Naples, I'd never felt better in my life. The sun was shining, the stage was set up, and thousands of sailors were waiting as I leapt to the stage:

It's a thrill to be here on the USS Crapgame.

The Navy calls it Shangri-La, *but that's just for the winners. I've never seen such action. I sat down at a mess table and the sugar cubes had numbers on them.*

And I've never heard of a chaplain wearing a green eyeshade before.

This is some raft. I heard that the guys stationed in Naples get a three-day pass and spend it on this ship.

As a taxpayer, I must admit I'm very impressed with this ship, our first seagoing bowling alley.

I don't know how you guys make out on a ship this big. Personally, I'd like a little shorter run between my bunk and the rail.

In Naples we have one of the command headquarters of NATO. NATO: That's a Latin term meaning "Get your cotton-pickin' hands off my border."

It's a coalition of twelve nations that've sworn to give up borsht.

It's a combined defense effort. The English are making jet planes, the Americans are making missiles, the Germans are making rockets, and the French are making love. But they're doing their share. If war is declared, they'll have the biggest army in the world.

I always look forward to visiting Naples, city of romance and love at first sight. On a three-hour pass you haven't got time for a second look.

Professor Colonna has been waiting all this trip to get to Naples. He comes every year for his booster shot of marinara sauce.

The streets here are a little narrow for cars. In fact, they're a little narrow for people. If it wasn't for olive oil, there wouldn't be any traffic at all.

But it's a great city and they paid me a great honor this morning. They made me an honorary Italian. Yes sir, it's quite a ceremony. The mayor of Naples tapped me on the shoulder with a bread stick and his assistant sprinkled grated cheese on my head.

★

Back in Burbank Jack Baker, our choreographer, put together a little soft-shoe number for John Bubbles and myself. But after my eye flew up and the doctor told me not to move my head too much I had to cool the dancing. But when we got to that big auditorium in Naples I was really up. After I finished the monologue I passed John backstage. I said, "Put on your dancing shoes, Bub . . . we're gonna fly tonight."

And Bubbles said to me, "Beautiful, baby . . . but what are we gonna do?"

I said to him, "It's too late to rehearse. We'll ad-lib."

And that's exactly what we did. I started throwing steps at John and he never missed a beat. And after we soft-shoed off Bubbles came over to me and said, "Man, you're crazy. You did six finish steps out there. From here on let's keep it simple. I don't have to audition. I'm already bigger than I wanna be."

John was one of our great sleepers of all times. Whenever I passed him on a plane or in a bus or in a hotel lobby, he'd be dozing. And when I'd kid him about it, he'd say, "I ain't sleepin', pops, I just keep my eyelids closed so the world don't see too much of me."

His Highness Constantine, King of Greece, Athens, 1963.

Yeah, '63 was quite a tour. The more I worked the better I felt. I was back to normal. And it was just in time. In 1964 we finally got the word from the Pentagon. We were about to make our first Christmas trip to Vietnam.

Subic Bay, Philippine Islands, 1964.

The last Christmas show

CHAPTER 15

Bombed in Saigon

We made our first Christmas trip to Vietnam in 1964, but it actually began in a Japanese dressing room in 1962. I had just come offstage and I found a young man waiting for me, standing off to one side almost in the shadows. He stepped forward and said, "Mr. Hope, may I speak to you?" He was wearing a red beret and Special Forces uniform I'd never seen before.

I went into a corner huddle with him. "I'm from Vietnam," he said. "I've hitchhiked all the way over here to Japan to see you. I've got a scroll under my arm with a lot of American Marines' names on it. We don't get many entertainment breaks in Vietnam, and I've been delegated by my outfit to fly up here and see if I can persuade you to come down and do a show."

Then he unrolled that scroll; it stretched quite a way. The Defense Department had already nixed a Vietnam trip that year, as you remember, but I started making phone calls. The answer was the same: no, the situation was still too sticky. But so was the memory of that soldier in the red beret. I couldn't get him out of my mind.

I tried again to get to Vietnam in 1963, but ended up in the Middle East. It wasn't till 1964 that the okay finally came through.

We started out in Korea, and this year it was more like Christmas should be: snow fell every day we were there. There wasn't a sign of the balmy golfing weather of '62. On one junket we made to an outlying base, the snow fell so thickly that it forced down one of the helicopters and delayed the director and some cast members right up to show time. For a while it seemed more like Alaska than Korea; the temperature went as low as six above. That wasn't so bad for the crew members, who could bundle up in parkas, but the girls in the cast had to appear onstage wearing sleeveless gowns in swirling snow. They always wore skins lightly sprinkled with goose bumps.

Our base anchor was Bangkok and when we left for Vietnam, we flew over the Gulf of Siam to avoid crossing Cambodia and came in from the south across the Mekong River Delta.

We had been provided with a fighter-plane escort that led us through a steep approach to land at Bienhoa, where we were going to give our first Vietnam show. That kind of approach was scary but necessary because of possible enemy ground fire. Wrecked planes all around the field gave eloquent testimony to the mortar attacks made by the Cong a few days earlier. The runway was pockmarked with craters big and small. During the show I managed to dig a joke or two out of the novelty of playing a golf course paved with concrete and with a lot more than eighteen holes. "We were greeted with a salute," I said. "A couple of them were even from our own side."

With all the fire fighting in the area, the holes in the runway and the wrecked planes and the fact that it could happen again at any time made it a dramatic show. And we had two MPs on either side of the stage. When you first looked down at them, it looked as if they were protecting us from us.

During the show I did a joke about the wonderful protection we were getting from the Military Police. How they had twenty-five men with machine guns guarding the girls and for the fellows they had a midget with a slingshot. From the time we stepped off that plane in Vietnam, we really *did* have security. There was an escort assigned to every member of the cast and that escort officer was armed. Whenever we moved *anywhere* in Vietnam, we moved in convoy. And in addition to armed drivers in every car, there were military police in jeeps ahead of us and behind us and around us.

During the show Eddie Fisher showed up. He was touring with John Bubbles, who had been with us the year before. Eddie was wearing jungle fatigues, crossed ammo belts, and two pearl-handled revolvers. Bill Larkin couldn't resist putting him on. "When did you first start wearing the guns, Eddie—after your first camp show?" Fortunately for Bill, Eddie was not too fast on the draw.

After the show we made a short hop to Tan Son Nhut, the Saigon airport. It was a turbulent year in Vietnam; Cong terrorists were running wild. General "Westy" Westmoreland was so busy he wasn't able to meet us. Instead he sent a delegation to represent him. After the greetings, Air Force buses, cars, and jeeps were quickly loaded to run us to our hotels in downtown Saigon. It was obviously no time for fooling around; the motorcade included guards with loaded rifles. We traveled with six thousand pounds of idiot cards, so it took Barney McNulty quite a while to get them off the plane. We had to wait ten minutes while he and the cards were fitted into the tail end of the convoy. Escorted by that security force of MPs in jeeps, we finally started out, but even with a convoy blocking for us, crawling through that human anthill was no easy run.

Ann Sydney, Anita Bryant, Janis Paige, Anna Maria Alberghetti, Jill St. John at Korat, Thailand, 1964.

Five minutes from downtown, we heard fire engines and got the word by walkie-talkie to stop on McNamara's bridge. I was riding with General Joe Moore, Air Force commandant in the Saigon region. He called one of the boys back from the leading jeeps and asked what was going on. The driver replied that there was a fire at the Brinks, a bachelor officers' hotel. The Brinks was catty-corner from the Caravelle and the Majestic, where we were staying.

After twenty long minutes we got the word to go forward, so we took off again for the city through Saigon's "back door," a roundabout route through back streets that were narrow and crowded. The fire made the normal wartime crowds and confusion even worse. People milled about, blue smoke hung in the air, and all the lower-level windows facing the street were broken.

When we got to the Caravelle Hotel we were hustled right to our quarters. When I entered my room our physical therapist, Freddy Miron, came rushing at me and poured out a wild story about a "bombing."

Bombed in Saigon   179

I must explain that Freddy is solid enchilada and when he gets excited it's not easy to understand what he says.

"Freddy," I said, "there was no bombing. Try to control your overdeveloped sense of drama. The MPs said it was a fire. Who knows the most about it, you or the MPs?"

And Freddy in a moment of Latin hysteria replied, "I don't care whether you're Bob Hope or not, it was a bombing."

As it turned out, Freddy was right. As Westy Westmoreland later told me, a Vietcong truck loaded with TNT and dynamite had driven up in front of the Brinks just before we were scheduled at the Caravelle across the street. The Cong drivers set a time fuse, got out, and ran like hell. Ten minutes later the truck blasted off and the hotel was gutted. Several people were killed and dozens were wounded.

If Barney McNulty had been ten minutes faster loading those idiot cards, our Christmas show would have been the wrong kind of smash. It's the only time I ever wanted to kiss Barney. Fortunately, I waited an instant and the need abated.

It all sounded melodramatic at the time. A few years later I received this letter indicating that we were actually the Cong's target.

HEADQUARTERS, II FIELD FORCE VIETNAM
APO SAN FRANCISCO 96266

19 February 1967

Dear Bob:

A few minutes ago I read a translation of a document we captured several days ago in which the VC were pointing out their weaknesses in conducting successful terrorist activities in cities. This quote should interest you: "Attack on Brinks BOQ missed Bob Hope by ten minutes due to faulty timing devices." I'm *not* kidding.

This reminded me that I still had not written to thank you for the autographed copy of your wonderful book, *Five Women I Love*. I thoroughly enjoyed it—and particularly your account of the golf game at the Royal Bangkok Sports Club. I was stationed in Bangkok a number of years ago and lost more balls in those klongs around the race track than I care to admit.

Your show at Christmas was tremendous, as usual, and I'm sure you know how much every man enjoyed it. It was a particular pleasure for me to meet and to have a chance to talk with Mrs. Hope. I am so glad you talked her into singing "White Christmas," which she did so beautifully.

Brinks hotel, Saigon, Vietnam, 1964.

I know I shouldn't single out one act or one participant, but as long as I live I'll never forget Anita Bryant's singing of "The Battle Hymn of the Republic."

Again, thank you for the autographed copy of your book which I will always treasure, for coming to Vietnam again, and for being Bob Hope.

With my warmest regards,

> *Sincerely,*
> JONATHAN O. SEAMAN
> *Lieutenant General, USA*
> *Commanding*

The Los Angeles *Herald-Examiner* reported our near miss this way:

CONG PLOT TO KILL BOB HOPE BARED
BOB HOPE 'SAVED' BY CONG GOOF

Saigon, March 16 (UPI)—It was discovered today that the Viet Cong leadership has rebuked some of its Saigon terrorists for failing to kill Bob Hope and his entertainment troupe during their Christmas tour of Vietnam two years ago.

A captured secret Viet Cong document released today complained that the Viet Cong bombs intended for Hope exploded ten minutes before the Hope group arrived.

The rebuke was included in a general criticism of terror acts that failed by the "Urban Sapper Movement." That was Congese for the Viet Cong terror squads that planted bombs in the cities of South Vietnam. The document, captured by the U.S. 25th Infantry Division on Feb. 6, 1967, was especially critical of the terror attack on the Brinks Bachelors Officers Quarters in the heart of Saigon on Christmas Eve in 1964 that killed two Americans and injured 50 Americans and 13 Vietnamese.

The document said, "In the attack on Brinks, the bomb exploded ten minutes before the set time. Shortly after the explosion the cars of the Bob Hope entertainment group arrived."

The document also criticized the Cong's sapper squads for failing to assess enemy countermeasures, for bad timing and for other errors, including a waterborne attack in which one swimmer "made too much noise."

From his Palm Springs home today Hope quipped, "It's hard to believe they were critical of my act.

"But they ought to get a tour guide because they bombed the hotel across the street from us. I think the Viet Cong are drinking a lot. This isn't the first time people have tried to do away with me. The same thing happened to me when I was in vaudeville. The audiences were always trying to get me.

"I thought it was a gag until I was notified by General Seaman by letter of the captured Cong documents. Now I want my kids to see that letter so I can prove I was a hero in absentia."

After Freddy left my room at the Caravelle there came a knock at the door. In walked Navy intelligence men to search me and my luggage. Of course, they didn't suspect me or any of the crew members of being terrorists, but they were afraid something might have been planted in our pockets or luggage en route. While the crew members and I tiptoed around inside the hotel,

Korat Country Club, Thailand, 1964.

military security people continued looking for bombs. They were walking around with metal detectors checking everything for anything. There were lots of questions and confusion about whether we were going to stay there or not.

I remember one high-level meeting with the project officers, intelligence officers, and the security police. Their first question was whether they should take our whole crew, put us on the plane, and get us out of the area immediately.

Their next question was whether the show the following day should be canceled . . . whether the delicate members of the cast had been exposed to enough emotional anxiety and terror. Can you imagine them calling me "delicate"?

Then they asked me if I had any suggestions. I had one. "We're due at a cocktail party at Ambassador Maxwell Taylor's in an hour. Forget the bombing, forget the terrorists. Get us the gowns and make-up cases off the plane for the girls or you're going to see fireworks the like of which you have never seen before."

Pleiku, Vietnam, 1964.

John Bubbles, Nhatrang, Vietnam, 1964.

184

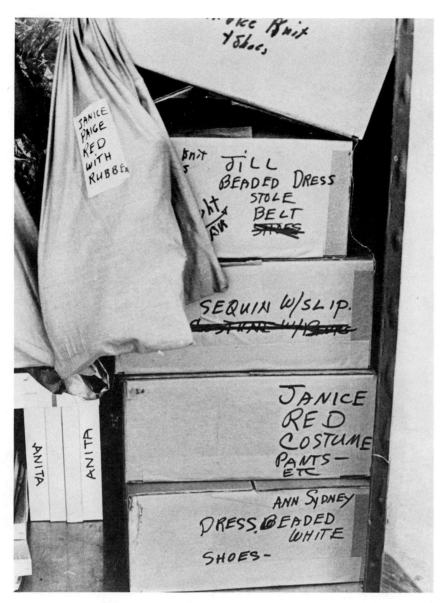

Loading ramp, Tan Son Nhut, Vietnam, 1964.

Then I went down the hall to talk to Janis Paige and Jill St. John. I was going out into the night and wanted reinforcements and they're my favorite kind. I asked them if they'd join me at Ambassador Taylor's. They said they'd like about a week to think it over and they intended to discuss the matter under their beds. I explained to them that there was nothing to worry about—that if a coward like me was willing to venture out, it had to be safe. And what angers me is that they bought it.

At the cocktail party we found out the extent of the casualties at the Brinks hotel. Those who had been injured had been taken to Saigon's one

Camera platform, gaffer: Bobby Comer; director: Jack Shea; camera operator: Harlow Stengel; assistant: Felber Maasdam; sound: Dave Forrest; cue cards: Barney McNulty, at White Beach, Okinawa, 1964. (U. S. Air Force)

small hospital. It was well run by the Navy Medical Corps, but it had limited capacity, and people were being killed and wounded in Cong terrorist attacks all the time—civilians, Vietnamese military, our own men. Westy's wife, Kitzie, was a good nurse's aide as well as a very dedicated person, and she had spent months working on a project to cope with taking care of mass casualties. The Westmorelands had a guest house just outside their villa, and Kitzie had come up with the idea of readying it as an emergency hospital.

It was only a few weeks after she had the hospital set up that the Brinks hotel blew with a bang. So the ambulatory patients in the regular hospital were moved to Kitzie's guest house and the Brinks wounded took their place.

Jill St. John, Anna Maria Alberghetti, Anita Bryant at Korat, Thailand, 1964. (U. S. Army)

The medical people moved in extra cots and dug into the emergency supplies stashed in Kitzie's guest house. The casualties arrived by the dozens, about seventy-five of them in all, some with serious injuries, some minor. Thanks to Kitzie's guest house there was plenty of room, and the staff was able to cope with the emergency victims.

The big explosion happened on Christmas Eve, of all nights. The Westmorelands had had a dinner planned for the cast, including Anita Bryant, Jill St. John, Janis Paige, Jerry Colonna, Anna Maria Alberghetti, John Bubbles, Miss World, Ann Sydney, and Peter Leeds. Kitzie Westmoreland was so tired she couldn't cope with all of us, but Westy decided to go ahead

King and Queen of Thailand, Onnie Morrow, Sil Caranchini, Les Brown at King's palace, Bangkok, 1964.

Tony Hope, Ann Sydney, Yongsan, Korea, 1964.

with the dinner anyhow. A stiff upper lip in the face of Cong terrorism seemed called for.

Before dinner we all sang Christmas carols to try to brighten our spirits. Then we went over and spoke to the patients in Kitzie's hospital, which was only a hundred feet away.

After I got back to Westy's party, Garrick Utley of NBC-TV News arrived at the door. He asked me if there was any chance I'd go to the regular hospital to visit the Brinks explosion victims. I grabbed Les Brown and Jerry Colonna and headed out the door.

Bombed in Saigon   189

They took me into the ward where they were picking broken glass out of some of the wounded. People who'd been taking showers or standing near windows were riddled with glass, and medics were plucking it out with tweezers. I shook hands with all the hands it was possible to grab. Some of the guys were on their stomachs having glass removed from their buttocks. One fellow, who was also lying on his stomach on a table, had his head down; a doctor was pulling glass out of it. Somebody yelled, "Bob Hope," and the wounded kid raised his head to see me through the blood that was streaming down his face. He said, "Merry Christmas." He meant it. He was smiling a great big smile through his blood. I'll never forget his "Merry Christmas." I still get a big lump the size of a grapefruit in my throat when I think of it.

Then I went back to the Caravelle, where a UPI reporter was waiting for me. He talked to me for a few minutes and shook my hand. Then he looked down and saw blood on my cuff. It had dripped there when I shook hands with the guys back at the hospital. The reporter's story was headlined here and there round the world: BLOOD ON HOPE'S CUFF ON CHRISTMAS EVE. To me it was sad and tragic; to the press it was sensational, and sensational does it every time.

Later on some of the crew and I went to midnight Mass in a big field at Tan Son Nhut Air Base. We had to go under military escort through the barbed wire and trenches in the street. It was one of the last years Cardinal Spellman was able to travel to Vietnam, if not the last. I sat in the front row because the cardinal's aide had reserved the seats, but it was a bad move. I may have looked as though I were meditating, but I was asleep. I admit it. I was absolutely done in after those two hospital tours. Luckily for me, I woke up before Mass was over.

A couple of days after this midnight Mass at Tan Son Nhut I met Cardinal Spellman at the airport. I said to him, "I want to apologize to you because I fell asleep twice at your midnight Mass," and he said, "That's all right, don't worry about it, I caught you at Loew's State."

CHAPTER 16

Playing the Palace—in Bangkok

Getting ready for the 1965 Christmas trip to Thailand and Vietnam, I had one of the toughest auditioning jobs I'd ever faced. Carroll Baker was the problem. Not that there was anything wrong with Miss Baby Doll herself—she was one of the most succulent dishes I'd ever put on the menu for those lonely GIs. But after she'd played the thumb-sucking nymphet in Tennessee Williams' sensational *Baby Doll* and appeared in *The Carpetbaggers*, she made a worldwide series of "very" personal appearances. The clothes she wore on those tours were so revealing that she became known as the "transparent blonde" even before she played the title role in *Harlow*. When we signed her up for the '65 tour it took me about ten minutes to prepare her act and about four days to audition her gowns. What you couldn't see through, you could see over, and what you couldn't see over wasn't there at all. She finally found a couple of gowns I figured wouldn't heat the war up too much, and might even let my TV show get on the air without an X rating.

What a cast we had that year: Joey Heatherton, Kaye Stevens, Dianna Lynn Batts (Miss World), and Anita Bryant. And because we were an equal-opportunity employer, we even had some men along—singer Jack Jones; those two classy tappers the Nicholas Brothers; my favorite straight man, Peter Leeds; Les Brown and his band; and Jerry Colonna and his mustache.

Joey Heatherton made me feel a bit dated; I knew her father, Ray Heatherton, when he was an actor and singer at Warner Brothers. But there was certainly nothing dated about Joey when she went into her Watusi routine. She'd gone along with me earlier that year when I'd hopped over to the Dominican Republic along with Tuesday Weld, Jerry Colonna, and Tony Romano to entertain the Marines. Joey took her mother on that trip, and Mom turned out to be one of the most dangerous gin rummy players since gin was invented. When she finished playing cards, I expected her to pull out three walnut shells and ask me which one had the pea under it.

Da Nang Air Base, Vietnam, 1965. (U. S. Air Force)

The last Christmas show

Naturally, Tuesday Weld, the great disappearer, one day found herself on the other side visiting the rebels. It was a strange kind of an altercation where you make personal appearances on both sides. Fortunately both sides knew her, so they called off the war for a few minutes, which, if you've had any experience with wars, you'll agree is a step in the right direction.

Vietnam was still a tinderbox, so the first stop on the Christmas tour was Bangkok, Thailand. We didn't stay long. We grabbed a shower, parked our bodies overnight at the Erawan Hotel, and then boarded some C-130s for a hop to a U.S. base called Udorn.

One of the fascinating things about the trips was watching the reactions of the first-timers when they got their initial glimpse of where the action was. So I kept an eye on Kaye Stevens. Kaye hadn't been too turned on by Bangkok—nice town and all that—but when she looked out the window of that C-130 and saw tanks, trucks, artillery, planes, and all those men waiting for us, she broke down and cried.

It was also a great experience for Carroll Baker. Primarily a movie star, she loved working on the stage in front of the crowds. We did jokes like:

BOB: Say, Carroll . . . I love the gown you're wearing . . . Is that a Schiaparelli?
CARROLL: I'm sorry, Bob, but I've forgotten where I bought it.
BOB: Mind if I look at the label?
  (*peers at label inside back of dress*)
CARROLL: What does it say?
BOB: "Off limits."
  (*indicating audience*)
How do you like this group of tigers?
CARROLL: Oh, they make a beautiful sight, Bob. It looks like one big dessert tray.
BOB: That's been left in the sun too long.
CARROLL: I want to thank you for bringing me. You had a choice of so many girls, yet you picked me.
BOB: Well, actually it was due to your agent.
CARROLL: Really?
BOB: Yeah. He hates to see a man cry!
CARROLL: Bob, how come you didn't invite my husband to come along?
BOB: What are you talking about? I begged him to come. I even gave him a boat ticket.
CARROLL: But, Bob, by the time he gets here we'll be home.
BOB: Not if he's a fast rower. Carroll, you're considered the sexiest gal in movies today, isn't that so?

CARROLL: Well, I'm rarely mistaken for Phyllis Diller!
    (*beat*)
But really, Bob, my pictures aren't meant to be that sexy. It's all in the mind.
BOB: It *is*?
    (*to audience*)
You're all under arrest!

Kaye was the first one onstage at Udorn. She went out there and sang a number called "Gee, But It's Good to Be Here," and she sang it as if she meant it. She tossed her gloves to a couple of soldiers sitting down front and

Jack Jones, Kaye Stevens, Carroll Baker, Anita Bryant, General Westmoreland at Tan Son Nhut, Vietnam, 1965. (U. S. Army)

The last Christmas show

then stretched her arms out to the ten thousand guys in the audience. They let out a roar you could hear all the way to Sacramento. When she came backstage, she told me, "That made me feel so good—like a woman. Like I was wanted and needed." She sure got their message.

A not-so-funny thing happened to us at Udorn and at a show at Takhli that same day. Les Brown's boys had left Los Angeles looking as if they'd spent a year under a rock. They were sitting up on that open stage in short-sleeved shirts with their pale faces hanging out, and they sat and sat. By the time we got back to Bangkok that night they were beginning to look pan-broiled, and the next day they puffed up like an actor's head. They ended up with sun poisoning, and poor Joey Heatherton ended up without part of her act for two days; the lead trumpeter, Don Smith, had burned his lips so badly he couldn't blow the high, hard ones she needed for her dance number.

Doing a show back in Bangkok, I had a painful accident myself. I was waiting on a five-foot platform in the wings when a guy I didn't know barged through the door. I stepped backward, and the next thing I knew, I was doing a tumbling act. A good thing for me I had a net; he turned out to be one of our security men, Robert Raft. He wasn't exactly a rubber raft, but he broke my fall enough so that all I hurt was my ankle. I picked up a golf club, waggled it a few times, and went back onstage. But that evening at the Erawan, a doctor found that I had sprained at least two ligaments in my leg. I didn't let on to the cast, and I got that doctor to tape it up good and tight. I was scheduled to play the Palace that night, and no good trouper missed a gig at the Palace. Ah yes, the Palace. That invitation dated back to 1960 when the King and Queen of Thailand paid an official visit to the United States. Like all good tourists they came to Hollywood and made the mandatory visits to the Farmers Market, Knott's Berry Farm, and "a Hollywood movie studio."

At that time Lucille Ball and I were collaborating on a movie called *The Facts of Life* for United Artists. The King and Queen visited us on the set and stayed for several hours. They turned out to be real movie buffs. They were fascinated by the technicalities of movie making and they asked us a lot of questions. The Queen in a careless moment said that if we ever got over to Bangkok to give her a call. At the time it was just a gracious invitation, but safe. How was I to know that my straw-hat circuit would eventually include Bangkok.

As soon as we arrived in Bangkok the word was passed through diplomatic channels to Their Majesties that we were approachable.

The next day the major, who was the King's equerry, called and said that the King would like to have us for dinner.

I said, "Oh, that's very nice. We'd be delighted to come."

He said, "How many is 'we'?"

And I said, "Eighty."

Playing the Palace—in Bangkok   195

He said . . . well, I don't exactly know what he said. There were several short words in Thai which I assume meant "How delightful," because shortly thereafter royal invitations to dinner at the Palace were hand-delivered to the cast and crew, and like all good peasants we were thrilled.

I'm not much on protocol, but that night with King Phumiphon and Queen Sirikit probably set diplomacy back about fifty years. I introduced Joey Heatherton to the King and she did all right—managed a little bow, said how d'ya do, and then backed off gracefully. Kaye Stevens did an all-out curtsy. And then I said, "Your Majesties, this is the young lady who represents the entire United States of America. This is Miss U.S.A., Dianna Lynn Batts." Dianna wrinkled up her nose, made two fingers on her left hand into a V sign, and said to the King, "Hi." Then she turned to the Queen and said it again: "Hi." I just about dropped my socks. The Queen, though, was an all-right lady. She took a look at Dianna, realized she was just a good-natured kid, and replied, "Well, hi yourself."

That set the tone for the evening. We did all the right things, you understand, standing when Their Majesties stood and sitting when Their Majesties sat and never crossing our legs. The Thais believe, rightly enough, that the sole of the foot is the lowest part of the human body. Taking it from there, they also believe that it's the worst kind of insult ever to show the bottom of your feet to anybody. But the mood was informal, to say the least. Kaye Stevens sat opposite some prince at dinner, and kept saying things like, "How do you like it here, prince baby?"

I was talking to the King, and he told me he had been born in Massachusetts. "Gee," I said, "that would make you eligible to be President of the United States."

"Yes," he said, "I thought of that. But I took the job of King here because I thought the work would be a little steadier."

The show had a few hitches, but nobody seemed to mind. The microphone broke and fell when Jack Jones tried to use it as a hand mike, and Joey couldn't dance because of blisters—on her feet and the band's lips. But then Les Brown began to play "Days of Wine and Roses," and before you knew it the King had his solid-gold saxophone out and was sitting in. You could tell he was just getting started, and there it was one o'clock. We had to get up at five, so we finally approached him and suggested that it was getting very late and it was time for us to go back to the hotel to bed. The King seemed surprised. "What time do you have to be up?" he wanted to know.

"Five o'clock," we said.

"Oh, five o'clock?" said the King. "Wonderful, we can jam until four and then you can go right to the plane."

Fortunately the Queen took pity on our pooped musicians and led His Majesty off to the royal pad.

We enjoyed their hospitality for five years in a row. Each year a totally

Harold and Fayard Nicholas, USS Ticonderoga, *China Sea, 1965. (U. S. Army)*

Anita Bryant at Tan Son Nhut Air Base, Vietnam, 1965. (U. S. Air Force)

198   *The last Christmas show*

different meal—each year a different palace. And we always had a fine time because they were a charming couple—a great host and hostess. They love the uncouth, the unwashed—no matter how many gaffs we made, no matter how limited our knowledge of protocol, they seemed to enjoy us.

And one time about four years later the King mentioned to me that he might be coming to America. I said, "Gee, that's wonderful; why don't you come and visit me?"

And he said, "Can I bring eighty?!"

At Tan Son Nhut airport in Saigon the next day I stepped up to a mike and recalled the previous year's blast at the Brinks. "Saigon is really a very friendly city. The last time I was here, a hotel came out to greet us." This time, Westy Westmoreland came out to greet us, and everything was done in proper military fashion—at least until Joey Heatherton, overcome by the general's good looks, threw her arms around his neck and kissed him. She was immediately followed by Carroll Baker, Kaye Stevens, and Jack Jones, who is nearsighted.

The ride into town was just about as hairy as in 1964. Once the caravan got going, with sirens wailing up front, it didn't stop for anything. When we got to the hotel, we didn't walk up to the front door, we ran. I've been in a lot of sticky situations, but I don't think I was ever as nervous as in Saigon in '65. Every time I went into that hotel I wondered whether some Cong with a contract on my life was going to pull the string. I kept looking out the window at the people in the street and wondering, "Which one?"

Christmas Eve, we took in Mass at the cathedral with Cardinal Spellman again, and the next day we went out to Tan Son Nhut to fly to Dian. That day, I got a small idea of the logistics trouble my gang could run into. There was a delay at the airport, and I went over and asked Johnny Pawlek, "Why aren't we set up? Why aren't we ready to go?"

"We've only got one plane," Johnny said.

"But the general just told me we can have anything we want," I said. "If you want two planes, you can have them. They're yours."

"Your friend the general may say we can have them," said Johnny, "but my friend the sergeant says we can't."

Westy was standing nearby, grinning from ear to ear. "That's the way the Army runs," he said.

We finally made it to Dian, played Bienhoa and Camranh Bay, and from there hopped out to the aircraft carrier *Ticonderoga*. The *Ticonderoga* was built in 1942 and is probably our oldest carrier, but she was still a grand lady doing magnificent duty in 1965. We arrived just after Cardinal Spellman had left. Captain Robert N. Miller, the skipper, said that "this is the greatest thing that's happened to the ship since the last typhoon."

Joey Heatherton was certainly the greatest thing that ever happened to Ensign Rich Tucker of Lombard, Illinois. They chose Tucker to escort our

luscious roundtop around his fighting flattop because he was one of the two bachelors in the squadron. But as one of the crewmen chimed in while Tucker and Joey sashayed toward the end of the flight deck, "He was also the one wearing a gun."

Anita Bryant and Jerry Colonna judged a beard contest. The professor kept his distance, but Anita snuggled up to each man's chin foliage until she finally found a texture that suited her. "This is it!" she shouted. The winner, Allen Boucher of St. Cloud, Minnesota, insisted that Anita was the first prize, but he finally settled for $50 and shore leave in the Philippines.

There's an unbelievable tension aboard a carrier when they're waiting for the planes to come in. Some come in with bombs and rockets hanging below their wings—the ones that didn't get away right. When you're belowdecks, you subconsciously listen. You hear the plane bounce, and then you can tell that it didn't catch the arresting wire and had to go around again. That was a terrible thing. One guy missed six times before he made it. Nobody said anything, but you could tell they were listening and waiting and listening and waiting. When he finally made it, there were deep sighs all around.

We were all fascinated by the technique of the landings, and Admiral Ralph Cousins, who was then commander of Carrier Division 9, suggested that we go up on the bridge and watch a squadron returning from a mission over enemy territory. It was eerie up there on the bridge as the planes streaked in out of the darkness, picked up the beam, and landed on the careening deck with meticulous accuracy. As fast as one plane would land they would tow it away to make way for the next.

Then it happened. The ship was pitching and as it came up a plane was landing. It caught its tail on the edge of the flight deck, missed the arresting wire—there was a shower of sparks as it skidded over the edge into the China Sea.

The pilot, Lieutenant W. S. Braugher of Newark, Ohio, hit his ejector button before his plane exploded in a ball of flame, but for thirty anguished minutes we were afraid the pilot was lost.

The carrier's escort destroyers, the USS *Turner Joy* and the USS *Swanson*, scoured the waters.

The tension was almost unbearable as they searched the seas in the dark. And then came word over the loudspeaker: the pilot had been sighted and plucked from the water by the angel, the helicopter that is always aloft when planes are taking off or landing.

What a scream went up in that boat when the copter landed. The medics rushed to the hatch, opened it, and helped the pilot across the flight deck to sick bay. Then the pilot struggled, fought with the medics, broke away, and ran back to the copter. He climbed in and kissed the angel pilot. I guess if you're a hero you can get away with that stuff.

Captain William H. House, the Navy chief of staff, and I drove golf balls

Kaye Stevens at Saigon, Vietnam, 1965. (U. S. Air Force)

Playing the Palace—in Bangkok   201

from the flight deck before the show started. Then we turned to and strutted our stuff in front of the *Ticonderoga*'s crew while the crews of the *Turner Joy* and *Swanson* watched through binoculars from off our beam.

Afterward, the *Turner Joy* messaged the *Ticonderoga*:

PLEASE RELAY TO HOPE TROUPE, MISS HEATHERTON, MISS BRYANT, MISS STEVENS, MISS USA—ALTHOUGH WE HAVE BACK-ROW SEATS, THE VERY THOUGHT OF THE NEARNESS OF YOU HAS DONE WONDERS FOR OUR MORALE. THANK YOU.

From the *Ticonderoga* we took choppers to Ankhe. Kaye Stevens' pilot let her listen in on the earphones, and she could hear voices in Vietnamese. It sounded to her like "Voing, boing, Bob Hope." She asked the pilot what they were saying and he said, "They're down there giving our position. For security, they need to know where we are every minute."

The biggest security problem in 1965 came on the ground at the Ankhe headquarters of the 1st Air Cavalry Division. We could see our soldiers in action to the right of the helicopter as we dropped down. Just before the show, a sergeant major stepped in front of the audience and made an announcement: "Keep an aisle clear on both sides of the stage in case of incoming mortar rounds. In case of VC attack, the left side of the audience will move out to the right. The center audience will move to the rear, and the cast of the Hope show will take cover in the foxholes immediately adjacent to the stage."

Reassuring, what? The action was so close to Ankhe that the commanding officer, General Kinnard, wasn't there to introduce us; he had to leave the field in the middle of combat and didn't get to the base until we'd already started. We never had to follow the emergency instructions, but later one of the security men told us that the Cong had been sitting out there within a mile of the show. I hope they liked the jokes. About five thousand soldiers saw the show; another thousand were positioned around the base in case of attack. Above us, four choppers circled on patrol and a forward air controller (known as a "fac" in GI slang) swooped low over the hills looking for VC troop movements.

They even had the radar turned on so they could detect incoming mortar rounds in flight. That wouldn't have done us any good if they'd been on target, but it could pinpoint the mortar crew and give our fighter planes and artillery a chance to zero in on it. The immediate perimeter of the show site, within two hundred yards of the stage, was protected by troops with rifles, machine guns, and wire-detonated mines. That was show biz in Vietnam; Broadway actors should have it so good.

None of that security got a workout at Ankhe, but we could have used a little during the second show we did that day, at Nhatrang, home base of the psychological warfare unit, the 5th Air Commando Squadron. The day before we got there, the VC had blown up a warehouse one hundred yards from the stage. During the show, Kaye Stevens was singing her opening number, and the lyrics went something like, "Frankly I feel right at home, this is champagne with all the fizz, this is where the excitement is . . ." At the end of that last lyric, воом! Off went a grenade. Kaye didn't know whether to cry, scream, run, or drop to the floor. Luckily, she didn't do any of these. About five thousand heads had turned in the direction of the blast, but Kaye is a real trouper; she went right back into the song and all those heads wheeled right back too.

Just as we were closing the show a captain stepped up to the microphone. It was completely ad lib and unprogramed, but more than that, I was thrown by his name tag. It said, "Cooley." And that was the name of one of my very closest friends, Charley Cooley, who got me my first job back in the old days when I was sweating it out trying to get started in Chicago. He traveled with me until he died several years ago. When I saw the name Cooley, I couldn't quite place it. Was this a relative, or what? Actually, it was mere coincidence. The man's name was Chaplain Cooley, and he asked if he might lead us in prayer.

It was just about sunset, and we bowed our heads. It was suddenly all very quiet. It was a lovely prayer, simply spoken, and thanking God for our nation, our heritage, and asking help and guidance and the strength to carry on our mission.

Just as he finished speaking there was a pause, and then three jets roared out of the sky, buzzed us, and roared off into the sun. It was a shockingly dramatic moment—either the wildest coincidence in the world, or somebody up in that big stage in the sky has the makings of a great director.

We did the Da Nang show the next day under some of the most miserable conditions since Moses played Egypt. Talk about mud! When our helicopters landed, there were soldiers assigned to carry the girls through that knee-deep red goo. The girls even got carried to the latrine. If you were a fellow and had to go you had to go it alone.

That Da Nang show was one of our few Christmas shows that had to be called on account of rain. It was drizzling pretty good when I came out, took a look at all those guys sitting up to their rumps in mud, and said, "What a delightful spot! How come they missed this for a GI housing tract? Don't just sit there—plant rice."

Then Kaye put on her $4,000 dress and her $30 shoes and a lot of mascara and went out to sing one of her numbers. "On a wonderful day like today," she warbled, "I defy any cloud to appear in the sky/I dare any raindrop to flop in my eye/On such a wonderful day." And down it came. By the time she finished, a great black river of mascara was running down her face, her false eyelashes had fallen off, and every GI in the crowd was doubled up laughing. But that was it for the day. As the band played "Thanks for the Memory" the audience slowly sank into the mud.

It was a shame too, considering the trouble my advance men had scouting the site for the show. Sil Caranchini and Johnny Pawlek had flown up there in a clucky old Caribou aircraft. Sil remembers that the maximum ceiling in that plane was twelve thousand feet, and they had to go up that high to get over a cloud bank that had socked in Da Nang. Then the pilot said he'd lost communication with the ground, so he'd have to go down and see where he was. He spotted an opening in the cloud bank and dropped like a rock from twelve thousand feet to seventy-five. Johnny Pawlek had a cold, and his ears just about exploded in that unpressurized clunker.

They were over the water when they finally broke out of the clouds, and Sil swears that the waves were lapping over the wheels. They circled around, trying to get their bearings, scurrying up and down the coast until a warrant officer said that they had better find a field soon because they were running out of gas. Just then they spotted an airstrip. It wasn't Da Nang, but the pilot figured it was better to land there than run out of gas somewhere worse, and he made a pass over the strip. They were just about to set down, when—oops—the pilot decided that it wasn't friendly territory and up he went. They were skimming over the treetops with the gas getting lower and lower when the pilot finally spotted the mountain at Da Nang. When they landed, the only thing in the tank was a drop of gas and a lot of prayers.

When the Da Nang show got rained out, I flew from there with a few troupe members to do a command performance for some of the men who'd been wounded in Vietnam and were being patched up in the hospital at Clark Air Base in the Philippines. We got aboard a couple of twin-engined jets with a few thermoses of orange juice (with just a splash of vodka) and took off. Thank heaven for those thermoses; if it hadn't been for them, I think I would have died of pneumonia right there on the plane. I was soaking wet, not so much from the rain but from wearing a raincoat in all that heat.

I remember that Dianna Lynn Batts was in about the same soaked condition I was; she looked like a week-old mushroom. Then our den mother, Anita Bryant, put Dianna's hair up in curlers. After a couple of hours in the air, Anita brushed Dianna's hair out. Talk about magic mushrooms! That wilted flower suddenly became Miss U.S.A. again.

At Clark we did a brief bit at the airport, then went over to the hospital. They had all the movable patients in the lobby, and we did a full show for them. Afterward we went through the wards to talk to the guys who hadn't been able to make it to the lobby. I remember I had a special message for

Tuesday Weld, Tony Romano, Dominican Republic, 1965. (U. S. Air Force)

one kid from his Marine buddies at Chu Lai. When I started in the door of his room, the doctor said, "I don't know if you should see him."

"I've got to see him," I said.

I went in, and they had that poor guy on a special vibrating pad, trying to keep his circulation going. He was incoherent. I kept trying to get through to him, but I don't think I ever did. All I could do was say a few words and leave the stuff from his buddies—a book and a picture with a lot of signatures wishing him luck. I was really down when I walked out of there.

Luckily, there was a cheerful postscript to that 1965 trip. At Westy Westmoreland's annual Christmas Eve dinner in Saigon that year our girls had gone on a kind of scavenger hunt for insignia. Kaye started it, I think. Before dinner, they began plucking badges, bars, and stars from every uniform in sight. I remember that Westy had one badge he was particularly proud of—something President Nguyen Cao Ky had given him for making a parachute jump with the Vietnamese airborne troops. I have a feeling it was practically a medal for bravery, but he only kept it for about half an hour before dinner. By the time we went into dinner, that badge and just about everything else was gone—including one of his sets of four stars, which Carroll Baker had collared. Every other officer in the room was stripped of everything those girls could unpin—one of them even filched a cross from a chaplain. She held it in her hand for a minute, looking at it, then she raised her baby blues and asked, "What rank are you?"

After dinner and a grand speech by the general, Kaye Stevens walked up to him and said, "You know, you're so beautiful with those stars and those stars are so beautiful . . ."

Westy said, "You really want them, don't you?" And he took them off and handed them to her. When I made my little thank-you speech afterward I called him "Gypsy Rose Westmoreland."

It took four years, but Westy finally got even when we happened to run into each other in Columbus, Ohio, in 1969. Westy was there to talk at the commissioning ceremonies at the Ohio State ROTC. I was there to get an honorary LL.D. from Ohio State University. That night the city fathers threw a shindig for Westy at the Wigwam Club just outside of town, and when I talked to him on the phone he asked me to come over.

I got there about eleven, and by eleven-thirty they'd twisted Westy's arm enough to get him to stand up and make a few remarks. He aimed them straight at me. He recalled a time when he and I had been at West Point for a graduation dinner. After the dinner, a lot of the people in the audience went up to the head table to talk and ask for autographs. Westy was wearing a white dress uniform and a chestful of medals, but one little old lady walked up and said, "I've seen you so many times on television. I never thought I'd get to meet you in person. Only somehow you don't look the way you do on

TV. You look much younger." She took a second look at Westy and added, "You *are* Bob Hope, aren't you?"

At the Wigwam Club, Westy added: "It took me days to figure out what brought on that attack of mistaken identity. Then it hit me: when that little old lady scanned my profile and got to my chin, she thought it was my nose."

But I voted for him anyway.

Phyllis Diller at Takhli, Thailand, 1966.

The last Christmas show

CHAPTER 17

And now a word from Betty Lanigan

For my 1966 trip to Vietnam I was able to persuade one of my all-time favorite funny girls, Phyllis Diller, to join the troupe. Also along were Reita Faria (Miss World), a very sexy Indian girl who was studying to be a doctor, Vic Damone, Anita Bryant, Joey Heatherton, and the Korean Kittens. The Kittens were three little girls who sang and danced as cute as they looked. To keep things twirling along, I threw in Diane Shelton, who made up for being an unknown by spinning a mean baton. Les Brown rounded out this fantastic group.

One of the wildest phenomenons of the Christmas trips was the volunteers. Each year as the trip approached they wrote or phoned from all over the country—secretaries, war widows, ushers, nurses, mechanics—they all wanted to go on the trip and help. They volunteered to sew or cook or work as dressers or porters.

I was in Palm Springs one November afternoon, when the phone rang and it was Lynda Bird Johnson calling from the White House. She said, "Bob, I'd like to go to Vietnam with you this Christmas."

I said, "Hey, great. Have you talked to your dad about it?"

She said, "Yes. He said, 'You're twenty-one, you've got to live your own life.' "

And I said, "Well, Lynda, we'll have a ball. I know they'd love to see you and I think it's great of you to volunteer."

The next day Clark Clifford, who was President Johnson's adviser, called and said, "What do you think?"

I said, "We'd love to take her—but you know the rules on these tours. She'll have to work. We can't take any tourists."

Clark said, "She'd love to work in the show. Remember she has to have

Korean Kittens, Da Nang, 1966.

The last Christmas show

half the laughs. She *is* the President's daughter." I promised and he said he'd clear it with Saigon.

About two days later Lynda Bird called me back and said, "Sorry Bob—it's off."

"Why?"

"General Westmoreland doesn't want to take a chance on that much security."

I know Westy was right but at the time we were disappointed. The guys overseas would have enjoyed knowing the President's daughter came to Vietnam to see them, and, let's be honest, it wouldn't have hurt the ratings on our TV show. Fortunately that show didn't need much help.

When we took off from Los Angeles International Airport my good-bys, for once, were not so wrenching: Dolores and my daughter Nora and son Kelly were scheduled to join me for some of the less hazardous legs of the journey. The first scheduled stop was Wake Island, but before we got there we did an impromptu radio broadcast for the 150 men aboard the Coast Guard ship *Klamath*. When I asked Vic Damone to sing something, he said he didn't know what to sing unless there were some Italians aboard the ship. The ship's answer flashed back: "Today we're all Italians, Vic."

Our Starlifter jet got a tuneful greeting at Wake from a small band of musicians dressed in airplane mechanics' white coveralls. The bandleader, Jesse Floriendo, had got himself up in a false mustache and a straw boater that exactly matched a cartoon of Jerry Colonna the group had drawn on a large hand-printed sign that read: WE MISS JERRY COLONNA. So did I. It was the first trip in years that the old professor was unable to make, and he never made another.

The crowd at Wake was bigger than usual—about 1,500 of the island's 1,800 population—but they had a couple of other reasons for being at the airport besides our gang. Just fifteen minutes before our arrival evangelist Billy Graham had taken off for Tokyo, and after we left, Cardinal Spellman was due to arrive. That took care of the topical part of my monologue: "Billy Graham is just ahead of me and Cardinal Spellman is just behind—that's the kind of book ends I like on a trip like this."

After I'd fed them as much of my humor as I thought they could take, I introduced General Emmett "Rosy" O'Donnell, the returned World War II Air Force hero who was then president of the USO. "Rosy kept the plane waiting in Los Angeles," I quipped, "because it took him so long to get the medals off his pajamas." Rosy took that one in stride and told the crowd he was glad to return to Wake since he was the first pilot ever to land there, on September 5, 1941, three months before Pearl Harbor. Rosy's mission this time was almost as vital as it had been then. He'd come along with us to inspect the USO installations at every stop to find out how to expand and improve service to the troops.

And now a word from Betty Lanigan   211

The show was a quick one because the plane was refueled and ready to carry us to our next stopover, Bangkok, Thailand. We weren't scheduled to do a show there, just take a little R and R before the rigors of South Vietnam. I'd planned a golf game with Marshal Dawee Chulasapya, then chief of staff of the Thai Air Force. The game almost had to be called on account of shoes; I'd left mine back in Hollywood. Clubs they had plenty of, but 10½Bs were scarce.

The military scurried around to see if they could borrow a pair from a big-footed member of the Royal Bangkok Sports Club. As luck would have it, they came up with three pairs. I almost wore them all, six holes per pair, like the President signing a new law with a fistful of presentation pens. It seemed that everyone wanted to say, "Bob Hope hooked his drive in these shoes."

Over the years, the cast of characters who went along to bring the servicemen a more Hope-filled Christmas grew and grew, along with some truly marvelous people in supporting roles. One of my strongest support troupers was Betty Lanigan, who represented public relations for NBC-TV. Her real role was to help us keep our sanity, be a friend to those who needed friends, and keep a perceptive eye on our progress.

A lot of what she wrote came out of her typewriter sounding official, such as, "Bob Hope's fifteenth Christmas spent entertaining American troops overseas took him on a trip of thirty thousand miles to Thailand, South Vietnam, the Philippines, and Guam. During the course of nineteen shows given for the soldiers, sailors, and Marines stationed in Southeast Asia, the indefatigable Hope was seen by more than half of all the American troops, and heard via Armed Forces Radio by thousands more . . ." You know the sort of thing.

Years later I discovered that Betty did a lot of other writing that was much more personal, human, heart-warming, and perceptive than any of the news releases she produced for the press. It took the form of diaries and letters home, and it contained some of the best accounts of what happened to us I've ever read. Betty's first trip was in 1966, and I'd like to share her remembrances with you:

A police escort took us from downtown Bangkok to the airport, an event in Thai history, since Bob was the first entertainer so honored. Well, that seventeen-minute trip may have been a great honor to Bob, but to me it was sheer terror. Bangkok traffic has to be survived to be believed, and even then it's unbelievable. Bob later quipped that "a national crisis in Thailand is when all three million people try to run the same traffic light."

The Air Force flew us to South Vietnam, and for security reasons we were not told our exact destination—Pleiku—until we were airborne. The military men on board tried to relieve the tension a bit by chatting with us en route. One Army major told me a poignant anecdote about his three-year-old back

Senator Stuart Symington, Colonel Bob Gates at Phuket, 1966.

in the States who kept asking his mother, "Why can't Daddy fight the war at home?"

Vic Damone and Bob went up to the cockpit of our plane as we approached Pleiku, home of the 4th Infantry Division. "What are those puffs of smoke down there? Artillery fire?" Vic asked. Bob answered, "No, they're just burning de Gaulle's picture." Actually, the smoke rising over the landscape came from brush fires farmers had started around their houses. They were afraid the Vietcong would hide in the underbrush and make their villages a target for allied ground or air strikes.

When Joey Heatherton and the Korean Kittens got off the plane in their miniskirts, the soldiers nearly fainted. What an impact! "Number one," they screamed (everything is either number one or—the worst—number ten; nothing seems to be in between). One soldier said to me, "Ordinarily, ma'am, I go for the more educational things. I'm really devoted to museums, temples,

And now a word from Betty Lanigan   213

Joey Heatherton at Udorn, Thailand, 1966.

Vic Damone at Chu Lai, Vietnam, 19

and all those things, but I'm willing to make an exception and watch Joey Heatherton."

We were supposed to take off immediately from Pleiku by helicopter to the foot of Dragon Mountain, where the GIs had dug out an amphitheater for the show. The takeoff was delayed, though, because the helicopters had to wait until fighter planes returning with empty bomb racks could land. An air strike was going on just four miles away.

That was pretty scary, but it didn't scare me away from the windows of the helicopter as we swooped over the countryside. Vietnam—even with all that fighting going on—was remarkably beautiful. It looked like Oregon, with

214   *The last Christmas show*

high mountains and lush vegetation. The camp at Dragon Mountain was pretty depressing, though—a combination of dust and mud. I don't know whether the GIs were depressed. They certainly weren't after we got there, even though they'd been sitting for hours in the mud. This was the troupe's first show, but the boys didn't seem to mind the rough spots. Everything Bob offered was appreciated, from the baton twirler on up.

A sketch that Bob used at every stop involved picking a boy from the audience to sing to one of the stars. At Pleiku, it was Reita Faria, Miss World. The youngster Bob picked was Tony Bruno, from East Orange, New Jersey. He was a doll, but he sang too well for the spot to be funny. It would have been better if he hadn't been able to carry a tune. Still, although he seemed sophisticated on the stage, his hand was shaking so hard afterward that he could scarcely write down his parents' address when I asked him.

The most moving thing in that grubby place was watching those ten thousand men listen to Anita Bryant sing "The Battle Hymn of the Republic." Swirls of red dust blew across the stage, moving her chiffon dress like a flag. The soldiers screamed their approval so loud it was shattering.

Back in Bangkok late that afternoon, I made a terrible ring around the bathtub at the Erawan Hotel with all that red dirt from Pleiku. But then I couldn't very well go to the royal palace with a dirty neck, not with all those exquisite Thai ladies in their jewels and silks. Bob was dapper and handsome in a white dinner jacket, and Dolores, who'd joined him by then, also looked stunning in white.

Phyllis Diller, believe it or not, looked absolutely *great*. Her hair was lovely, her dress was chic. She looked so good that she had to redo her whole act, since she couldn't rely on her usual material that pokes fun at her appearance. She took about three lines each from fifteen different routines to fit the way she looked, and she was still funny. The outdoor setting looked like the Tivoli Gardens in Copenhagen, but it was terribly uncomfortable because of the heat and the humidity. The Thai ladies all had fluttering fans, while the American girls were stuck with limp hairdos and glistening foreheads.

It was a lovely evening just the same. I couldn't imagine how Queen Sirikit managed to sit so straight for a whole evening without ever touching the back of her chair. His Majesty, who loves to play the saxophone, did something rather touching. He'd painstakingly learned "Thanks for the Memory" to honor Bob and joined Les Brown's band to play it. The Queen just sat there and smiled and smiled and smiled.

The next morning got off to a great start. First, Rosy O'Donnell told Dolores that he thought the affair at the palace was "quite a formation." No wonder Rosy has such rapport with the troops; he will never leave the service in spirit. Phyllis Diller was complaining over breakfast that she'd put elbow cream on her eyes by mistake, so they didn't blink, they bent. The rest of us were busy teasing Les Brown. The only untoward incident in Vietnam

Vic Damone and His Eminence Cardinal Spellman at Saigon, 1966.

the day before had been when the jeep he was riding with the Korean Kittens caught fire. "I don't know how it happened, Les," someone said. "You're not *that* hot."

So spirits were pretty high when we set out for the show at Takhli Air Base, home of the 8th Tactical Fighter Wing, where we were greeted by a big sign saying SNOOPY SAYS, "HAPPINESS IS BEING HOME FOR CHRISTMAS." The treat of the day came when Bob introduced Dolores, who was in the audience. The troops applauded so hard she was forced onstage, where Bob asked her to sing "White Christmas." She looked completely startled and told him she didn't know the words. He said he'd feed them to her and to sing anyway. So she did, and by the time she got to the second chorus she had mastered the lyrics perfectly and had even altered the last line to say, "And may all your Christmases be at home." While she sang, the kids were as silent, respectful, and attentive as they would have been in church. It was deeply moving, and I think we were suddenly all a little homesick.

After lunch on the base, Bob held a brief press conference. He told the newsmen that his audiences don't change over the years; the warmth remains, and they still come at 8 A.M. to see a 1 P.M. show. "Besides," he cracked, "I got hooked on box lunches back in '48."

On the way to the afternoon show site at Korat Air Base, our cavalcade of jeeps stopped at the foot of a jet plane that had just landed. Captain S. D. Mathison stepped down, thus completing his one hundredth mission over North Vietnam. He had thought nobody would meet him because he had seen all the people gathered for the Hope show when he flew in. Instead, Bob and all the girls greeted him, shared the champagne the other pilots had bought him, and cheered him as he donned his new coveralls with the "100 mission" patch already sewed on it.

That evening, on the plane back to Bangkok, Dolores told me how much the soldiers had moved her: "I could take every one of them and give them a hug and a kiss—and a good plate of spaghetti. Then I'd send them off for a good bath and see to it that they joined other young people for a good time. They verify what you think you know about American youth. People who criticize the young people today are like reviewers who comment after reading only a third of a book. If you saw them hooting and screaming at the glamourpusses on the show, you'd think they were a bunch of sex maniacs. Then they turn around and cheer and applaud for Anita Bryant singing 'The Battle Hymn of the Republic.' They're so much more than people give them credit for."

To the delight of the men in the cast, we had two unexpected passengers the next day on the flight to Camranh Bay—a pair of perfectly gorgeous Pan American stewardesses who had been in Bangkok on a forty-eight-hour layover. They offered to help out with our wardrobes just so they could be in on such a glorious experience.

We arrived at the field to find twenty thousand troops sitting on the sand, with only a slight breeze keeping the place from turning into a frying pan. It was so hot that Barney McNulty, who had picked up a bug in Acapulco, passed out, and our director, Mort Lachman, found himself up on the ladder handling the cue cards until the medics revived Barney. When Bob got a look at the size of the audience and heard the first roars of laughter, he was delighted. Backstage he said, "My God, it's like the Hollywood Bowl out there!" Mort went backstage to make sure the sound man was prepared for the onslaught of sound that always greeted Joey Heatherton. Mort doesn't miss a thing. He was afraid the GIs would break the equipment with the sheer volume of their enthusiasm.

And now a word from Betty Lanigan 217

The equipment survived, so did we, and we headed back to Bangkok for an early night. Next day we were scheduled to play Udorn Air Base and Nakhon Phanom Air Base, both in Thailand. Nakhon, which is nicknamed "Naked Fanny" (the service never changes!) is way up near the border of Laos. Bob was a big favorite with the pilots because he was so interested in everything they did. After we landed during a thunder and lightning storm, he addressed them British-officer fashion and said, "Good work, men. Take three or four dollars out of petty cash."

There were so many signs in the audience at Udorn that Bob quipped, "They've got more idiot cards than we have!" One air-rescue group called the Jolly Green Giants had a sign that read THE JOLLY GREEN GIANTS WILL PICK UP JOEY ANYTIME. The Korean Kittens, one of the most popular acts in the show, really broke it up with their dancing. Nora Hope, who was watching them from the wings, would rather dance than eat, so she was practically drooling at the great music. When I told Bob I thought Nora was jealous of the Kittens, he laughed and said, "Yeah, she'd have her eyes slanted if she thought I'd let her get out there and dance."

It turned out that Nora didn't have to get her eyes fixed at all. After Dolores sang "White Christmas," Bob introduced Nora and Kelly. On impulse, he said to Nora, "Go ahead and dance for them." She whipped around to the band and said, "Give me a beat," and then did the wildest Watusi you ever saw. She looked cute as a bug in her bright yellow dress and yellow scarf hat.

We ate lunch between shows at the Nakhon Phanom mess hall. The Thai workers had been told that some big American TV stars were coming, and you should have seen the puzzled looks on their faces when they got a load of Phyllis Diller. She was in full make-up between shows, and her hair was teased way out around her head. They were peeking out from behind posts and around doorways in utter confusion.

The high point of the afternoon show came when Anita Bryant sang "The Battle Hymn of the Republic." The troops rose to their feet and cheered, and for the first time, Anita wept. Before the tears of the rest of us had time to dry, Bob was presented with a beautiful teak carving of a stack of elephants. The plaque on the base read: "To Bob Hope, whom the elephants and the troops in Thailand will never forget, Christmas, 1966."

Back in Bangkok, it was hard to sleep that night. I kept thinking about Tan Son Nhut, our show site the next day. The Tan Son Nhut show was the core of our trip, the place where we were most needed. The base was filled with Christmas loneliness, and more. There were no dependents to help pass the long days, there was constant tension because of terrorist raids, and the hospitals were filled with wounded, often dying men.

To brighten our spirits on the flight from Thailand to Vietnam, we had a Christmas tree trimming party on the plane. Everybody put an ornament

Joey Heatherton, Reita Faria, Phyllis Diller, Korean Kittens at Cu Chi, Vietnam, 1966.
(U. S. Army)

or a piece of tinsel on the tree, and we took pictures of Bob, Dolores, Nora, and Kelly around it. Then Major George Dawson brought us down to earth— or as down to earth as you can get on a plane—with the following briefing:

"We have no reason to believe there is more danger from terrorists on this visit than there was on your last two trips to Vietnam. But just in case there is a mortar attack on the show site, lie down flat to reduce the target. If your hotel is under attack, lie on the floor and cover your face and eyes. The greatest danger is from flying glass. Your best protection from that is to cover yourself with your mattress. Do not go to the window. Do not run toward an explosion if you hear one. They usually set off two bombs. One goes off first and attracts a crowd; the second gets the crowd. So run in the opposite direction. And if you see a package anywhere, it is not a Christmas present. Call the demolition squad in a hurry."

We were also warned not to have dinner in large groups, but to go only with two or three people since a crowd makes a good target. These were

And now a word from Betty Lanigan   219

sobering words, further reinforced when armed guards in machine-gun–mounted jeeps met us at the plane. We traveled by convoy to the show site with those armed jeeps interspersed in the caravan.

Some ten thousand troops had gathered in the hot sun to see the show. There were even hospital patients whose dressings had to be changed at some point during the performances. The Army had parked ambulances at the back of the site, so the bandages were changed on schedule. The patients then were hurried back to laugh and applaud at Bob's sallies and whistle at the pretty girls. The intense heat was hard on everyone, but particularly on the band. The medics said they expected a lot of cases of heat prostration, so hospital towels were cut into thirds and soaked in garbage cans filled with ice water. Nora Hope acted as runner for the iced towels, and not a single member of the band passed out.

The heat, however, wasn't our only problem. Vic Damone, dressed in an Air Force uniform for a sketch with Bob, was barred from the area and told that backstage was "for cast only." Fortunately, someone grabbed him in time to make his entrance. Just after that the backfiring of the motor operating an air conditioner brought an MP rushing to the spot, shoving a magazine into his M-16 rifle.

When the show was over the cast went to the Third Field Hospital at Tan Son Nhut. Bob had a blister on his heel (a souvenir from his borrowed golf shoes) fixed so he could keep up his rapid pace. It was just as well that he stopped for five minutes, because this hospital visit was really rough. Although Bob never let the patients sense his dismay at their wounds and their pain, in the moments when he walked from one ward to another he would be white around the mouth from anger at the thought of what they were undergoing. His deft, sympathetic (but not sentimental) manner with the patients was fantastic. Some of the other members of the troupe were getting their introduction to visiting the wounded. Nora Hope went along, and before entering each ward she would take a big gulp of air, then charge in smiling, saying softly, "I'm Nora Hope. How do you feel today?"

Vic Damone also began to come into his own during the hospital visit. His warmth and feeling for the sick and wounded was obvious in his every move. The hospital visit reached inside him, and he was obviously shaken. Phyllis Diller, who said she was more pained than most of the patients during the visit, nevertheless did it well. The kids loved her. She said marvelously shocking things to them, so they giggled and guffawed like the teen-agers most of them are. We asked her to pose with one boy because his profile was so great. "His *profile!*" she shrieked. "His whole *body* is great!"

Reita Faria, a fourth-year medical student, was not appalled at the sights. In fact, the hospital didn't seem to upset her as much as the sight of the thousands of lonely soldiers on the hillside at Pleiku. After the tour she said, "Imagine doing this for someone else's country!" She wept all the way back in the plane until Bob told her, "Reita, we're not doing it for someone else's country, we're doing it for the world. As Miss World you ought to know that."

Back in Saigon, the streets were thronged with people celebrating Christmas Eve the way we celebrate New Year's. Thousands of them wearing masks and paper hats and blowing horns brought traffic to a standstill. Though curfew had lifted for the civilian population wanting to attend midnight Mass, the city was still scary. Any pedicab or jeep could have held a terrorist, so you never felt secure. You had to walk in the middle of the streets because no one was allowed on the sidewalks near the buildings for fear of bombs.

I would have liked to have spent the evening in my hotel room, but Army photographers had processed the pictures we'd taken of Bob and his family and I had to find out if AP or UPI was interested in wirephotoing them back to the States. I took off with an armed escort, and because of all the crowds I didn't get back to the hotel till 12:30 A.M. I couldn't take a sleeping pill because the water wasn't safe, and there was no phone in the room to call for bottled water. So I just lay there until morning and wondered what the rest of the world was doing on Christmas Eve.

The first show on Christmas Day was at Dian for the 1st Division—the big red "one"—in a nice little theater built in the middle of what appeared to be a grassy mud puddle. The whole area was protected by tanks equipped with dozer blades, MPs with rifles every three or four feet, overhead air cover, and dozens of other security measures.

Backstage they had fixed up a buffet table with all kinds of good things we felt guilty about eating, since we knew that many of them—such as fresh oranges—were things the GIs had not had in months. Besides, we were due to have Christmas dinner at Cu Chi before the afternoon show. But the soldiers' good will was so obvious, we just had to sample everything and tell them how wonderful the food was. We kept saying thank you to them, and they kept saying thank you back to us, so it was all very Christmasy in a nicely awkward way.

Choppers flew us to Cu Chi after the morning show, and the military there told us that for the benefit of the enlisted men, they had split us into groups of three or four, so each detachment of men could have someone from the States as a guest at Christmas dinner. The group with whom Bob had lunch bade him good-by at two-thirty when we left for the show. At two-forty they killed two VC and captured a third who had sneaked in through the perimeter. During the show we could hear the sharp crack of rifle fire, but it was three quarters of a mile away, so it didn't seem scary. The artillery began to roar as things heated up near the Iron Triangle, but the shooting was going the other way, and it didn't seem nearly so frightening as being in Saigon. At least you could tell where it was coming from.

The show was a happy show. The famous "Tropic Lightning" 25th Di-

General Rosy O'Donnell (in white shirt) at Ankhe, Vietnam, 1966.

222   *The last Christmas show*

vision, home-based in Hawaii, was a great audience for Bob. But the thing about it which most of us still remember and which Bob still laughs about was his introduction by General Fred Weyand.

> WEYAND: Bob, I'm here for one very simple reason, and that is to thank you on behalf of all these women and men who are here at Cu Chi with the 25th Division.
>   (*cheers and applause*)
> You wonder, at least I do, why would a man like this . . . ah . . . come all this way . . . volunteer on Christmas Day to appear here with us. And you sort of wonder if maybe he's committed a crime in the United States, or . . .
>   (*laughter*)
> . . . or maybe he's ducking the draft . . .
>   (*laughter*)
> . . . or maybe he's just some kind of a nut. You can't tell.
>   (*cheers and applause*)

For the second day in a row some crew members made a hospital visit immediately after the show. It was pretty rough because there were a few patients who'd been caught in the "truce" and were in very bad shape. One boy, who didn't want to spoil the pleasure of the others at having visitors from home, folded pieces of cardboard and clenched them between his teeth so he wouldn't scream. Phyllis Diller saved the day. Her laugh became Number One on the Tape Recorder Hit Parade at the Twelfth Evacuation Hospital. Every boy wanted his own tape of her wild cackle, and she obliged, over and over again.

Meanwhile, Bob and four or five people in the camera crew were being flown by helicopter into one of the self-help villages (the pacification program in which the Army was so vitally interested) to see tangible evidence of the "other war" being waged for the hearts and minds of the Vietnamese. Bob got an opportunity to see firsthand what the villagers had accomplished for themselves in becoming self-sustaining. He was buoyed up by the experience and raved about the visit on his return. "This is what has to win it," he said. "Wonderful, what they're doing. If it could only be repeated over this whole country."

The day after Christmas, our show at Ankhe was held in the proverbial "sea of mud." It poured, it rained, the heavens opened up. The kids sat doggedly in the mud, where many of them had spent the night rolled up in ponchos so they wouldn't miss the show. Big brooms were used to sluice water off the stage, and giant rolls of canvas were spread to dry it off enough so that our girls could dance. Five minutes before the show started, it stopped raining. (The band claimed that on one Christmas trip, Bob looked up at the heavens when it started to rain and said, "Not now!" and it stopped. At Ankhe, I became a believer.)

Diane Shelton started her baton-twirling number and kicked off her shoes about midway so she wouldn't fall on the slippery stage. The Korean Kittens heated up the stage so much that I swear it dried out while they were singing their crazy version of "Bill Bailey, Won't You Please Come Home?" That song wouldn't have struck me so funny if the Kittens had been able to pronounce *l*'s. Some of us had been dubious about taking Asian girls to entertain troops in the Orient, but we should have known that Bob wouldn't have signed them up unless he was sure they were sure-fire.

Every year before the Christmas trip, Bob's house turns into a miniature post office as scores of wives and relatives send Bob messages and gifts for their men overseas. Naturally the odds against our finding any of the guys are very high, but occasionally there's a happy coincidence and we play a base and are actually able to deliver one of the messages. That was the case at Ankhe that day. And here's a transcript of what happened:

(*Hope onstage*)

BOB: Is Specialist 4th Brian H. O'Connell here? Where is he? Would you come up, please? This fellow is from Studio City, California . . . and he's the proud father of twins . . . do you know about this?

(*laughter from audience*)

O'CONNELL: I know something about it.

BOB: I hope you do. Just before we got on the plane, his wife brought this over to us. Here's a picture of twins. His twins that he's never seen. Right here.

(*yells and applause*)

MUSIC: "*Rock-a-bye Baby*"

BOB: Oh, we have arrangements for everything. We also sell Pablum on the side. Isn't that nice, though? How old are they? When were they born?

O'CONNELL: November 16.

BOB: November 16? And you have never seen them, huh?

O'CONNELL: Nope.

BOB: Where you been, in the rough, or something?

All we want to say is congratulations. That's wonderful. And they're beautiful kids. Here's a picture of them. Just pass it around. Let everybody see it. Congratulations.

(*he exits*)

MUSIC: Playoff

Billy Graham and Joey Heatherton at Qui Nhon, Vietnam, 1966.

The weather cleared for our second show of the day at Qui Nhon, and everyone's spirits began to lift. Bob told the troops he was wearing his "Sunday-get-shot-at" clothes. They loved the line about how nice it was to be back "after my fifty-week pass." Another well-received line was brand-new: "They told me the next war was going to be a pushbutton war, so I'm glad to be here with all you pushbuttons."

After the show we were flown to the USS *Bennington* to spend the night and do two shows—one on the *Bennington* and the second on the *Franklin D. Roosevelt*. Almost all of us were violently seasick, which detracted from the charm of the crisp sheets, the good mattresses, and the great food.

And now a word from Betty Lanigan   225

Next morning broke bright and sunny, but very windy. Several of the cast were green of face. At the beginning of the show the wind was so strong that the sheet music on the stands of Les Brown's band whirled in the air like dry leaves. Sailors chased the music wildly down the deck of the *Bennington*, and most of it was recovered.

I was intrigued to see that one officer brought his own chair to view the show—an aluminum rocker with fat plastic cushions. He sat there contentedly rocking away, happy as a clam, while Bob quipped, "What's the name of this island? It looks like a floating L.A. freeway." Bob was tickled by a hand-printed note he got, which had been written in second-grade fashion by some wise sailor: "Dere Mistur Hope, Can you and Joey come over to our hous for Chrismus?"

In the afternoon, the show moved on to the *FDR*, which had steamed up near the *Bennington* during the morning. Helicopters deposited the cast and crew on the deck of the ship, but the wind was still blowing with such force that everyone was relieved to find that the show would be done on the hangar deck under cover. The decision to have the show indoors had been made at the last minute, and the men had worked all night long to build the stage. That was no mean feat when you consider the welding of scrap iron that went on, the measuring, the carpentry, and all the rest. Having it indoors cut down on the number of men who could attend, but the carrier had closed-circuit television, so most of the men could watch on that. I loved Bob's line about doing the second show of the day on the *FDR*: "I feel like a wetback Avon lady." He looked the part in a saffron yellow jacket with a seal on it reading "Tonkin Gulf Yacht Club."

Fifteen thousand troops sat in a cold rain to greet us the next morning when we flew back into Da Nang. In the past ten days there had been four-teen inches of rain. It was the middle of the monsoon season, but men had been brought in from as far away as sixty miles, rain or no rain. Bob told the Marines on hand that he brought them greetings from their "real leader, Gomer Pyle." He also explained to the non-Marines that the Marines were so tough that when they "get a three-day pass, they go to Hanoi."

After the show the troupe was again split into groups. Vic Damone joined Reita and me on a tour of the hospital. Vic has always been good, but that day he outdid himself. He even had to sing unaccompanied because his guitarist had stayed behind. I asked a young doctor in the intensive-care ward if it was okay for us to be there, and he said, "Don't you know what you can do for these men that I can't touch with pills and plasma?" I guess he was right, because when Vic asked gingerly if they wanted him to sing, they begged him to. He stood alone in the middle of the ward and sang "Strangers in the Night."

Next day we took off for Clark Air Base in the Philippines. We were play-ing Clark mostly for the hospital patients, not for the troops stationed there on permanent duty. Their needs were pretty much taken care of since there were about ten thousand dependents on hand.

Bob's opener for the afternoon show brought roars from the audience of seventeen thousand: "The war is costing entirely too much. Wouldn't it be awful if we ran out of money and they repossessed the war? The next thing you'll hear about is a coin-operated machine gun." Then he rattled off a little rapid-fire comment on drafting women: "We may still have a swinging war. If we can't end it, we might as well enjoy it."

When the final applause faded away, Bob headed for the hospital with Colonel William Hernquist, the chief of staff. One of the first patients Bob visited had had his face shattered by shrapnel during the truce, and his right hand was heavily bandaged. Bob said to him, gently, "Hand me your ping-pong paddle."

After Bob toured the wards Colonel Hernquist asked him to go to the air-strip to see an air-evacuation plane take off for the States. There were 80 patients—40 in litters, 40 in seats. The surgeon estimated that close to 2,500 patients fly out of Clark each month. The ones who are going to recover quickly are sent to Yokohama and then returned to their outfits; others with more serious injuries or illnesses go home. He said that the high-velocity weapons inflict wounds far worse than those of World War II. Even a scalp graze from a high-velocity weapon can deal out a serious injury. A lot worse are the wounds from land mines—they are horrible.

As Bob was about to leave, another planeload of wounded came in from Vietnam, and he went aboard to say hello. One of the soldiers, evidently a victim of battle fatigue, was led off the plane by a nurse. He staggered and shambled vaguely as she gently guided him. Another of the wounded held a paperback book over his head and never stopped reading the whole time they carried him off the plane. There's a kid I could understand.

The next day, at Guam, thirty thousand troops were waiting for us. The days and weeks must get long even on a lovely island like Guam, with towering jungle cliffs, turquoise surf and pale, powdery sand. It must be like a stuck record, playing a bit of melody that you can't stand because you've heard it, and heard it, and heard it . . . The constant moaning of the wind could get a little wearing too. The isolation of that base made it seem doubly worthwhile to bring a touch of the States to so many lonely men, and they screamed themselves hoarse. It was a nice finish for the trip.

And now a word from Betty Lanigan   227

*Phil Crosby, Raquel Welch, Barbara McNair, Madeline Hartog-Bel (Miss World),
Elaine Dunn, and Earl Wilson on USS Ranger, China Sea, 1967.*

CHAPTER 18

Hurricane Raquel

There was no question in my mind about where I was going to be at Christmastime, 1967, but apparently there were some nasty rumors about where I wasn't going to be. While the show was still on the planning boards, I got a letter from a paratrooper in Vietnam:

Dear Mr. Hope,

This letter is coming to you with mistakes and all. It's the last piece of paper I could scrounge without the usual dirt and grime you find on any infantryman's stationery. Have talked with my fellow paratroopers and the rumor is that you won't be coming to Vietnam with your regular show troupe this Christmas. I just want to know if this is true. So I'm sitting in this muddy hell of a paddy trying to keep the paper dry and clean to get the answer. Anyway it's getting dark and I can't see any more—also have to get ready for Charlie. Answer if you can. If not, I still understand.

Sp/4 JOHN WATERS

The size of our cast was getting bigger and bigger, and I got so hung up with the logistics of the trip that I didn't get around to answering John until we had taken off from Los Angeles and were on our way to the usual refueling stop at Wake Island:

Dear John,

Your answer climbed aboard a big C-141 Starlifter jet this morning. We're on our way. Sixty pressure-packed gypsies at 35,000 feet, rehearsing, memorizing and fighting over who'll get the best punch lines. Charlie Solomon, our wardrobe man (this is his fourteenth trip), has trunks full of miniskirts not for me. I haven't switched. But for a great bunch of gals . . . Raquel Welch, Barbara McNair, Elaine Dunn, and the new Miss World, a beautiful twenty-one-year-old child from Peru. They're all nervous about our show. After all, it's their first time around. Wait till they play to one of those audiences in Vietnam—Pleiku, or Ankhe, or Da Nang. They'll be hooked for life.

Most of our crew—the production staff, the guys in the band, our cameramen—are veterans. Some of them have Christmas holiday hash marks all down their sleeves. Some of them haven't been home for Christmas since we started these annual gigs in 1954.

That's our answer, John. We're on our way. We'll be there if we can find you.

So pass the word to all the group and leave a welcome mat out in front of the foxholes. We should be seeing you in a couple of days. Meanwhile, don't forget to duck. I don't want to lose any part of an audience.

Best,
Bob Hope

Like a weather watcher, I take a certain pride in being able to detect hurricanes before they happen, and that year I really called one: Hurricane Raquel. Up to that time, Raquel Welch had appeared mainly on European magazine covers. She had grunted her way through a paleolithic production called *One Million B.C.* and had gone along for the ride in a science-fiction film called *Fantastic Voyage*. She'd played in five other movies, but she was best known for an appearance in which she never spoke a line, or even moved—a publicity poster for *One Million B.C.* in which she just stood there in a furry Stone Age bikini.

Standing still, Raquel could outperform most so-called sex bombs at their shimmiest. A lot of her build-up was the result of a publicity campaign directed by her then manager-husband Patrick Curtis, but Raquel certainly helped. When Curtis multiplied it out, her 5 feet 6 inches came to 37–22½–35½. I don't know why he bothered with those half-inch figures; her shape wasn't fractional to me, and I figured it wouldn't be to Sp/4 John Waters or to his buddies either.

Barbara McNair was also on her way up. She'd sung her way through a lot of guest appearances on TV with Dean Martin, Ed Sullivan, and Carol Burnett, but her own TV show was still in the future. Phil Crosby, Bing's second son (or third, depending on whether you counted him or his twin brother Dennis first), went along to do a bit of crooning and some stand-up routines with me. This was Phil's second trip, but I didn't get to see much of him on the first—it was that 1963 expedition to the eastern Mediterranean when I saw most of the world through glasses, darkly.

Also along was Elaine Dunn, a young singer who'd toured Europe, North Africa, and Iceland with me before, and was making a name for herself in

The last Christmas show

Martha Raye arriving at Tan Son Nhut airfield, Saigon, Vietnam, 1967.

General Hay at Lai Khe, Vietnam, 1967.

road companies of *Bye Bye Birdie* and *Sweet Charity*. Miss World that year was Madeline Hartog-Bel, the daughter of a Peruvian cattle rancher. She'd made beauty contest history that year by not bursting into tears when she won her title in London. Instead, she fainted dead away.

Earl Wilson, the Broadway columnist, joined us, so we had no shortage of acting talent.

As was becoming usual, our first stop was Bangkok, Thailand. We landed a little after midnight and clocked some shut-eye at the Erawan Hotel. That afternoon I played golf with Thailand's Air Marshal Dawee Chulasapya and our own General Hal McCown. Les Brown went off to visit some stateside friends who were having a traditional Thai house dedication. Nine Buddhist priests chanted, sprinkled holy water, and went through an elaborate ritual. When I asked Les why he didn't play golf with me at the Royal Bangkok Sports Club, he answered with one of those straight-faced conversation stoppers of his: "You can play golf any time, but how often do you get invited to a Buddhist house dedication?"

Our first show the next day was at Da Nang. The Marine who introduced me, Corporal Donald Laedtke of the 1st Force Reconnaissance Company, had won both a Bronze Star and a Purple Heart. He won the first decoration when he was radio man on an eight-man patrol that had been hit hard by the Cong. His lieutenant and sergeant had been killed and he'd had to take command himself. He won the Purple Heart when he and others in his patrol were hit by a grenade burst.

After the show, Corporal Laedtke wrote a letter home. It was forwarded to me by his folks and I gratefully include it here.

Dear Mom and Dad,

Today was a real thrill for me because I was given the job of introducing Bob Hope to the sixteen thousand Marines in the audience when he gave his first show in Vietnam for Christmas 1967. To tell you the truth, there were some Navy and Army guys in the crowd, not all Marines, and the Lord only knows who was up on the sides of that mountain, hanging from the trees and climbing on top of telephone poles. If it was Charlie, he must have liked the show because we didn't have a bit of trouble.

Some of the guys were called back to duty during the performance, but most of us got to stay all the way through. Good thing, too, because some of the guys were there at 5 A.M. waiting for the show to begin at 2 P.M. I don't know how those guys found out so fast, to know how to get to the show site so early, because they only told us the night before. Guess they wanted to keep the news secure.

All my life, you know, Mom and Dad, I've watched Bob Hope on television and in the movies, but I never saw one of his shows. Let me tell you the guys aren't going to forget this one in a hurry. He had Raquel Welch with him and she was wearing some kind of skirt that was even shorter than a miniskirt and this blue and white dress was knitted or something because it sure let you know how she got to be a pin-up girl.

Mr. Hope had a lot of jokes made specially for us, and the guys liked it when he said Da Nang was better known as Dodge City, or the terminal of the Viet Cong rocket line.

Barbara McNair was terrific, and they had a little tiny black-haired girl from Peru (Miss World) who wore a sparkly dress and even stockings that sparkled. Boy, what a cute Christmas tree.

Bing Crosby's son Phil sang and the guys liked him too. He's not a bit put on and he jokes with Bob about his dad when the two of them are onstage together.

I guess even a big television show or a show for the servicemen like Bob Hope's can't have everything go smoothly and they had a funny thing happen today. Mr. Hope had a girl in the show, a black-haired singer and dancer named Elaine Dunn, and she was going to do a song in a costume that had a couple of layers. First it looked like an evening dress, then like a short evening dress, and finally like a shiny white bathing suit sort of thing. I guess it had hooks in the back or something, but whatever held it together started to give way and she was smiling and dancing and holding it together. But finally everybody came rushing from backstage to see if they could fix the costume, because they sure couldn't put it on television if the poor girl had a big gap in the back of her costume. I asked somebody backstage later who was trying to help and they were laughing their heads off. They said it was the prop man, the hairdresser, the wardrobe man, the unit manager, the sound man, Les Brown, and finally when he realized backstage that everything had stopped, Bob Hope came rushing out to see what was the matter and even he was trying to snap her up. The girl was blushing bright red and honestly, Mom, it wasn't planned, it really was an accident. I saw her face when she came offstage. Later when she visited the hospital some of the guys presented her with a pair of big safety pins. They had heard from guys who could get out and go to the show what had happened.

Well, it was quite a day. Not one I'll forget too soon. Mr. Hope told us that we saw a lot of things in the show that nobody will ever see again because they will cut them out. Then he said, "Playing here is better than New Haven, anyway." I guess that's where they try out Broadway shows. All I know is we loved it and life would be a lot brighter and it would pass a whole lot faster if we had something like Bob Hope to look forward to once in a while. Don't forget to write.

Love,
Don

After the Da Nang show, the troupe split into three parts to visit field hospitals. All of Raquel and I were coptered to the U.S. hospital ship *Sanctuary*, a kind of floating camp follower. When a kid got hit in the jungle, whether by mortar, sniper, or land mine, he was plucked from a paddy field by a chopper and rushed to the *Sanctuary*. Her crew of 350 technicians, orderlies, doctors, and nurses went into action with their skills. From the field to the hospital ship was only a matter of minutes, which is one reason the medics had a spectacular record in wound recoveries. The *Sanctuary* has beds for 683 patients, but this had been a good Christmas; only 150 beds were occupied. One kid even had red and green tassels on the toe of his leg cast.

I've been in plenty of hospitals, and each time I've had to make myself go through those ward doors. But Raquel was beautiful; she didn't falter for a minute. She didn't have to do any fancy steps or quick patter. All she did was walk from bed to bed, flash her smile filled with strong, pearly teeth, and sick men started to get better.

One kid in particular really got to me. He'd tangled with a land mine on patrol and three of his buddies had been killed. He was the lucky one, relatively speaking, but he'd lost both legs and had a big hole where a lot of his stomach had been. Naturally he was worried, but—get this—not about himself. The *Sanctuary* had a radio station on board and he was scheduled to talk to his parents that evening. As far as he was concerned, his biggest problem was to get through that phone call without upsetting his mom and dad.

The other segments of our troupe weren't faring much better. Madeline Hartog-Bel, Miss World, found the contrast between her appearance in a silver lamé gown before sixteen thousand Marines at Da Nang and the grim reality of visiting the wounded at the Naval Support Activity Hospital almost too much. She made it through the GI wards but when she was taken to the Children's Ward tears streamed down her face and she had to duck out. It was her first time but we'd run into these cases in many camps. They were Vietnamese infants from three to five who were "adopted" by the hospital. Some needed plastic surgery to correct birth defects. Others needed orthopedic surgery for hip and leg deformities. They were not in the hospital officially and somehow there just wasn't any paper work on them. They were desperately in need. We had the equipment and the highly skilled surgeons. And who's going to turn a three-year-old away?

We all pulled ourselves together for two shows in Thailand the next day, one at the Royal Thailand Air Force Base at Udorn and the second at Nakhon Phanom. The following morning, security being what it was, the cast got orders at the Erawan Hotel to "wear clothes for hot weather and carry clothes for cool weather."

No destinations were named, but the first one turned out to be Chu Lai, a great sandbox of a place that looked more like a World War II base than anything I'd ever seen in Vietnam. By 1967 the United States had finally realized that the war in Indochina was going to take an all-out effort, and we were building up the kind of supply and base system that kind of war required.

On my first tour of Vietnam, Chu Lai had had a kind of country-club atmosphere. In those early days it had an unspoiled look, as it says in the tourist brochures; only a few battalions of Marines had discovered what looked like a beautiful beach resort, nestled on the shore of the South China Sea. Even then, the facilities weren't exactly luxurious—many of the foxholes were without running water except in the monsoon season, and the black-pajama-clad natives weren't too friendly.

By 1967, the resort had been discovered by the great unwashed, and 15,000 of them were there waiting for us, all members of the Americal Division and all very weary of the war. About 150 of them had spent the night on the

General Palmer, General Nguyen Ky, and General Westmoreland at Long Binh, Vietnam, 1967.

benches to be sure of getting good seats. Many of them were patients, some pretty badly wounded. One boy who had been almost totally blinded three days before by a land mine just wanted to hear the sounds of laughter and music. He had to be led in his blue pajamas and robe to a seat backstage.

The soldier who'd been chosen to introduce me was Specialist 4th Mike Esmond of Philadelphia, who had recently won the Silver Star. He had been on patrol when his platoon came across an infantry battalion that had been pinned down by enemy fire. Esmond had jumped from his half-track to help the wounded. When he got back into his vehicle, it was hit by shrapnel and he picked up a piece himself. I asked him if he had gone to the hospital. "No sir," he said. "We were pretty busy, so I had it taken out and went back to duty." Today that kid is a big hit lighting up metal detectors at airports.

The reason for the cool-weather clothes was our next stop, the aircraft carrier *Ranger*, two hundred miles at sea. Usually we transferred from shore to carrier by helicopter, but the *Ranger* was so far out we had to make the trip by fixed-wing aircraft. None of us had ever landed on a carrier that way before, so we were a little antsy about the whole procedure. Les Brown told

The last Christmas show

writer Bill Larkin that he'd never seen me so nervous. "I know," Bill said. "He's over in the hangar right now, calling a cab."

I admit it—the idea of landing on the deck of that carrier with nothing but arresting gear to keep us from polluting the South China Sea had me a little tense. It didn't help when they handed out the life jackets, studded all over with little pockets labeled "shark repellent" and "flares." In the same vein, one of our brave troupers sat down in his seat, pulled the barf bags out of the pocket in front of him, and began labeling them with a marking pen: RIGHT LEGS, LEFT LEGS, ARMS, and LEFTOVERS. As it turned out, the landing was quite a neck snapper. As he got off the plane our drummer, Lloyd Morales, said to the pilot, "Man, you've *got* to do something about those brakes."

At each base we did a little interview spot with Earl Wilson asking the questions of "the oldest serviceman on the base." Then I'd stagger out in some beat-up fatigues with hash marks running up and down both sleeves and

Earl Wilson on hospital ship Sanctuary, *China Sea, 1967.*

Hurricane Raquel   237

a bunch of medals and carrying a shovel. If it was an Army base I'd be a dog-face. If it was a Marine base I'd be a gyrene. On board the *Ranger*, I was a sailor, of course, and the spot went something like this:

EARL: Thank you, fellas! . . . You know, back in the States we've heard the civilian and naval experts' opinions of the war. But I've been asked by my newspaper editors to find out the facts from the one man who would really know what's happening out here—the average seaman. So I asked your personnel officer for the enlisted man who had been stationed on the *Ranger* the longest. And I'd like to talk to him now.

> (*beckons off*)

Won't you please step out here?

> MUSIC: *Country bumpkin type*
>
> (*Earl takes out reporter notebook and pencil*) (*Hope comes shuffling out in beat-up fatigues, his chest is covered with medals, and dragging a mop*)

BOB (*sloppy salute*): Okay, Mac . . . what do you want painted?

EARL: Why would I want anything painted?

BOB: That's the way it is in the Navy, Mac. We paint it, and if we can't paint it, we polish it, and if we can't polish it, we promote it.

EARL: Sailor, this isn't a work detail. I'd like to ask you a few questions. First, what is your job?

BOB: I'm the head painter.

EARL: You mean, you're in charge?

BOB: No, I mean I paint the heads.

EARL: I'm not too familiar with service insignia . . . What is your rank?

BOB: Apprentice Seaman.

EARL: Apprentice Seaman? But what are all those stripes?

BOB: Whip marks.

EARL: How long have you been stationed on the *Ranger*?

BOB: Twenty years.

EARL: How's that possible? This ship's only ten years old.

BOB: No wonder I couldn't find a hook for my hammock!

EARL: And what is your naval occupational specialty?

BOB: I told you—I paint.

EARL: And what do you do after you paint?

BOB: That's a naval secret.

EARL: Sailor, I have a top-secret clearance . . . answer my question . . . what do you do after you paint?

BOB: I scrape it off.

EARL: That's the stupidest thing I ever heard of.

BOB: You think that's stupid . . . you're paying for it with your taxes.
(*applause*)
MUSIC: *"Anchors Aweigh"*

And if you think actors are hokey, let me tell you a little about columnists. On our first outing before our first gig, Earl was backstage pacing up and down nervously saying, "Bob, I'm not sure I can do this. Maybe we should skip it." The second day he was waiting for laughs. The third day he was signing autographs. And the fourth day I caught him in make-up . . . at eight o'clock in the morning. There's a little bit of it in all of us and a lot of it in Earl.

GIs and Raquel Welch at Cu Chi, Vietnam, 1967.

Hurricane Raquel   239

On the USS Ranger, *China Sea, 1967.*

At dinner aboard the *Ranger* the cast split up; I ate with the officers while the girls had chow in the enlisted men's and petty officers' mess. I always knew the Navy belonged to the swabbies and the petty officers. Afterward we watched catapult launchings up on the flight deck. When the planes came back and were safely landed, Madeline Hartog-Bel took over the ship-to-plane radio and gave them their final sign-offs. You should have seen the dazed looks on those pilots' faces as they climbed down with that dulcet "over and out" still ringing in their ears.

The next morning Madeline went to the ship's hospital to talk with a Spanish-speaking pilot whose back had been injured when his plane had been shot up over Haiphong and he'd had to eject into the ocean. "Did you radio for help?" Madeline asked in Spanish. I don't know what the Spanish is for "You bet your life," but it really broke Madeline up. By the time we were ready to transfer from the *Ranger* to the carrier *Coral Sea*, the crew had elected Madeline an honorary argonaut. If a bunch of sailors ever get to give away an aircraft carrier, Peru will be the first country to get one—provided Madeline makes admiral.

The only thing more shattering than landing on a carrier is being catapulted off one. The catapult is operated by a giant blast of steam and you hit 185 m.p.h.—and I mean hit—before you reach the end of the flight deck. They tell you to take off your sunglasses, remove your hat, secure any loose objects, and strap yourself down with *six* heavy webbed and buckled straps. Then you brace your feet on the seat in front of you. A crew member yells "Here we go!" and it feels as if you're headed for the moon. One guy in the band forgot to take his glasses off and he never found them again. I was lucky; I got my head back just in time to land on the *Coral Sea*.

What a giant operation our carriers are! On the *Coral Sea* they scramble up five thousand eggs for breakfast and sizzle up six thousand doughnuts just for the guys on the midnight to 4 A.M. watch. The crew works a sixteen-hour day, with only eight off for sleeping, eating, cleaning quarters, caring for uniforms, and watching my TV shows. No wonder they were glad to see us; they got to "stand down" for a whole day.

After the shows on the carriers we took a day of R and R in Bangkok and then played the King's palace. Things were a lot more easygoing than the first time we did it. It was like old home week. All of the officials who stood so high on protocol on the previous trips were going around slapping band members on the back like long-lost relatives. The royal housekeeper, who'd tried to keep people in their places back in '65, was giving everybody guided tours around the palace and the gardens. The King was really relaxed. He brought out his clarinet instead of his saxophone, and after he'd sat in for a few numbers with Les and the boys he even let us get to bed at a decent hour.

The next day we did our Christmas Eve show by daylight—not because of any lack of yuletide spirit, but because we were at an old French rubber plantation at Lai Khe, surrounded by the kind of trees the Vietcong love to shoot from behind. Being in that kind of situation after the sun goes down can be very fatal. The officers of the 1st Infantry Division were relieved to hear that our show took only two hours; it meant they could get those ten thousand troops back to safe positions by nightfall.

A truce was supposed to start that evening, but as we did the show you could hear artillery pounding in the hills around the old plantation, and we sure felt far from the old folks at home. A battalion of search-and-destroy troops was out stalking the jungle around us, and you could hear the chop-chop-chop of helicopters as they patrolled the perimeter looking for uninvited guests. Just two weeks before they'd lost fifty-eight men in an ambush two miles from the show site. When Barbara McNair wound up with "Silent Night" and I slid into "Thanks for the Memory" the applause was almost drowned out by sighs of relief.

That evening we split up again. The troupe was scheduled to spend Christmas Eve at Phanrang Air Force Base and I scurried off to Saigon for a quiet dinner with Westy Westmoreland. By that time Mrs. Westmoreland was living in the Philippines, so it was just the two of us. Westy reminded me that he had first seen me work at Bad Kissingen in Germany during World War II. He was a young lieutenant colonel and I was a young comedian. It's amazing how he aged.

Last week I ran into Westy in Palm Springs and we talked about that Christmas Eve together in Vietnam. He has almost total recall and he put his recollections down on paper for me:

> After dinner, Bob said, "I have to go to Mass; if I don't Dolores will never forgive me." So we got in my car and we went down to the cathedral on the main square. When we got out, the place was absolutely jammed with people. Our security men tried to weave us through the mass of humanity, but after a while we couldn't move. We were stuck in the crowd. How many of them were Vietcong there was no way of telling, and I was quite concerned. We were the only Americans in that sea of Vietnamese. The only thing to do was get back in the car. It took us an awfully long time to get out of there without running over anybody, but we finally worked our way out of that totally Asian environment. Once we'd made it, I suggested to Bob that we go down to the Third Field Hospital, where there was a Catholic chaplain. When we got there a midnight Mass was in progress. Afterward, tired as he was, he went through the hospital and talked to every patient. By the time he'd finished, a long queue of men had formed, and he spent an hour signing autographs.

What Westy left out of that letter is that *he* went from bed to bed with me and how thrilled the guys were to meet him in person. At that time he was not only head of the entire operation, he was on the cover of *Time* magazine as "Man of the Year." He's a strong-looking guy. He's got the kind of face that was born to be on a dollar bill. I used to say to him, "Are you going to run for President from Vietnam or are you going to wait until you get back to South Carolina?!" As it turned out he did wait until he returned to South Carolina to run for governor—and he was booby-trapped.

I used to tell the guys what a thoughtful general he was . . . how he always had a chicken standing by in case I needed blood. And what a brave man he was . . . how when the shots were firing and the bombs were falling he wasn't hiding under the bed, and I was in a position to know.

Next day we played the biggest audience we ever had in Vietnam—thirty thousand men, all packed into a natural amphitheater at Long Binh, forty miles outside of Saigon. What a noise when our girls walked out on that stage. The scream must've stopped traffic on the Ho Chi Minh Trail. The soldier who introduced me, Specialist 5th Bruce D. Gaub of Seattle, got almost too many laughs for comfort. "Welcome to the Land of Rising Commitment," he said.

One of the highlights of our show in Long Binh was the talk spot with Raquel. What a reception she got!

BOB: Here she is . . . Miss Raquel Welch!
    MUSIC: *Playon for Raquel*
    (*applause*)
    (*she enters*)
BOB (*during applause*): At ease . . . Faint if you like. It's not Mom's apple pie, but you'll have to settle for it. Stop drooling . . . you're just increasing the humidity. All right, you fools . . . land . . . land!
RAQUEL (*looks down at floor*): Bob, am I standing in the right place?
BOB: Honey, don't worry . . . If you're not . . . we'll move the base. Raquel, on behalf of those assembled, I'd like to welcome you to our little ready-room.
RAQUEL: Well, thank you, Bob. I'm most happy to be here and see all these boys.
BOB: They were boys before you came out. Now they're old men.
RAQUEL: Bob, are these men really so starved for affection?
BOB: Of course not—they have their sergeants.
RAQUEL: Well, why don't we do what Israel does—draft girls along with the men?
BOB: It wouldn't work here. The Israeli Army finishes its wars in

Hurricane Raquel   243

five days . . . and oh, that weekend! Raquel! That's an unusual name. What is it—French—Hungarian—or Russian?
RAQUEL: It's pure San Diego.
BOB: I thought it had a strange, exotic ring to it.
RAQUEL: Bob, why are we talking about me? You're the real hero here.
BOB: Who told you that?
RAQUEL: You did.
BOB: I'd rather not discuss it.
RAQUEL: Oh, don't be so modest . . . I think everybody should know about your being a Green Beret in disguise!
BOB (*trying to stop her*): Forget it, Raquel . . .
RAQUEL: I *won't* . . . not after you risked your life for me last night . . .
BOB (*worriedly*): Oh, they're not interested in that.
RAQUEL: Not everyone would be brave enough to come to my room at four o'clock in the morning and offer to protect me from a Cong attack!
BOB: I was sleepwalking.
RAQUEL: I don't believe it.
BOB: I don't either, but that's all I could think of.

After the talk spot, she did a number in which volunteers came up onstage to dance with her. And what I learned was very reassuring—fellows still like girls. I was sure of that when guys with their legs in casts would throw away their crutches and hop onstage to join in the Watusi.

Not only did we have an all-star cast, we had an all-star audience. Westy had brought Ambassador Ellsworth Bunker, and Bunker's wife Carol Laise had flown over from Nepal, where she was U.S. ambassador. I introduced the Bunkers to the audience, and they kissed each other onstage. I couldn't resist. "That's the first time I've ever seen two ambassadors kiss each other and really mean it," I said.

Westy, bless him, had also invited South Vietnamese Vice-President Nguyen Cao Ky to the show and had asked him to bring a gift. It turned out to be a black mandarin costume, like those worn by Vietnamese elders. It consisted of a long black robe and an oddly shaped black hat, and Westy asked Ky to bring the biggest outfit he could find, Vietnamese elders not being particularly noted for brawn. When the show ended, Ky got up and said, "All my comrades in arms join me in expressing our deep appreciation for your gestures. We know how big your sacrifice, how big your dedication. I'm sure a generation of Vietnamese today and to come will remember you with gratitude. Come back next year, when my country and people will have peace back and freedom."

Eddie Fisher at Bienhoa, Vietnam, 1967.

Barbara McNair at Camp Bearcat, 9th Division, Vietnam, 1967.

Then he draped me in the robe. It was a mite snug, but the troops kept their cool—until he put that black hat on my head. It looked like an overdone peanut on a bowling bowl, and it took every bit of balance I could muster to keep it from toppling off. Dignity, Hope, dignity, I told myself—and the stiffer I stood, the harder it was to keep from breaking up. Finally, the audience did it for me; they burst into a thirty-thousand-man guffaw that practically blew that Vietnamese skimmer right off my head. I called on all my vaudeville training, caught it deftly in one hand, and made a bow to Vice-President Ky. By that time he'd broken up too, and we ended up grinning at each other.

Our next stop was a supersecret base in Vietnam. Its official name was Camp Martin Cox but everybody called it Bearcat. I laugh every time I think of "Bearcat."

About two weeks before we left on our Christmas trip, I was having dinner out in Santa Monica at the Miramar Hotel. A big freckle-faced GI just back from Vietnam shouted across the room, "Hey, Bob, you're going to play Bearcat."

I hustled over to the GI and whispered to him, "Cool it, will you. That's top secret. And it's just a rumor."

And the kid boomed, "No, you're going to be there. I just left Bearcat and I built the stage for you."

Well, the secret was out. If there were any Cong in Santa Monica we were finished. For three weeks we had kept this information top secret. We had talked with the Defense Department and our advance party only in code. Long Binh, Bearcat, Da Nang were names that were never mentioned. They were Able, Charlie, and Baker one year, Harriet, Helen, and Grace the next. We made the guys on "Mission: Impossible" look like a bunch of boy scouts. Bearcat was a bigger secret than Zsa Zsa Gabor's age.

And now everybody in Santa Monica knew we were going to visit the 9th Infantry Division. I swore the entire dining room to secrecy.

"They really overdo security here," I told the ten thousand guys in the audience at Bearcat. "When I stepped off the plane, General Westmoreland said to me, 'Welcome, stranger.'"

Near Bearcat was the headquarters of the Thai division in Vietnam, the Queen's Own Cobras. I stopped in on the way back to our Chinook helicopters and arrived as those very tough fighters were celebrating a victory over the Cong. They had suffered heavy casualties, but were still so full of high spirits that they not only made me an honorary member of the division but an honorary Thai as well. There's only one problem about being an honorary Cobra—you never know when you're going to meet an honorary mongoose.

Just because Westy Westmoreland had me to Christmas Eve dinner didn't mean that he'd forgotten the rest of the cast. From Bearcat, our helicopters lifted us directly to the roof of the American Embassy for a full-scale Christmas party. Even that little hop had a bit of excitement to it—one of the choppers must have got lost in Saigon's downtown traffic, because it missed the Embassy and landed instead on the roof of the presidential palace. It was instantly surrounded by a squad of very trigger-happy guards. By rights, they could have shot first and asked questions afterward, but I guess the sight of the ashen face of our cameraman, Jack McCoskey, peering through the chopper window convinced them that anybody that scared couldn't have nasty designs on the life of the President.

We spent the night at a place laughingly called the New Saigon Hotel. A better name for it would have been The Sign of the Stopped Toilet; by the time our weary road company had finished trying to wring a little hot water out of the showers and get the johns to work, they were really pooped. Still, they found enough energy the next day to pay a visit to the Third Field

Hurricane Raquel   247

Hospital in Saigon and do two shows, one in the morning at Phuket Air Base and another in the afternoon at Camp Holloway, near Pleiku, for the 4th Infantry Division.

Pleiku was in the Vietnamese central highlands, and I remembered the camp there as a peaceful, picturesque spot that consisted of a few huts, a couple of copters, and a round or two of ammunition. Most of all, I remembered the Montagnards, or Vietnamese mountain men, who lived in the area. The Montagnards were not only fiercely independent, they were savage fighters. Theirs was a positive negative philosophy: they hated every other group in Vietnam—Buddhists, Catholics, Chinese, Communists, nationalists, Vietcong, lowlanders, and city folk. The only people they liked were the other Montagnards in their own village. They were not even too thrilled about the Montagnards who lived over the hill.

A tattered group of them had come to our truck-stop show years before, banging pots and pans and bamboo sticks. They must have been tired out from all that hating because they put friendship bracelets around our wrists. I was hoping things would be as peaceful this year at Camp Holloway, but since it had been mortared and overrun by the Cong three weeks after our previous visit, I wasn't at all sure what I'd find.

As soon as we landed, I realized that the scene was entirely different. The men of the 4th Infantry Division had the situation well in hand. The central highlands bristled with American military machines and armor of every kind. Everywhere we looked were trucks, tanks, and fighter copters—hundreds of them.

This time we entertained more than twelve thousand troops, instead of playing to a couple of hundred guys from the back of a truck. And there were as many more out in the fields all the way to the Cambodian border.

As usual, the troops were a great audience. When you're up to your tailbone in a rice field and someone behind a bush is trying to kill you, when your next step may be your last, you don't have much choice. You can laugh or cry. The best GI humor is a gallows combination of both. The only way I can explain it is to recall a classic joke, the story of a murderer who had been sentenced to the electric chair. His lawyer came to tell him that every appeal had been exhausted. The governor had turned down his plea for clemency. "What should I do?" the condemned man asked. The lawyer was reduced to one final bit of advice: "Don't sit down."

We had come to Vietnam to bring a few laughs to the servicemen, but they almost didn't need us. Evidence of their kooky minds and swinging spirits was already everywhere. It's hard to top them. For example, the 12th Air Commando Squadron at Bienhoa, which specializes in defoliation, had a motto worthy of my best gag man: "Only we can prevent a forest fire." There was a sign over a one-man bunker outside Camp Holloway that read, "Occupancy by more than one coward is prohibited by law."

Sergeant O'Connell, Ankhe, Vietnam, 1967.

I tried to carry some of their humor with me the next morning when we flew to Takhli in northern Thailand to do a show for five thousand gung-ho pilots, crew chiefs, and technicians who had never been heard about. Officially, they didn't exist. The base was so secret that they didn't allow the bugler to blow reveille. A sergeant just went from man to man whispering, "The general's up . . . How about you?" Their mail from home was addressed "Shhhhhhh." They didn't have to join the Foreign Legion to forget; nobody was going to remember them.

We met about one hundred mission pilots who hadn't had their names on paper since they made the yearbook at the Air Force Academy. If you think war is hell, try winging your way home with a tailful of lead and being listed as a diplomatic secret. Or, worse yet, having to lie to your wife and trying to explain to her that those aren't bullet holes in your leg, they're mosquito bites.

Hurricane Raquel

The previous night our number one bird, President Johnson, had landed at nearby Korat Air Base to do his best to remedy the situation. In an informal ceremony—and that's really the word for it—he awarded a Distinguished Flying Cross to a twenty-four-year-old pilot from Alabama, Lieutenant George H. McKinney, Jr. The medal was awarded in an officers' club bar. There was no press present, and the entire visit was shrouded in secrecy.

I was curious about what it takes to win the DFC, so that afternoon, when I got to Korat, I found George and got his story from him. The whole history of the war might have been different if we'd only let George do it. He'd had a couple of adventures, only a few days apart:

"We had just dumped our load on the railroad yards near Hanoi when Charlie poured everything at us—flak, SAMs, MIGs, all at the same time. We took a four-foot hole in the left wing, and we had various other problems. But we managed to bring our plane back to Thailand and steered it to an uninhabited area where we were able to eject.

"Another time, we were flying cover for some F-105s in a strike northwest of Hanoi when the flight leader called to say he had a MIG on him. We caught the MIG firing at our last 105. He turned back and thought he was going home, but we tucked in behind him and hit him with a two-and-a-half-second blast. He burst into flame from the aft section and spiraled onto the ground."

By the time George had finished his second tale of high adventure, a few of his buddies had joined us. I decided to find out from some real experts what some of their slang meant. First I asked about "body snatching." It means hovering over the jungle in a "Jolly Green Giant" (rescue helicopter) and lowering a "penetrator" (a hook attached to a seat or a litter) into the "green stuff" (forest) to fish up a pilot using a "beeper" (electronic homing device). All the while "Charlie" (the Vietcong) was throwing everything he had at the chopper and the downed pilot—rockets, rocks, and "37s," "50s," and "60s." The caliber wasn't too important, however; all our boys had to remember was that if one of them hit them it was going to sting.

Aerial tankers were called "wet nurses." Hanoi was simply "downtown." Every broken-down house, Quonset hut, or "hootch" was called the "Chu Lai Hilton" or the "Hilton East" or the "Hilton" something. Aircraft carriers were "bird farms." A "lifer" was any GI with longer time to put in before rotation home than some other GI. A soldier with only ninety days to go was described as being "too short to carry on a long conversation."

The point of that last one didn't sink in till several days later, after we'd played Cu Chi, Phanrang Air Base, and Camranh Bay. When our sixty-seven pooped pigeons climbed aboard that big C-141 Starlifter at Anderson Air Base in Guam, we really knew that we'd traveled more than twenty-five thousand miles in fifteen days. We'd traveled in everything from jeeps to aircraft carriers to choppers. We'd done twenty-one full-blown shows, toured

GI and Joey Heatherton, Guam, 1967.

six hospitals, and logged eleven hours in combat zones. We'd been dusted, baked, soaked, wind-blown, and catapulted. By rights, we should have been snoring in our seats as the big jet droned along toward Midway. But the trip was still too fresh in our minds, and the flight home seemed too short to cover everything we had to say to one another. Most of us stood in knots up and down the aisle, rehashing the trip. For each member of the cast, it meant something different.

To Johnny Pawlek, the sound engineer who has made twenty-two Christmas trips with me, it was "the look on the faces of those combat troops at Lai Khe. Three thousand of their buddies had been sent out to the hills just before the show. But the guys who stayed behind were so intense. Their eyes never left the stage."

For some the greatest memory was a reunion with friends or relatives. Betty Lanigan had met up with her nephew Captain Thomas Anthony. Dick Hannah, one of the cameramen, found his brother-in-law, Steve Morehead. The head cameraman, Harlow Stengel, who made these trips with me for seven years, met his son Peter in Pleiku. It was the greatest Christmas present he has had in his lifetime. The trombonist, Joe Howard, made the whole trip hoping against hope that he might see his son Dave, a combat engineer. They met at Bearcat. They didn't say a word; they just grabbed each other and hung on.

Phil Crosby said he'd never forget one kid at a field hospital in Da Nang: "He was torn up from head to toe, but he managed to get his right thumb up and wink at me." For Joan Maas, the production assistant, nothing in her seven trips touched a kid she saw in the hospital at Clark Air Base in the Philippines: "This poor kid had a brain injury. He was just relearning to talk; yet when I said good-by to him, he grinned and made a circle with his thumb and index finger." Raquel Welch, our dazzler, and Herb Ball, our photographer, and everybody else who visited a hospital ward said they'd never forget those kids waiting to heal so they could go back to action.

Les Brown looked at things in a lighter, man-of-the-world vein. He said he'd never forget Barbara McNair singing "I'm a Woman."

The only sour note I heard about the 1967 trip came from Raquel Welch after we got back. She was quoted in *Time* magazine as saying instead of entertainers we should take over a planeload of hookers. That's what the guys really wanted.

I have to disagree with that. I don't know why she said it. Certainly nothing the audiences ever said or did would warrant her feeling that.

We've played to some of the toughest troops in the world. And the guys have never been anything but courteous. Of course, I don't know what they were thinking. If you could be arrested for that, we'd all be in jail. In my case, it would only be a misdemeanor.

We just take pretty girls to remind the guys what they're fighting for. I took an apple pie and mom once, and two divisions, including the chaplain, went over the hill.

I don't think sex is the only thing that our boys over there think about. I know an insurance salesman who really packed 'em in—Cardinal Spellman. Of course, he represents a pretty good company—Mutual of Vatican City.

CHAPTER 19

If we lose another motor, we'll be up here all day

My number one It girl of 1968 was Ann-Margret. A beautifully packaged bundle of dancing dynamite, she had seventeen movies to her credit, including the film version of the Broadway musical *Bye Bye Birdie*. Linda Bennett was my featured singer. She'd been born and raised in Bountiful, Utah, which certainly lived up to its name. She was lovely to look at, with a singing voice that was perfectly suited to the sad and beautiful songs of *Brigadoon*, in which she'd appeared with the New York City Center's Light Opera Company.

We always liked to have a heavyweight on the show but I think we overstated our case when we added Rosey Grier. Rosey had just left the Los Angeles Rams to become the first guitar-playing three-hundred-pound rock-'n'-roll singer. And he was really popular . . . who was going to criticize him? When Rosey got on the plane and asked our ninety-eight-pound weakling, assistant director Clay Daniel, where he was supposed to sit, Clay said, "Any three seats you want. Just don't step on me."

Honey, Ltd., turned out to be a singing group with talent unlimited. All of them college seniors from Detroit, the four Honeys had descended on Hollywood that year with little more than a promo record and a lot of nerve. Both worked. They'd so impressed Jerry Lewis that he'd carved a four-minute niche in one of his TV shows to make room for a bit of their blues-rock sound.

Penelope Plummer, an eighteen-year-old blond Australian, was that year's Miss World. To give those thousands of GI eyeballs a rest from going back and forth across all those curves, I signed up Dick Albers, one of the world's greatest trampolinists. That way the boys could watch something going up and down—that is, if they could bear to take their eyes off the ever lovely Les Brown and His Band of Renown.

Santa Rosy O'Donnell, Rosey Grier at Los Angeles Airport, 1968.

Back in those days, Greg Garrison, producer-director of TV's Dean Martin show, spent a soul-satisfying part of each year auditioning for a dozen girls between the ages of eighteen and twenty-two to be the singing, dancing Golddiggers. One day at NBC he stopped me in the hall and said, "Hey, Bob. Your Christmas shows are the greatest but why don't you take the Golddiggers with you?"

I stared at Greg as if he was simple and said, "Don't be ridiculous, Greg, these planes only hold so many people. It's not a subway, you know. You can't cross the Pacific hanging on a strap."

That afternoon I was talking to our project officers in Washington and I mentioned the Golddiggers. They stared at me on the phone as if I was simple and I said, "Wouldn't it be a great lift to see those twelve beautiful dolls walking into a hospital? Think what that would do for morale."

I guess that intrigued them. All I know is the next day we either had a bigger plane or they had stretched the old one, because suddenly we had seats for twelve Golddiggers.

They went with us for three straight years and each one was a delight. The girls were beautiful and talented and tireless. I wish I could remember their names. I'll try. Let's see. There was Pamela Beth, Nancy Bonetti, Kathi Brimer, Lezlie Dalton, Diana Gaye Liekhus, Susan Lund, Deborah McFarland, Lynn Cheryl Steiner, Debbie Thomason, Mary Kathleen Wright, Peggy Hansen, and Brenda Lynne Powell. Amazing how that sort of thing comes back to you.

I remember one time at Long Binh. We had just finished a show and we were headed into the post exchange for a binge of toothpaste and jockey shorts when ten GIs came running up to the Golddiggers and said, "What time's your show? We just got off work." The girls stopped right there and did their whole routine on the PX porch. I stood by in case they needed a monologue but somehow my name didn't come up.

Our itinerary in '68 took us west to the East: Japan, Korea, Taiwan, Thailand, Vietnam, Okinawa, the Philippines, and Guam. You'll never guess what we took along to eat on the first leg of our trip to the world's rice bowl—six hundred pizzas! By the time we got to Midway, Rosey Grier was so full of dough he couldn't deplane—he was bigger than the island. We would have planted a flag on him and claimed him for America.

Fortunately for Rosey, Japan turned out to be big enough and so did the Tokyo Hilton, where we bivouacked. Our first tour of duty was just that— a tour through the U. S. Naval Hospital at Yokosuka and the 106th General Hospital at Kishine Barracks. About half the patients at Yokosuka had been wounded in skirmishes with the Cong, and I tried to spend most of the time cheering up the ones who looked as if their uphill climb had just begun. One fellow, covered with a cast from head to toe, had spent the whole day before we got there learning how to smoke a cigarette with a complicated contraption made of wires. It was such a painful process that he didn't waste a demonstration on me, but he sure lit up for Penny Plummer.

From Yokosuka, we flew to Kishine in Chinook choppers. Mine had a big sign on the side: WELCOME BOB-SAN. The copters were so noisy we all had to wear giant plastic ear muffs that made us look like Mouseketeers. We couldn't talk to each other, so we spent most of the time looking out the windows. Mount Fuji is usually covered with clouds, but that day it made one of its rare, spectacular public appearances. To show he was keeping his cool, Mort Lachman passed me a note: "You've seen one Fuji, you've seen them all."

WELCOME BOB-SAN was fine, but the sign that greeted me at Kishine was a bit hard to take. WE LOVE YOU, BING, it said. "Aha!" I snorted. "I've fallen in with a bunch of Commies!" I reassured the crowd at the landing pad that the United States was still there despite the uproar at the Democratic National Convention in Chicago. Nixon, I said, was the first Republican President who'd been elected by a Democratic convention.

The patients who could walk were hanging from the fire escapes and coating the stairways. I'm sure they were waiting for a glimpse of me, but Ann-Margret and Miss World may have had something to do with it. One old-timer greeted me with, "Hi, Bob, I haven't seen you since New Caledonia in 1943." I whipped back, "1944." As I passed, I could hear him telling his buddies: "He's right, you know. It *was* 1944."

One line I often used to get me over the threshold of orthopedic wards was "Don't bother to get up." At Kishine, though, the cats in casts beat me to the punch line. Over the beds of all those plastered guys was a sign that really fractured me: WELCOME BOB HOPE. WE WOULD STAND UP AND SALUTE, BUT AT THE MOMENT WE'RE ALL HUNG UP.

A lot of the patients had substituted fancy Japanese kimonos, or "happi coats," for their regulation hospital bathrobes. It sure brightened up the scenery, but I couldn't resist ragging one guy in a really elaborate brocaded number. I turned to the film crew that was trailing behind me and said, "Have you met the hostess here?" In addition to the guys who'd been wounded in action against Charlie, I met one soldier who'd been badly banged up in a truck accident. "You could have stayed home and got into that kind of trouble," I told him.

The head doctor, a colonel, walked up to me in the hospital and said, "Would you go in through the burn ward? I don't want everybody to go in but if you would go in I think maybe you could give these guys a lift. They're in pretty bad shape."

To paraphrase *The Godfather* it was the kind of offer you couldn't refuse. I had been up half the night in Tokyo trying to find a co-signer so I could go to a nightclub. To say the least, I wasn't a ton of muscle that morning. I didn't actually say okay, I just nodded slowly and followed the doctor into the burn ward.

I'm afraid I lack the words to describe that ward and I don't think I could use them if I had them. Many of those guys were beyond hope . . . they were sitting around with just a towel over their privates because they couldn't lie down with some of these burns they had. A lot of them died of pneumonia. And to see kids with half their faces burned away is unbearable. You have to fight not to turn away. What can you say to them? I'd say, "How you doing?" "What are they doing for you?" and hurry on.

We had so little to give, and they gave so much.

We choppered back to Tokyo for a quick dinner and our final dress rehearsal at the Pearl Ballroom. What a place that was; it looked like a Japanese Las Vegas. Ten chandeliers hung from the ceiling, and each was decorated with 200,000 real pearls. My only worry was that several members of the troupe were coming down with the 1968 version of Asian flu—including Ann-

Ann-Margret at Da Nang, Vietnam, 1968.

Margret, who couldn't speak above a whisper by the end of rehearsal. I wasn't
worried. When I went up to Harrah's at Lake Tahoe to look at her act she
had no voice but her looks and talent could be heard for miles.

Next day, at Camp Zama south of Tokyo, they were. We flew down by
helicopter, and although Tokyo can have smog that makes Los Angeles look
like a health spa, there was none that day. Tokyo can be one of the loveliest
cities on earth, and just to look at the women is enough to make any normal

If we lose another motor, we'll be up here all day

Westerner feel grubby. All our gals complained about feeling clumsy and provincial in comparison to those exquisite and sophisticated women.

The 2,200 men at Camp Zama didn't seem to see it that way. They really went wild when Honey, Ltd., came out in silver lamé miniskirts. The only way to calm the GIs down was to come on with my monologue. "I know we're in Japan because the smog comes in slanted. I got a wonderful welcome at Tokyo airport—then my kimono fell off, and they realized I wasn't Shirley MacLaine.

"Back in the States," I told them, "we're making progress. Last year they were burning draft cards. This year it's our schools. Who ever thought that an eraser would be a Molotov cocktail?"

Linda Bennett wore a beautiful flesh-colored, high-necked gown all beaded with crystal. She had a marvelous figure, and I got it straight from the wardrobe mistress that it was all hers. Also, as it turned out, I needn't have worried about Ann-Margret. Besides loud dancing, she displayed a kind of kittenish sexiness that turned on the boys much more than any blatant bump and grind could have.

After the show we did another hospital tour. One imaginative patient had a sign over his bed: QUIET. BONE GROWING. Another had so much spunk and spirit when sick that I'd hate to meet him well. He chatted head to head with Linda Bennett for so long that I quipped, as I passed his bed, "Sergeant, you're monopolizing that girl."

He shot back: "It's the best I can do in the condition I'm in."

Rosey Grier was in top form that day. He was wandering in and out of the wards strumming away on his guitar when he came up against a badly wounded guy lying under a small white tent.

"What happened, man?" asked Rosey.

"They shot my leg off."

"Did they sew it back on?"

The kid grinned. "As a matter of fact, they did."

"Well, kid," said Rosey, "start steppin'."

We were the ones who had to start steppin'—back to Tokyo for an early night. We were scheduled to take off at 8 A.M. the next morning for Korea. A good thing we knocked off early, too, because we ended up doing seven (count 'em—seven) shows the next day. I thought I was out for a little handshake tour of some remote bases up near the demilitarized zone, but half the stops turned out to be capsule shows. I got a little suspicious when some of the guys said, "So long, see you later," but I didn't find out what they meant until the whole cast got together for the big show of the day at 2nd Infantry Division headquarters. We had a huge crowd—thirteen thousand screaming, whistling GIs—and as soon as I got a good look I realized that I'd seen a lot of them earlier that day at those handshake stops. They'd been flown to division headquarters for a second go at me.

Admiral John McCain, Cu Chi, Vietnam, 1968.

If we lose another motor, we'll be up here all day   259

It's hard to say just how lucky they were, but I guess they were luckier than many of their buddies who weren't there. In the previous two months a lot of North Korean infiltrators had slipped across the demilitarized zone and had killed about ninety of our boys from ambush. The troops had had to draw lots to decide who could be off duty for the show.

Backstage we swapped a few anecdotes about our morning handshake tours. At a Hawk missile site, Ann-Margret had made quite a hit in a miniskirt, knee-high boots, and a sable coat. The site commander was a dead ringer for Jack Palance, grim-reaper look and all. After Ann-Margret met him, one doughface whispered to another, "Man, we ought to have her up here every day. The colonel is actually smiling. I didn't think he knew how."

On every trip there's somebody who keeps slipping behind schedule, and that morning it had turned out to be Rosey Grier. Once he got to rapping with the soldiers at one of the outposts, he stuck to them as if they were carrying the ball for the San Francisco 49ers.

Les Brown, Dick Albers, and the four Honeys were awarded special certificates for having flown north of the Imchin River, *very* close to the demilitarized zone. The area they flew over was a hostile-fire zone, the only one in the world outside Vietnam and a combat area in every sense of the word.

Looking back over the script, I see that some of my material sounds pretty dated now. For instance, when I mentioned to Ann-Margret that I'd heard she was discovered by George Burns at the Sahara Hotel in Las Vegas, she replied, "Yes, and I think he is just the world's funniest comedian."

I did a long, slow burn, and then grumbled, "Well, he's all right—but he's no Spiro Agnew." Remember when Spiro Agnew was funny?

We rounded out that long day with another full-scale show for three thousand troops at Collier Fieldhouse at Yongsan Compound. It was a number one show. "In Korea," as I told the audience, "number one means the best and number ten means no good—which kind of pulls the rug out from under the Ten Commandments." For me, the number one moment backstage was when a little Korean orphan named Ho Minh Paik was brought to see me by Captain Fred Baird Smith of the Salvation Army. Little Ho had been abandoned by his widowed mother on a street in Seoul, but he'd been taken in by the Salvation Army's Seoul Boys' Home. He brought me a present and I gave him a toolbox in return. He was a beautiful rosy-cheeked boy who looked at me with immense round eyes in a dead-serious face. I thought for a minute about cracking him up with a joke or two, but I realized that it would be more likely to make him cry than laugh, so we exchanged gifts very solemnly. It was one of the most touching moments on the trip.

After those seven shows, it was a tired group of troupers that returned to Seoul to get ready for Okinawa the next day. The weather in Okinawa had been nothing but solid rain for the three weeks before we got there; the local anti-U.S. press, which was trying to talk Uncle Sam out of the islands we'd won from the Japanese in World War II, blamed American helicopters. The choppers were actually up there to take pictures of small crowds of demonstrators (the anti-Yankee press claimed they were huge), but the newspapers insisted that the helicopters were causing the rain to fall just to be mean to the Okinawans.

The day of the show we lucked out again. The weather was sunny and warm, seventy-six degrees, and those nineteen thousand troops really soaked it up. In view of the touchy relations between our military and the Okinawans who wanted them to get out, I'm afraid that bits of my monologue bothered some of the brass. "Okinawa," I said. "That's Japanese for 'How do you feel about another Pearl Harbor, Yankee dogs?'" The troops, who were not exactly overjoyed at the reception they were getting from the local populace, loved it. Considering their mood, I can see why another quip tickled their sense of outrage. "Okinawa is seventy miles long—which is nothing if you're being chased by a wild pig."

After the hostility in Okinawa it was something of a relief to fly to a warm welcome of sweet-smelling garlands and military bands in Bangkok, Thailand. Even the Erawan Hotel, our base of operations for the Thailand and Vietnam shows, looked almost like home. Security was even tighter than it had been in previous years—a couple of reporters who had joined us in Bangkok to do a series of exclusive stories for the London *Times* were refused permission to fly into Vietnam aboard our military aircraft.

We had three major shows scheduled our first day in Vietnam—at Bienhoa, Camranh Bay, and Long Binh—and the first of these almost turned out to be the last. About three hundred miles out of Bangkok, I was up in the cockpit gassing with the crew. The navigator, Vic Peck, got up to say something to the pilot, and I grabbed his arm, stopped him, and began telling him an airplane joke. "An airliner was on the way to Moscow," I said, "when suddenly the pilot came on the public address system and said: 'Ladies and gentlemen, we just lost one motor. But don't let that bother you, because this plane can fly on three motors. However, this will delay us for half an hour.' A little later he came on again. 'Ladies and gentlemen,' he said, 'we just lost another motor. But don't be alarmed, because this plane can fly on two motors. However, we will be delayed an hour.' A few minutes later he came on a third time. 'Ladies and gentlemen, we just lost another motor, but don't be alarmed. We can fly on one motor. However, we will be delayed an hour and a half.' The loudspeaker clicked off, and there was a long silence. Finally, a guy in the back of the plane spoke up. 'That stupid pilot,' he said. 'If we lose another motor, we'll be up here all day.'"

All the while I was telling the joke, I was holding on to the navigator's arm. I wouldn't let him go. When I finished, he didn't even laugh. He gave me a hard look, pulled his arm loose, and walked over to the pilot, Major Emmet H. Musser. The navigator leaned down, pointed out the window,

Dick Albers at Okinawa, 1968.

and said, "That motor's on fire over there." We all looked out, and sure enough, the left inboard engine was smoking. They had to feather the prop and turn on the extinguisher.

They'd also noticed our little mishap back in the cabin. Brenda Powell, one of the Golddiggers, was the calmest one in the bunch. She said very quietly, "I knew this was going to happen. I'm psychic, and I had a vision of this last week. I knew we'd lose an engine."

My public relations man, Bill Faith, was very interested. "You envisioned this exact situation?" he quavered. "What happened to us?"

The baby-faced Golddigger nodded calmly and shrugged. "Oh," she said, "we made it."

That broke the tension, and the gang all burst out laughing. Barney McNulty stopped making paper gliders out of his cue cards and Rosey Grier said, "If I'm ever going to fly, this may be the time to start practicing. The Lord sure gave me a long runway and a head start." I wasn't worried—with Ann-Margret, Linda Bennett, and twelve Golddiggers I knew it would be a soft landing.

The incident with the motor gave me some great material for the thirty thousand GIs on hand for the show. Ten thousand of those guys had been flown in from combat zones. One of them, out on a seven-man patrol, said that all he knew in advance was that he was ordered to draw straws with the six other guys. When he won, a helicopter suddenly appeared out of the sky, swooped him up, and carried him to Bienhoa—helmet, weapon, sweat, and all. He got a special reserved seat.

I stepped onstage and announced:

★

One of our motors went out on the way in, and I had quite a laundry problem.

I was carrying a cross, a St. Christopher medal, and a Star of David. When I go, I'm going to blame everyone.

Everything's fine back home. Nixon captured Washington and Jackie Kennedy got Greece. So everything's in good shape.

If you wonder why I'm here in Vietnam—well, Humphrey bumper stickers are a lot harder to get off than I thought.

Actually, I'd planned to spend Christmas in the States, but I can't stand violence. Besides, it was the perfect time to come to Vietnam —the war was moved to Paris.

We flew over the Ho Chi Minh Trail and there was nothing moving—worst traffic jam I ever saw.

There are three kinds of weather in Vietnam: hot, hotter, and Oh my God, Harry, the air conditioner's melted.

I met your commanding officer—first time I ever saw a three-star camel.

★

What the Lord giveth, the Lord taketh away, I supposeth. Or maybe I was challenging the fates with my wisecracks about the dry weather. Anyway, as the Golddiggers came out for their finale at Camranh Bay, the skies opened up and their bright red chiffon dresses were plastered to their skins. It created quite a pleasing effect to my eyes and to those 35,000 G-eyes, but it drove our perennial wardrobe mistress, Rose Weiss, up the nearest palm tree. She had to pack those costumes damp, and she was afraid that when she un-

If we lose another motor, we'll be up here all day

Golddiggers on USS New Jersey, *1968.*

packed them the next day at Nakhon Phanom Air Base in Thailand, they'd be completely mildewed.

It was a beautiful day at Nakhon Phanom, and the Golddiggers' costumes came out of their trunks in splendid condition. Come to think of it, the Golddiggers' trunks weren't in bad shape either.

I told one of the Air Force sergeants who met me about our plane trouble the day before, and he soothed me in a Tennessee drawl as thick as redeye gravy. "Why, those planes are really very forgivin'," he said. "They allow for all kinds of pilot error, and never act up. Very forgivin' planes."

That put me in a forgivin' mood myself, so I dropped all those plane jokes from my monologue.

264   *The last Christmas show*

Here we are in beautiful Thailand. In October you get the monsoons. In December you get me.

Nakhon is near the border of Laos, a neutral country. (This really cracked those Air Force guys up; they knew just how "neutral" Laos was.) Really, Laos is as neutral as you can get. In case of peace, both sides have refused it.

This base is pretty isolated. At rehearsal I saw a soldier winking at a TV camera. I asked him what he was doing and he said, "When you've been here ten months, if it's got legs, you wink at it."

Headquarters hasn't heard from you guys lately. What's the matter, did you lose the drum? I tried to talk to your medical officer, but it was hard. He was busy sacrificing the goat.

Things are so tough in Thailand that one cobra had to lay off three flute players.

Rosey Grier, though, is having a great time in Thailand. They give him a cut rate at the elephant wash.

★

A mite weary from four big shows in two days, we flew back to Bangkok that night for a dinner party and mini command performance at Air Marshal Dawee's.

That night, out on the lawn of his lovely house, we feasted on shark's fin soup, melon soup, roast duck, an exotic shrimp dish, and on and on and on until 12:30 A.M. At that point I was getting so woozy I began to see sharks' fins cutting through my melon soup, so we called it a day. We had a 6 A.M. start to make on our trip to Da Nang the next day, and we certainly didn't want to miss it.

In honor of Christmas Eve, we were greeted at the helicopter pad the next morning by a big "ho ho ho" from Santa Claus—one of the Golddiggers, Diana Liekhus, holding up her blond wig as a beard. We needed a little cheering up. Charles Lee, one of my writers, was so out of sorts that he walked around snarling, "Anybody who's up this early and doesn't have a bakery route is crazy."

The choppers lifted us to the Da Nang show site, a hill coated with twenty-one thousand troops. All during the show, more copters kept arriving, bringing in Marines from the combat zones. The area was protected by ditches and barbed wire, but it sure didn't stop those late arrivals. They parked their weapons and ammo and clambered over the wire as if it wasn't there.

Keeping an eye peeled to make sure that none of those Johnny-come-latelies

If we lose another motor, we'll be up here all day   265

were Charlie-come-latelies, I teed off with: "Da Nang. That's an R-and-R center for Cong rockets. If you're not carrying a piece of shrapnel around here, you're a tourist. This base has been shelled three times—once by the Cong and twice by the USS *New Jersey*." My one-liners got a warm reception, but not half as warm as the one that Marine Pfc Tommy Wright got from his sister Kathy, one of the Golddiggers. Kathy—and her mascara—dissolved into tears so tender that she had everyone in the immediate vicinity moist-eyed. The other Golddiggers looked on enviously. "Now I know where all our good-looking guys are," said one. "They're all over here."

After the show we clambered through the mud to helicopters for a couple of short hops—first to an evacuation hospital, where Ann-Margret, Linda Bennett, and I went through the intensive-care ward, and then to our next show stop, Chu Lai. About one thousand of the fifteen thousand guys waiting for us had been flown in by special airlift, but the good-seat ingenuity prize went to a couple of dentists who had pulled up in a mobile dental unit at 8 A.M. They had staked out good places, then had cleaned and filled teeth for chopper pilots (non-airborne variety) until show time at 2 P.M.

After the show, we had a date with our own chopper pilots to be airlifted to the deck of the carrier USS *Hancock*. It was our third major show of the day and we were a little weary, but the Navy helped with a bit of good old-fashioned hospitality. The officers had moved out of their quarters and into sick bay so we could sleep in their rooms. The food was fine, and after Da Nang and Chu Lai the hot showers and clean towels were even finer.

Captain Howard Grier, who introduced me at the show, said that "The troops always want to know two things. Can we have the Bob Hope show for Christmas? And can we go to Australia for leave? Well, we've got Bob Hope—and [here his eyes rolled toward Penny Plummer] a choice bit of Australia for Christmas. Now, I'd like to introduce one of the great showmen of the century—"

"Take your time, Captain," I interjected. But he didn't. He just said:

"Bob Hope!"

"Welcome to John Wayne's canoe—or Kennedy Airport with pontoons," I said. "Jackie Kennedy doesn't have one tenth this much yacht, and you didn't have to marry the captain to get it. The *Hancock* is not a new ship, but I didn't realize how old it was until I saw 'John Paul Jones' carved in the mizzenmast." The hijacking of the USS *Pueblo* was still in the news then, so I talked a little bit about the ransom we had to pay the North Koreans to get the crew back: "I don't know what kind of a deal they made—but we're really not going to miss Alaska. At one point we even asked the Russians to help us get our men back. Asking the Russians for help in getting our men out of a Communist prison is like asking de Gaulle to help us name a good California wine."

While Les Brown accompanied Honey, Ltd., onstage, Rosey Grier danced

Linda Bennett at Chu Lai, Vietnam, 1968.

with the Golddiggers backstage. Seeing Rosey outnumbered so badly, one Navy lieutenant who had been assigned to take pictures dropped his camera and joined in. After the show, we split up and attended Christmas parties all over the ship until it was time for midnight Mass. Barney McNulty, Bill Faith, Betty Lanigan, and I went to Mass down on the anchor chain locker. I have a feeling the Golddiggers danced till dawn.

If we lose another motor, we'll be up here all day   267

Utapao, Thailand, 1968..

268   *The last Christmas show*

They even did an encore the next morning. Up on deck waiting for the helicopters, they started taking snapshots as the destroyer *Decatur*, which had been doing escort duty for the *Hancock*, passed in special salute with the crew drawn up at attention on deck. The *Hancock*'s band was playing, so I said, "Stop taking pictures and *dance*. Those guys couldn't see the show, and waving at them is nothing." The girls lined up on the flight deck, went into one of their numbers, and really gave the *Decatur*'s crew an eyeful. When they finished dancing they crowded together and sang "We Wish You a Merry Christmas." Three cheers came ringing back across the water. Not to be outdone, the destroyer *Wedderburn* pulled alongside and got a second Golddiggers show.

The choppers hopped us to the deck of the battle wagon *New Jersey*, newly pulled out of mothballs for Vietnam duty. When I landed, the ship's trumpeter piped a terrific solo of "Thanks for the Memory" through the public address system, and then followed up with a few bars of "Hello, Dolly!" when the girls landed.

It's not easy to work a battleship. There's no place to put the audience. They were hanging from every gun, every turret, every porthole. I started firing monologue jokes in a 360-degree circle, hoping to catch somebody.

This is either a big Chris-Craft or Wake Island with a rudder. It sure was nice of you to take it out of mothballs just to give me a twenty-one-gun salute.

This is the last battleship in the world in commission. Just think— all of this to fight off a skinny Cong with a bag of rice and a bazooka.

I understand your captain is the son of a Methodist minister, so I've reworded fifteen of my jokes. But I couldn't do anything about the girls' costumes. You'll just have to pray for their souls.

This year for the first time in five years we were allowed to visit the Mekong Delta country. There we played for the "Riverines" and the "River Rats," who were in constant patrol up and down the rice paddy. In the middle of the monologue I found out why we hadn't been allowed there. I sensed I was losing the audience, which is not difficult if you've had as much experience with failure as I've had. The entire audience was looking over my shoulder. I turned to look and there on an island in the middle of the river was a full-fledged fire fight.

The bad guys were firing at the white hats and the white hats were firing at the bad guys but I was the one that was dying.

If we lose another motor, we'll be up here all day   269

I hurried on to mail call—a segment that looks simple, but takes a tremendous amount of preparation and coordination.

BOB: Every year before we leave home we get stacks of mail from all over the States for GIs at all the bases. So the first letter we have is to Jerry Long . . . a gunner's mate at Dong Tam . . . Hey, Jerry, are you there? Jerry?

(*he enters*)

How're you, my boy? I just wanna tell you I understand you know a Sharon A. Self. Is that right?

LONG: That's right.

BOB: She claims she's your fiancée. Do you know anything about this?

LONG: I hope so.

BOB: Well, how come you haven't mentioned it to the girls here? Sharon says your mail is kinda late . . . The last mail she had from you was to wish her Happy Halloween. But she wants you to write a letter right now—on television. Go ahead . . . dictate a letter to Sharon.

LONG: Hi, honey.

BOB: Hi, honey. Yeah, what else?

LONG: Miss you, love you.

BOB: Miss you, love you. We won't listen . . . go ahead, everybody turn your back, will ya? Wanna say something else?

LONG: No, I believe that's all.

BOB: Wanna say anything about the countryside? What a beautiful country club you're working in here and all that? You want to seal it with a kiss or anything? Right in the camera. She'll be watching. Go ahead, blow her a kiss. Blow it in the camera, not to me!

(*he blows a kiss*)

I'll bet he's a killer on a front porch, huh? Thank you, Jerry Long. Thank you very much. Nice to see you. Sharon'll get that, I guarantee you. Next we have Lieutenant John Howard. Come out here, John. Yeah!

(*he enters*)

Yeah, John, how are you?

HOWARD: Fine.

BOB: Nice to see you. We have a letter from your mother back in Covina, California. And she wants to know a couple of things. Now, are you wearing your rubber galoshes? Are you going out with girls? And remember her talk the night before you left. She says if you have any questions to write with 'em—to write home to her with 'em, and there's one more thing. She wants to send you a kiss, and she doesn't trust you with any of the girls and she wants me to kiss you.

> (*he kisses Howard*)
> (*audience applauds*)
> (*back to Hope—he spits*)

Can you get a Bronze Star for that? Well, don't hang around. We're not engaged, you know. That's all. Nice to see ya.

HOWARD: Thank you.

BOB: Right, my boy.

> (*he laughs*)

Now I have a note from Mrs. . . . Mrs. Wise, of Columbia, South Carolina, who claims her son is one of the best singers in all history. Lou, where are ya? Lou Wise.

> (*he enters*)

How are ya? . . . Yeah . . .

> (*cheers from audience*)

Yeah. Nice to see ya, Lou . . . and what song ya going to thrill us with today?

WISE: How about "White Christmas," Bob?

BOB: Wh . . . I've been stabbed. You remember the Crosby song? He's got Charlie written all over his tonsils. Les, can anybody back there make a noise like "White Christmas"? Let's give this disaster area a chance, huh? Go . . . I'll give you eight bars to make your fame and fortune. Otherwise, it's back to the swamps. Go.

> MUSIC: *White Christmas*

WISE: I'm dreaming of a white Christmas
Just like the ones I used to know.
Where the treetops glisten
And children listen

BOB: I hope Irving Berlin will forgive him.

WISE: To hear sleighbells in the snow.
I'm—

BOB: You know, Crosby's got kids everywhere.

WISE: With every Christmas card I write.
May your days be merry and bright
And may all your Christmases be white

> MUSIC: *Out*

BOB: Hey, how about that?

> (*applause*)
> (*audience shot*)
> (*back to stage*)

Very beautiful, fine.

Cartoon by Wayne Stayskal, 1968.

Thank you very much, Lou. Thank you. I think we found a secret weapon. If that won't drive 'em out of the delta, I don't know what will. Thank you, General Wise.

This 1968 trip probably set an all-time record for illness in the cast. By the time we hit the *New Jersey*, Linda Bennett was down with flu; she missed the next show at Phuket and had to ride a litter back to Bangkok. Rosey Grier came down with gastritis so painful that the *New Jersey*'s doctor was afraid he would pass out. "If he did, we'd need a crane to lift him," he said. "So I decided to keep him on his feet."

Rosey held out till we got to Bangkok, though, and then perked up enough to do our remaining shows in Cu Chi and Dong Tam, in Vietnam, and a farewell to Thailand in Korat. By the time we were headed home via Guam he was in fine shape, and later he felt good enough about the whole tour to put it in his own special kind of perspective.

Here's how he sums it up: *Even though I was against the war, I thought we ought to let the soldiers know that we were not deserting them, to let them know that they were our brothers and our sisters. The anti-war battle we were fighting at home was not against the soldiers and the nurses; it was against the power that sent them there and the attitudes that sent them there. I went with Bob because I felt he was doing something I could relate to. I wanted to show the servicemen we cared about them. That we didn't care why they were there, we cared about them. I wanted the soldiers to know where I stood. Even though I didn't approve of the war, I approved of them as human beings, doing what the government asked them because they were citizens of our country. And I approve of that.*

So do I, Rosey. So do I.

President and Mrs. Nixon, Vice-President and Mrs. Agnew, White House, 1969.

The last Christmas show

1969

CHAPTER 20

Some firsts at the White House

By the time 1969 rolled around, I'd done so many Christmas tours that I was almost convinced that nothing new could happen on one of them. How wrong can you get?

It was my first round-the-world Christmas tour and the first kickoff dinner and command performance at the White House with the entire cast and crew. It was also the first time I went to Vietnam and performed for an audience that was colder than Thule.

But first things first: just imagine, me and seventeen gorgeous dames traveling around the world together. Take that, Hugh Hefner. Along again were that dancing dozen, the Golddiggers (actually, there were thirteen of them; they came equipped with a spare). As I remember roll call, it went like this: Barbara Sanders, Sheryl Ullman, Debi McFarland, Susan Lund, Rosetta Cox, Sheila Mann, Jackie Chidsey, Peggy Hansen, Michelle De La Fave, Susie Cadham, Nancy Bonetti, Paula Cinko, and Patricia Louise Mickey. Thirteen —count 'em—thirteen.

We had a wonderfully balanced cast that year. Our Hollywood sex symbol was Romy Schneider. Granted she wasn't from Hollywood, but in every other respect this stunning Viennese pastry certainly filled the bill.

Our singer was Connie Stevens, which is the understatement of this chapter. If you've seen Connie in Vegas you know that she does it all—she sings, she dances, and of course, one of the things I enjoy the most, she is superb in comedy sketches. We did a sketch in which I was a lonely GI and she was a rough, tough lieutenant on a desert island. She treats me like a prisoner on the island, making me march and clean up the area, and refusing to let me eat in the "officers' club." While we are alone on the island, my enlistment period runs out. She tries to get me to reenlist by becoming very provocative. She holds the paper and pen up in front of me and indicates that all will be well between us if I would just sign. The guys in the audience became so involved that they were all standing up and shouting: "Don't sign . . . you'll be sorreeeee!"

And we had a lovely gal and a great dancer, Suzanne Charny. If you saw any of our shows in which she appeared I don't have to tell you how she lit up the stage.

Our Miss World of 1969 was also from Vienna. She was the beautiful and statuesque Eva Reuber-Staier.

Irv Kupcinet filled our quota of journalists; in fact, he left a little hanging over. Hector and Ted Piero were the perfect opening flash act. They just dazzled the kids with their fantastic jazz juggling act.

The White House provided quite a few extra firsts all by itself. For example: for the first time the President and Mrs. Nixon signed autographs during dinner; for the first time a pair of torn pants was mended in the closet of the state dining room; for the first time a dancer stepped on a presidential toe while she was performing.

When the party started, it looked like any other presidential banquet for a crazy, mixed-up bag of hoofers, chanteuses, baggy-pants comics, and trombone players. I stood in the reception line with the Nixons and made a few identifying wisecracks of introduction as the cast and crew filed past. Despite the President's political affiliation, it was a democratic party: we drew numbers out of two silver bowls—one for men, one for women—to decide at which table we would sit. A good thing we did too; it would have taken the time allotted for the whole trip to figure out whether an assistant cameraman was supposed to sit on the left or the right of a saxophone player, and whether an idiot-card man got to sit down at all.

I didn't let democracy get completely out of hand, though; I sat beside Mrs. Nixon and was just getting absorbed in my Beef Bordelaise when I glanced up and saw one of the Golddiggers holding out her menu to President Nixon. I'd warned everybody beforehand that you're not supposed to ask for seconds at the White House, so I couldn't figure out what was up. It all came clear in a few seconds when the President pulled out a pen and signed the menu. Pretty soon half the people in the room were lined up in front of him, and I'd turned the color of the Tomatoes St.-Germain I was eating. One of the military aides tried to call a halt to the stream of autograph seekers, but the President just waved him off and kept on signing. I started apologizing to Mrs. Nixon, but she interrupted me—by holding out her menu and asking for my autograph! Before I knew what was happening, the whole place had turned into an autograph hunt, with everybody taking turns asking everyone else for signatures. Harlow Stengel, one of the cameramen, even cornered two waiters in the butler's pantry to add their names to the President's.

My embarrassment was nothing compared with Carlos Acosta's, the assistant cue-card man, who slipped on the stairs to the dining room and ripped a vital seam in his trousers. Since I didn't know what had happened, I thought the whole party had gone bananas when I saw one of the maids slipping him into a linen closet. Suzanne Charny, however, won the red-face award of the evening. During her exotic dance number, she landed right on the President's foot. She was in shock when she came offstage. "My God," she said. "I stepped right on Mr. Nixon's foot. I don't know how I ever finished my dance."

What an audience, though. In the front row in the East Room were the Nixons, the Vice-President and Mrs. Agnew, Defense Secretary Melvin Laird, Westy Westmoreland, and Secretary of State William Rogers. Behind them were Attorney General John Mitchell, Major Charles Robb and Lynda Bird, David and Julie Eisenhower, the Henry Fords, General Rosy O'Donnell, and a whole caucus of senators and congressmen. The President introduced me and said some kind words about my upcoming Christmas tour. He also stunned Les Brown by announcing that they were old friends since they'd been at Duke University at the same time. He quickly wiped the smug-young-sophomore look off Les's face by adding "some thirty-five years ago."

After the show the Marine orchestra played and Les Brown listened. I guess after thirty-five years the President had had just about enough of "Sentimental Journey." We didn't overstay our welcome; the President had a war to run, we had a war to visit, and our plane was scheduled to take off from Andrews Air Force Base for Berlin shortly after noon the next day.

General Rosy O'Donnell and Melvin Laird came out to say good-by at Andrews, so we did a forty-minute minishow in the hangar. I introduced the members of the cast, and they all said a few words or warbled a few bars from the songs they'd be doing along the way. We had to cut it short, though; we had a tight schedule, and we had to be airborne by 2 P.M. For once we made it: all aboard at one forty-five (even Barney McNulty) and wheels up at one fifty-five.

We made one quick stop at Rhine-Main Air Base to pick up a pilot qualified to take us through the East German air corridor to Berlin. Actually it's no problem. It's plainly marked—you just stay between the tracer bullets.

It reminded me of the airlift days of 1948. As we approached Berlin we couldn't see a thing through the windows of the plane—just a thick white blanket of snow. I expected the pilot to repeat the crack the other pilot had made twenty-one years before—the one about the soup being so thick that he'd just passed a noodle. But this pilot was great. He made a beautiful landing in somebody's back yard. I believe they call it Tempelhof Airport.

It was 7 A.M. when we landed, but Major General R. J. Ferguson, commander of the U.S. forces in Berlin, was on hand to present me with a Berlin-shaped plaque and ask me "to carry our admiration to our troops in Vietnam." I knew I wouldn't have much trouble keeping that promise.

That afternoon we did a full dress rehearsal in Deutschlandhalle, a giant convention hall that reminded me of the old Madison Square Garden— with just a soupçon of sauerkraut. It took us five hours, in which half the time was spent trying to find Barney McNulty with the cue cards—the other

Connie Stevens, Piero Brothers, Golddiggers at Andrews Air Force Base, Washington, D.C., 1969.

two and a half hours were spent trying to separate the local photographers from Romy Schneider. They've all lived together for a long time but for some reason that day it was love at first sight. Not that the press overlooked me. At the height of the flashbulbs one of the photographers turned to me and said, "Would you mind holding her coat, whoever you are?"

That night we decided to take in some of the celebrated Berlin night life. We headed instantly for the Resi. In the kindest of terms let us put it down as Ma Bell's answer to a swinging single's club. There is a telephone on every table and every table has a number. If you see somebody that attracts you at the neighboring table then you just dial the number. If you have the right personality, the right style, a touch of wit and humor, a hint of sexuality, you will never have to learn to live alone and like it.

I didn't want to seem pushy, so at first I waited for someone to dial me. Then I thought, "Oh, what the hell . . . I'll dial a few numbers."

I could go through one of those long and agonizing stories, but I know you'll beat me to the finish. At the end of a frustrating three hours, I ended up with a tab for $153 and Les Brown.

The audience at the Deutschlandhalle show the next afternoon gave us a warm reception. I was greeted by Willy Brandt's successor as mayor of Berlin, Klaus Schuetz, and again by General Ferguson. This time, in less official surroundings, General Ferguson let on that he was also tainted with show business; he'd been a technical adviser on Ronald Reagan's first movie.

Funny, the things you remember about a show always turn out to be the things that were either the most ridiculous or the most moving. They had folding seats by the camera stand, in full view of the audience, for members of my staff. They were built like the seats in the newer U.S. movie theaters that fold up automatically whenever you take your weight off them. Judy Binder, Mort Lachman's assistant, did just that somewhere about mid-show; when she sat down again without looking behind her, the result cracked up the audience. As she sprawled on the stage, all 6,500 U. S. Army and Air Force men gave her a standing ovation.

General Ferguson threw a reception for us after the show at Columbia House at Tempelhof, and at 8 P.M. we took off for Rome. The trip only took a couple of hours, but then we fell into the clutches of a bus driver who didn't know the way from the airport to the Cavalieri Hilton. The bus ride took almost as long as the flight, and we finally pulled up at the hotel at 2:30 A.M. It didn't take me long to get to bed, but others had a bit more trouble. When Suzanne Charny answered a knock at her door, she found an assistant manager waiting on the threshold. Without a word, he solemnly swept her into an ardent embrace and kissed her smack on the lips. Then he stepped back and announced: "That is a token of our admiration of Mr. Hope." I could have delivered that message myself, and I might even have skipped the tip.

We were scheduled to leave the hotel for our first show at nine-thirty the next morning, but that didn't stop our sight-seeing fanatics. At 6 A.M. the Golddiggers were up and on their way to the Vatican. Their miniskirts left the guards gaping, but only for a minute; when the girls tried to go inside the cathedral the guards stopped them and informed them, with gestures, that there was too much of them showing for sanctity's sake. Luckily, it was chilly that morning and the girls had taken sweaters with them. They calmly tied the arms around their waists, let the long part of the sweaters serve as a wrap-around skirt, and advanced on the Pietà.

The girls were still full of tales of their adventures as we boarded buses for the sixty-five-kilometer run to Gaeta, the port on the Mediterranean where the Sixth Fleet was riding at anchor. We drove through some intermittent showers along the way, but no one paid much attention since the scenery was so spectacular.

But it began to pour. By the time we boarded the motor launches to ride out to the aircraft carrier *Saratoga*, we seemed to be *in* the Mediterranean, not on it. Weather isn't usually too much of a problem on a carrier; you can always move the show from the flight deck to the hangar deck, which is pretty much weatherproof. But the stage they'd built for us on the *Saratoga* was a massive affair, so solidly bolted together that it would have taken three hours to dismantle and move it. What's more, we were on a very tight schedule; we had only two hours to do our thing and move on.

If I hadn't seen what happened next, I never would have believed it. A warrant officer surveyed the problem, then mustered five hundred volunteers. He positioned a couple of hundred sailors under the stage, and the rest around the edges. Then he climbed on top with a bullhorn and hollered out: "On the count of three, lift and move!" He'd count three, the sailors would lift, move the stage about five feet, then rest. He'd count again. Each move nudged the stage closer to the giant elevator that carried planes from the hangar deck to the flight deck. That stage must have weighed close to thirty thousand pounds, but it took them only about forty-five minutes to move it to the elevator, lower it, move it off the elevator, and set it up again. It was like watching the Egyptians build the pyramids strictly on manpower, working together. Those sailors got a reward no Nubian slave ever dreamt of: front-row seats for the show. Since there were about six thousand sailors—including men from nine other Sixth Fleet ships—crowded onto that hangar deck, they were pretty happy with their close-up view, especially since they couldn't quite straighten their backs.

We were welcomed aboard by all sorts of people—and things. First Vice-Admiral David C. Richardson, commander of the Sixth Fleet, and Captain Warren O'Neil, captain of the *Saratoga*, gave me a large white flag bearing a patch from each of the fifty ships in the fleet. Then CS/2nd Ralph Marx and CS/2nd David Galloway went their commanders one better by presenting me with a three-hundred-pound cake baked in the shape of the *Saratoga*. Flattops are incredible, but I'd never seen one that was edible—and that one was incredibly edible. It even had WELCOME BOB HOPE SHOW frosted onto the top. I torpedoed right into it, and passed the first piece to Eva Reuber-Staier. It was so good she almost ate the tiny plastic model airplane perched on her slice of flight deck.

The success of the show just goes to show you that our men enjoy something more than just a pretty face. In Germany, I'd recruited a team of Argentine jugglers to go along to Italy with me and all those girls. The Piero Brothers, they called themselves, and they were fantastic; even with all that feminine competition, they stopped the show and won a standing ovation.

When we'd wound up the show, we got another hint that our gang was a

Connie Stevens at Camp Eagle, Hue, Vietnam, 1969.   *Teresa Graves, Utapao, Thailand, 1969.*

big drawing card. A message came booming over the loudspeaker: "Now hear this. Now hear this. Will the unannounced visitor from the USS *Waldron* please report to the quarterdeck immediately and identify himself?"

We left the *Saratoga* around 9 P.M. and headed back to Rome and a 1 A.M. flight to Incirli Air Force Base in Adana, Turkey. We put on an afternoon show in the hangar at Incirli for about 4,500 men, including Turkish military and government personnel. The base commander, Colonel Robert B. Clark, introduced me, adding that the huge WELCOME, BOB HOPE banner stretched across the back of the stage was the same one used for my last visit there in 1963. "We knew you'd be back," he said, "so we saved the banner and changed the three to a nine."

I appeared on stage wearing a native costume—baggy Turkish trousers, a cap called a kasket, with worry beads strung around my neck and a string bag of oranges dangling from my hand. The audience's reaction was like a shot of adrenalin. They were yelling and screaming, "Choke Cosell! Choke

Some firsts at the White House   281

Cosell!" Naturally I looked around to find Howard, but then I found out they were yelling a couple of Turkish words: *cok guzel, cok guzel*, which means (unless somebody was pulling my leg), "the greatest." Not one to waste an opportunity like that, I slipped right into my monologue:

★

How 'bout this. They gave me Gleason's old pants.

And I want to thank him very much for these worry beads. I'm going to send these to my stockbroker.

I love this outfit. You can't tell whether you're coming or going.

Thank you, ladies and gentlemen. Here we are in Incirli, Turkey. Incirli . . . that's a Turkish word meaning, "Don't knock it . . . it beats Vietnam!"

I visited the mosques when I was here six years ago and this trip I plan to visit them again. I'm not overly religious, I just wanna get my shoes back.

★

They must have loved me in Incirli; Colonel Clark presented me with two historic coins, a gold Ataturk minted in 1923 and a two-thousand-year-old silver coin bearing the head of Alexander the Great. Quickly stowing our loot, we headed for the airport.

We were facing a fifteen-hour flight to Bangkok. We had to go by way of Sharjah Royal Air Force Base on the Persian Gulf since neither India nor Pakistan would give us permission to fly over their territory.

We weren't scheduled to do a show at Sharjah, but to those tommies everything that wasn't a sand crab or an Arab was a show—particularly our gaggle of glamorous gals. The welcome was warm, to say the least. When our big C-141 Starlifter landed, the RAF leftenant on duty warned all our lovelies that the desert base was womanless, and had been that way for some time. "Ye gods," he said, with understandable emotion, "I have not seen the likes of these women in two years, and neither have my six thousand men. In fact, we have not seen *any* ladies in two years. So watch yourselves."

Even though he wasn't kidding, we had no problems. The base, you see, was veddy British—hawf Air Force and hawf Army—and you know how proper the British are. They unwound just enough to help us with a triple surprise birthday party for one of the Golddiggers, Colonel Joe Smith (the project officer on the tour), and Onnie Morrow. By the time we finished the champagne and the birthday cake the plane crew had baked, no one wanted to leave. There was a rumor afloat that the RAF was going to sabotage the plane to keep all the girls there over the holidays. When the all-aboard was regretfully announced, one of the junior officers called out a bit wistfully, "Women and children last."

We took on two more cast members in Bangkok—Teresa Graves, the bubbly star of Rowan and Martin's *Laugh-In*, and Neil Armstrong, the world's (and the United States's) first man on the moon.

Teresa was a comparative newcomer in those days but there wasn't any question that she was going to be a big star. She had a combination of singing and dancing and comedy that was uniquely hers. And in the most literal sense of the word, she was a show stopper. This year she has her own program on television—a dramatic show in which she plays a hip undercover police-woman. I saw the pilot for it and as they say in the song, "This Could Be the Start of Something Big."

Since Neil's legs weren't much to look at, I decided to keep him out of hot pants and just have him do a skit with me—and then maybe field some questions from the audiences in Vietnam and Thailand. I was a little worried about how he'd do onstage, since he was trained to do most of his work in a capsule.

We had quite a schedule for the week ahead: Lai Khe, Utapao, Cu Chi, Chu Lai, Camp Eagle, Da Nang, Nakhon Phanom, Korat, and Long Binh—not to mention the USS *Sanctuary* and *Ranger* and the traditional command performance for Their Highnesses, the King and Queen of Thailand.

As it turned out, Neil was the last performer I had to worry about. Even the cast and crew looked on him with a kind of awe and wonder. His skit about being a man on the moon wasn't terribly funny, and he was a pretty rigid actor, but—oh, wow—the reception he got! All I had to do was introduce him, call him the Christopher Columbus of space, and the whole audience would stand up and cheer, and cheer, and cheer. The shortest standing ovation I clocked was four minutes, the longest twelve. All those guys who knew what it meant to put your life on the line really loved him.

Yet strangely people did not recognize Neil on the street. When he and I would go walking in Bangkok, it seemed as if everybody knew me. Of course, I've had my puss hanging out for so long on the screen and on television that I'm difficult not to know. But people would stop me in the street and ignore him and I'd point to Neil and say, "This is Neil Armstrong." There'd be an embarrassed moment when they'd stare at him. And I'd say, "Neil Armstrong. The first man on the moon." And then it would hit them and they would kiss his shoelaces and touch his clothes and forget about me. And then I'd think, "Why did I introduce him? He's the first man on the moon. Let him get his own introductions."

When Neil came out at the end of the shows for the question-and-answer free-for-all, the GIs wouldn't let him go. We had mikes set up in the audience, and they bombarded him with questions:

Neil Armstrong at Da Nang, Vietnam, 1969.

The last Christmas show

BOB: Now, who would like to ask Neil Armstrong a question? . . . about the moon trip. You in the back there. Will you stand up? What is your name, son?

CAVAGE: Cat Cavage.

BOB: Cat Cavage? Cat Cavage played for Baltimore. You're a different Cat Cavage. What's the question?

CAVAGE: What was the first thought when you stepped on the moon?

NEIL: A number of experts predicted that we were gonna get into serious trouble up there. Besides not being able to keep our balance, they said we'd probably find that the dust was very soft and very deep and we'd probably sink in. And so that's the thing I was worried about when I climbed down the ladder and stepped off. But . . . ah . . . I was sure glad that those guys were all wrong.

BOB: Right there—yes, stand up, son.

PARSONS: Sir, my name's James Parsons.

BOB: Where you from?

PARSONS: Goldsboro, North Carolina. I would like to know when you're planning on your next mission to the moon.

NEIL: If I'm planning to go back?

PARSONS: Yes.

NEIL: Well, I'll tell you. I had a great trip to the moon. I enjoyed every minute. I particularly enjoyed coming back. But I'd like to go to the moon again. I left a few things up there.

PARSONS: I'd like to go with you, you know.

NEIL: I'd like to have you.

(*applause*)

BOB: Right there. What's your name, son?

JONES: Airman Jones, sir.

BOB: Where you from?

JONES: Georgia, sir.

BOB: Question for Neil Armstrong.

JONES: Did you get TDY [temporary duty] pay while you were on the moon?

NEIL: Did I get TDY pay while I was there? Yeah, as a matter of fact I did. But they deducted 30 per cent for government quarters available.

(*applause and laughter*)

And they deducted for government meals available, and by the time I got done for the whole trip to the moon and back, quarantine, and eight days down at Cape Kennedy for work flight, I got forty-three dollars.

(*applause*)

BOB: Right there—is that two girls or one girl with two heads? What is it, darling?

GIRLS: We'd like to know when you're going to take the first woman to the moon?

BOB: Hey, wait a minute. When do you want to go?

NEIL: We welcome you with open arms. I really think that we'll have some women in space some of these days—I'm lookin' forward to it.

BOB: I'm sure they'll go when they find out they can go up there and be weightless. Right behind ya. What's your name?

THOMAS: Jim Thomas from Olathe, Kansas.

BOB: What's your question?

THOMAS: Okay. Did . . . ah . . . did it bother you being cooped up? In the ship on the way up there and on the way back?

NEIL: Well, it always bothers me a little bit being cooped up, but we could . . . we could look out the windows and we had some beautiful sights to see. And I'll tell ya, coming home wasn't . . . it wasn't any problem at all.

(*Neil laughs*)

BOB: Can I tell one joke that . . . I have . . . lucky enough to have Wally Schirra on our program with Walt Cunningham and Donn Eisele of the Apollo 7 group, Neil, and I gotta tell ya this joke . . . I think I can tell it to ya, but Walt Cunningham was flying . . . orbiting the earth at seventeen thousand miles and he had to go to the can . . . he had to do number one, so he floated down to this tube, down in the capsule, and he was doing number one, and he looked over and there was a window there so he pulled the shade. Wait a minute. Wait a minute, ace. Right over there.

DUPANG: Frank Dupang from Honolulu, Hawaii. I want to know why you are so interested in the moon, instead of the conflicts here in Vietnam?

(*cheers*)

NEIL: Would you say that question again.

BOB: That's good.

DUPANG: I wanna know why the U.S. is so interested in the moon instead of the conflict here in Vietnam?

(*cheers*)

NEIL: Well, that's a . . . that's a great question, and one which . . . ah . . . which you here may feel there's a good deal of contradiction. We don't feel that that's the case. The American . . . the nature of the American system is that it works on many levels in many areas to try to build peace on earth, good will to men. And one of the advantages of the space activity is that it has promoted international understanding and enabled cooperative efforts between countries on many levels and will continue to do so in the future.

BOB: Right there. What's your name?

ANDERSON: Jerry Anderson, Chickasha, Oklahoma.

BOB: Hey, Okie, what can we do for you?

ANDERSON: Mr. Armstrong, in your travels to the moon and around the world do you feel that the space program will help world peace?

NEIL: Yes, I do. People around the world have been given hope that difficult problems can be solved if you can identify the goal that you're seeking and work together to reach that goal. And I think it'll work in a lot of areas other than just getting to the moon.

ANDERSON: Sir, we in Vietnam would like to thank you for your contribution to world peace.

NEIL: Thank you very much.

    (*applause and cheers*)

BOB: Right there. There he is. Yeah. Stand up.

    (*laughs*)

You're livin' in a crouch, aren't cha?

GI: Yes, sir.

BOB: Where you from, son?

GI: Jacksonville, Florida, sir.

BOB: Yeah. Yeah. Ya got a bottle of Gatorade on ya? What . . . what's your question?

GI: Mr. Armstrong . . . ah . . . being from your experience on the moon and the knowledge that you have of it now do you think it's possible that one day humans could live on the moon?

NEIL: Yes. I think . . . ah . . . I think they will. We will see a scientific base being built on the moon. It'll be a scientific station manned by international crew, very much like the Antarctic station. But probably there's a much more important question than whether man will be able to live on the moon. I think we have to ask ourselves whether man will be able to live together down here on earth.

    (*applause and cheers*)

Normally, when we finished a show, all the GIs would rush onstage to talk to the girls, get their autographs, and take their pictures. You know the sort of stuff—anything to get to stand next to a girl instead of another GI. Well, this time round, the soldiers rushed the stage to talk with Neil, even after the question-and-answer period. The poor girls just clumped around looking like the losers in a deodorant commercial.

Some firsts at the White House   287

Cu Chi, Vietnam, 1969.

Our first stop in Vietnam, Lai Khe, was unnerving for a couple of reasons: (1) before we arrived, Vietcong rockets were discovered aimed directly at the show site, and (2) I heard some scattered boos from the audience. My hosts, the 1st Infantry Division (the Big Red One) took care of the first problem. Troops swept the perimeter of the base on the morning of the show, found six Cong rockets and nine Cong. They dismantled the rockets, disarmed the Cong, and brought everything into camp. Their quick action saved my life (for which I'm ever so grateful), the lives of our cast, and the lives of a lot of the ten thousand soldiers who'd started gathering early for the show.

288   *The last Christmas show*

Bob Hope and worry beads, Incirli, Turkey, 1969.

Major General A. E. Milloy, commander of the Big Red One, gave us a warm welcome and I jumped right into the monologue.

I couldn't quite believe my ears a few minutes later when I heard boos coming from the audience. My voice went ahead with my monologue, but my mind was racing back over what I'd said. I'd been talking about the show at the White House and reported, "The President said to me, 'I have a plan to end the war.'"

It didn't take long for me to realize that those few guys in the audience weren't booing me. They were sitting in Vietnam; they didn't want to be there; they wanted to be any place where there wasn't a war, and who could blame them? Their boos were just a way of answering the President. They were too tired, too worn out, too disillusioned to believe that anyone had a plan to end the war and get them out of that hot, steamy, rotten jungle. They'd heard that song before.

They were the coldest, most unresponsive audience my show had ever played to. The GIs were completely deadpan; they didn't laugh at anything. I tried to cope, but it was tough going—I just couldn't get through to them, and I couldn't figure out why.

After the show I tried talking to some of them face to face to find out what was going on. The story came out. They were all in a state of shock. It had been a wipe-out day for a lot of them. They had lost a lot of friends, and then had been rushed in from a fire fight to catch my show. After a morning like that, who could expect them to be in the mood for laughing it up at my jokes?

Eventually it came out that they had all been looking forward to the show as a chance to escape the dreariness of fighting that war. But we came on the wrong day. They wanted to be with us, they knew we wanted to be with them. But not that day; any day but that day. As I was leaving, one of the worn-out soldiers reached out and put something in my hand. A Zippo lighter. It wasn't much, but it was all he had.

The whole booing incident was nothing, really, but it got blown up way out of proportion back in the States. All that ever got reported was that I was booed at Lai Khe—not that a couple of guys out of fifteen thousand resented vague promises to end the war their buddies were dying in. As it turned out, Nixon did end it and did bring them home.

We started out with our longest show at Cu Chi for the fifteen thousand troops of the 25th Infantry Division. Cu Chi is about twenty miles northwest of Saigon, and the division was entrusted with the vital role of protecting the government of Vietnam in Saigon from attacks originating in nearby border areas. That afternoon we had a pretty impressive visitor in the audience, Admiral John McCain, commander of the Pacific area.

MCCAIN: Bob, on behalf of this command, I want to tell you the supreme appreciation we have. Let me tell you fellows something. They got a bunch of boys running around the streets back in the States and they're carrying signs, "Make Love Not War."

(*cheers*)

Well, you're in a fraternity that's big enough to do both. Get on with the business, goddammit.

(*cheers*)

Singing "Silent Night" in the rain at Da Nang, 1969.

Some firsts at the White House   291

I wanna tell you something. I never thought in my wildest whatnots that I'd be standing on the stage with Bob Hope and these good-looking gals that are right behind me. But also I wanna tell you there's room enough for you, too, if you wanna come on up here, boys.

BOB: Admiral . . . Admiral, sir. Do you want to get us trampled to death?

MCCAIN: Sorry about that, Bob. Now one other thing, men, I wanna say to you. Merry Christmas and a Happy New Year to ya. And I'm proud of every damn one of you. Good luck and God bless you.

Following the show, we did a two-hour handshaking, autograph-signing tour of the nearby three-hundred-bed Twelfth Medical Evacuation Hospital. As the motorcade pulled up to the Quonset huts that made up the hospital, a medical evacuation helicopter landed on the adjacent emergency pad. It was carrying eight injured Vietcong, and they got the best care the surgical emergency ward had to offer.

Shortly before we left the Cu Chi area to return to Bangkok, Terence Cardinal Cooke showed up. We all gathered round to greet him, along with Major General Harris W. Hollis, commander of the division. We wanted to give Cardinal Cooke our best wishes, since he was taking over the good work of his late predecessor, Cardinal Spellman.

We had to cancel our big show on the hospital ship *Sanctuary* because of rain, but when the weather cleared, Neil, Teresa, Connie, and I went aboard for a minishow. The shows at Camp Eagle, just south of the so-called de-militarized zone, for the 101st Airborne Division, and at Freedom Hill, Da Nang, for twenty thousand Marines, went off without a hitch. After a day off in Bangkok—if you can call a command performance for royalty a day off— and two shows in Thailand, things began to pick up.

Finally there was just one show to go—at Long Binh, in Vietnam. After that it was a hop to Guam, then home. As I was wrapping up the Long Binh show and getting ready to give the cue for "Thanks for the Memory," the colonel in command came up to me and said, "How long will it take you fellows to get your stuff loaded and move out?" I haven't had such a cool question since my days in vaudeville.

"What's your hurry?" I asked.

"Well," said the colonel, "there's a little fire fight coming in here. It's about six or seven miles away, and moving in pretty fast."

That did it. We were out of there in fifteen minutes flat.

I was worried about the girls, of course.

1970

CHAPTER 21

The pot boils over

As the fellow says, virginity is only a problem the first time, and I guess it's the same way with taking the Hope troupe all the way round the world. Having survived it in 1969, I was ready to try again in 1970. The captain of the West Point cadet corps, Tom Pyrz, had written to ask that I do a show there, so I scheduled a final dress rehearsal at the Military Academy. From there our course lay due east: a NATO air base at Lakenheath, England, an armored division headquarters at Hanau, Germany, the aircraft carrier *John F. Kennedy* in the Mediterranean off Crete, and then across the Middle East to Thailand, Vietnam, Korea, and Alaska.

Our sex goddess of the year was Ursula Andress. Like Venus on the half shell, she made her first hit in a sea picture, emerging from the ocean in the arms of Sean Connery in the James Bond picture *Dr. No*. And then there were the photos her once-upon-a-time husband John Derek took of her frolicking under a waterfall in the altogether. When I saw them in *Playboy* magazine, all I could say was, "I'd hate to have her water bill."

Lola Falana came along to do some of the steamy dance sequences that had made her famous on Broadway when she was in *Golden Boy* with Sammy Davis, Jr. We had two all-American girl singers along—a high-cheekboned blonde named Gloria Loring, who got her start singing in church choirs and the Playboy Club in Miami Beach, and Bobbi Martin, a country-and-western singer who wrote her own songs and played her own guitar. Miss World that year was Jennifer Hosten from Grenada in the British West Indies and Mr. World Series was Johnny Bench, the catcher for the Cincinnati Reds who had been voted the most valuable player in the National League. He turned out to be a pretty good player in any league. We took the Golddiggers along again and, of course, the Ditchdiggers, also known as Les Brown and His Band of Renown.

In all, we had seventy-six troupers along, and with that number there were bound to be some hitches along the way. The first one struck even *before* we

The pot boils over   293

were along the way. One of the Golddiggers, Liz Kelley, carefully set four alarm clocks to wake her in time for our departure from Van Nuys Air National Guard Base. They woke her up all right, but when she sat down to put her make-up on she made the mistake of resting her head on her arms on the dressing table. She dozed so long that her cab had to chase our plane as it was taxiing to the end of the runway. The pilot was in no mood to stop, but he had to get in the mood fast when the taxi cut in front of him. It was probably the first time in history that an Air Force plane ever got caught in a traffic jam behind an L.A. cab.

Poor Liz—she missed our then mayor, Sam Yorty, in one of his rare Los Angeles appearances. I guess he considered my leaving part of his anti-pollution program. Jack Benny played Santa Claus—with a switch. When he left, his bag was full. A few tykes turned up claiming to be my grandchildren. What a blow to a handsome young leading man!

Five and a half hours later we landed at West Point—which isn't easy, because they don't have a runway at West Point. Actually, we settled for Stewart Air Force Base, about thirty miles south of the Point. It almost took us longer to go those thirty miles than it took to fly the three thousand miles from Los Angeles. The New York State Police who escorted us were afraid of ice, so we crawled along at 20 m.p.h.

The pace picked up by show time at 1400 hours the next day. The cadets marched handsomely into the fieldhouse and were joined by a distinguished galaxy of guests—Army chief of staff Westy Westmoreland; West Point commandant Major General William A. Knowlton and his wife Peggy; General Alfred Gruenther, then head of the American Red Cross; General Lyman Lemnitzer; and, of course, former Air Force general Emmett "Rosy" O'Donnell, the USO boss who had helped start me on all those trips.

Tom Pyrz introduced me, and I tried to melt down a little of that brass:

★

Here we are at West Point. I just want to say, "At ease." Laugh if you like. I hate an audience that salutes jokes.

It's a beautiful sight. I haven't seen so much gray since I passed out at the letter carriers' convention.

And I love these collars you wear—they're something else. From the back, this place looks like the whiplash ward on "Medical Center." I suppose that's what comes of eating muleburgers; they pack an awful kick.

This place is a factory—an officer factory. Don't knock it; it's the only product that Ralph Nader hasn't put down.

★

There was a lot of talk about marijuana that year, so I eased into a pot joke:

★

Speaking of Johnnies, our own Johnny Bench has really got it good. Baseball's a great sport. Where else can you spend eight months a year on grass and not get busted?

★

That one really broke up the cadets. Tom Pyrz thanked me on behalf of all of them with what he called an "Academy Award." It was a regulation cadet bathrobe, trimmed with a varsity A and eight stripes on the sleeve. The most any member of the corps can earn is six, so they threw in a couple of extras—I guess to grow on. It tickled me so, I picked up a golf club and putted right off the stage and onto the plane.

By the time we were airborne on our way to Lakenheath, it was obvious that just about every Golddigger had a secret ambition to be a Bench-warmer for the Cincinnati Reds. And why not? Johnny was twenty-three, a bachelor, and an all-around good guy. When I said that for a catcher Johnny Bench could pitch pretty good, Mort Lachman reassured me: "Don't worry," he said. "Catchers seldom get to first base."

About 6,500 troops were waiting in that chilly Lakenheath hangar, so I tried to warm them up a bit:

★

Hey, I have a message from your wives and sweethearts back in the States: "Go home, Yank!"

I understand you guys love it here because it's so well located. It's just a stone's throw to beautiful downtown Mildenhall. I hear it's a real wild town. On Saturday nights they sell fish-and-chips till one o'clock in the morning.

You men will be enjoying a real Old English Christmas—the yule log blazing on the hearth, plum pudding bubbling in the oven, and the beer heating on the stove.

★

Back in the States, I told them:

★

The Nixon administration had made things pretty tough for me. Now I've got over three hundred comedians on TV to compete with —including Agnew and Fulbright.

We're having a little recession back home. A little recession—that means if it gets any worse, we're going to reapply as a colony.

It also means two chickens in every pot. But you have to be on pot to see the two chickens.

The British have given us a sight that makes us think we must be stoned even when we're not: Engelbert Humperdinck.

The first time I saw him I thought he was wearing a full-length mink coat under his clothes. It turned out that his sideburns were so long, they came down through the cuffs on his pants.

★

I lost some of the attention I was getting the minute that Ursula Andress made her first appearance in purple velvet shorts and a tight-fitting, long-sleeved top that was zipped way, way down. I made a note to see my tailor as soon as I got back to Hollywood.

Nobody can top Ursula, but one of the Ding-a-Lings sure tried. The Ding-a-Lings were a dancing group that had spun off from the Golddiggers, and one of them was a beauty from Brighton, England, named Wanda Bailey. Wanda had magnificent elbows, which she used to good advantage when the top part of her costume came apart in back. She pinned what was left of her top to her sides with her elbows and danced into the wings, where the wardrobe mistress, Rose Weiss, sewed it together. Rose must have used break-away thread, though; when Wanda wandered back onstage the top gave way again, and she finished the act without her usual low bow. The only way I could top that was to announce loudly: "I'd like to tell you what we do for fun, but I make more money selling slides."

I felt a little better at the reception at the officers' club after the show when I found out that they called the place the Bob Hope Service Club. The name had been suggested by the chaplain, Lieutenant Colonel Walter Bauer. Before we took off for Rhine-Main Air Base near Frankfurt I went over to thank him. I know somebody up there likes me, but before an airplane ride I like to check in at the branch office.

WILLKOMMEN IN HANAU, HERR HOPE read the sign that greeted us at the Fliegerhorst Kaserne in Hanau. Even more *willkommen* were the shoulder patches on the sleeves of the five thousand V Army Corps and 3rd Armored Division soldiers in the audience. The patches looked just like Chrysler Corporation emblems, and guess who was sponsoring the Christmas trip TV show?

I'd got myself up in a gray loden-cloth outfit, complete with knickers and an Alpine hat.

★

I'm delighted to be here in Hanau. For a minute I thought the Pentagon had said Hanoi.

The whole cast, Hanau, Germany, 1970.

Ursula Andress, Stumpy Brown at Hanau, Germany, 1970.

But I knew I was in Germany when I looked out the plane window and saw a field of liverwurst down below.

No mistaking this hangar, either. It looks like the Astrodome with Sauerbraten.

And the people! The Germans are so plump, this country looks like a Jackie Gleason factory.

It just goes to show you that Germany is a prosperous country. No doubt about it, we gotta lose the next war.

People seem so gay here. But I guess we'd be happy too if we put beer in our Wheaties.

They never touch water here. Even my bath had a head on it.

Then, news from the home front:

Fashions have really taken a turn for the worse. They invented the midiskirt to give equal time to bowlegged girls, but us guys can't see anything any more. Girls look like duffel bags with heads on them.

A lot of women are wearing leather pantsuits. When they bend over, they look like lumpy billfolds.

The only way the men can retaliate is with Sunday afternoon football games on TV. A woman can walk through the room in the filmiest black negligee she owns, and the man won't even notice unless it has a number on the back.

You show me a man who doesn't watch football on Sunday, and I'll show you a man whose wife could play tackle for any team.

Students are being almost as big a problem as women. There's so much bombing back home it makes you guys look like draft dodgers.

Before the show I'd had a little chat with Ursula Andress. Since she could neither sing nor dance, she didn't know what to do with herself once she got onstage. I reassured her: "Just stand there; the audience will do the singing and dancing." Well, when she slithered onstage in those lavender tights, she caused more flashbulbs to pop than anyone else in the show. The troops were running down the aisles, waving their cameras, shouting, whistling, and I was right—all she had to do was stand there; the vibrations took care of the rest.

298   *The last Christmas show*

By the time the show was finished a heavy fog had settled over Hanau, and we all had to hop aboard buses for the long slow drive back to Rhine-Main Air Base. Then we had a three-and-a-half-hour flight to Souda Bay, Crete. We were supposed to be shunted from Crete to the USS *John F. Kennedy*, the next show site. The nation's newest and biggest conventional aircraft carrier, the *Kennedy* was anchored with the Sixth Fleet off Crete. For some reason there was a shortage of big helicopters, so it took until 3 A.M. to get all the cast and crew transferred by small chopper and launches.

At about 10 A.M. the next day men from the neighboring ships—the *Leahy*, the *Caloosahatchee*, the *Bang* (a wonderful name for a submarine), the *Nitro* (a munitions ship), the *Brumley*, the *Purvis*, and the *Roan*—began filling the 1,051-foot length of the *Kennedy*. For the supposedly sunny Mediterranean it was darned cold, but by our noontime show time about seven thousand sailors were covering every surface in sight—cherry-picker cranes, the bridge, anyplace they could get a grip and hold on. They'd also hooked up a closed-circuit TV system to all parts of the ship. Even the nuclear fire party, on watch belowdecks for the outbreak of fire anywhere on board, could catch our act.

Unfortunately, in the hurry-scurry of the night before, two band instruments had been left ashore on Crete. So we had to hold off for twenty minutes while they were choppered over. When they arrived, they were greeted by a booming message over the loudspeakers: "Helicopter Squadron 2, Detachment 67 has saved the show!"

When I stepped onstage, signs were sprouting throughout the audience like beards at a radical convention. My favorite was WELCOME, URSULA, THE GOLDDIGGERS, AND BOB WHO?

About that time, the Russians had caused quite a stir by moving a large fleet of warships from the Black Sea into the Mediterranean, so I opened with:

★

For the benefit of the other ships in the area this show is being broadcast in Russian.

There are a few Russian ships out there . . . A few? At night you can hear "Red Sails in the Sunset" all the way to Gibraltar.

★

From Souda Bay, our Starlifter headed east, bound for Bangkok, by way of Dhahran, Saudi Arabia. After six hours in the air, we were glad to take a coffee break at Dhahran, even though we were warned before we got off the plane that we couldn't set foot on Saudi Arabian soil if we were carrying cameras, alcoholic beverages, or worldly publications like

Playboy. Moslem law forbids such things, and Saudi Arabia, which includes Mecca, is very strict about upholding religious law. It's probably the only country left where pantyhose haven't replaced chastity belts.

As we taxied toward the terminal, Mort Lachman, our director, announced the deplaning order. "Cameras and press first . . . stars last . . . Jews in the middle."

When we reboarded, someone had pinned up a sign saying TOTAL STATUTE MILES FROM VAN NUYS TO BANGKOK: 15,114. What that sign didn't say was that Bangkok was still six weary hours away. We were all so beat that we spent most of the next day sleeping, then headed out the morning after to Utapao, a Royal Thai Air Force base and one of the busiest. United States air tankers and B-52s took off from there, and though their destinations were secret, you could tell they weren't charter flights; there was never a tourist on them. "In case you're wondering where Utapao is," I said, "it's just a few miles from Satahip. So much for educational TV." An immense amount of building had gone on since my last visit, so I added: "It looks like down-town Peoria was drafted. They have a wonderful mess hall here. It's the first time I've ever seen—"

At that point the words about the mess hall had sunk in and I was greeted by a chorus of ten thousand boos. "All right, let me finish this line, will you?" I said. "It's the first time I've ever seen Spam wrapped in a banana leaf."

Silence. "See?" I said. "Aren't you glad you waited? This is the only base in Thailand that has a beach, but some of you have been complaining that it's just not like the beaches at home. So every six months the Navy's going to dump an oil slick on it."

That first stint in Thailand was what they call "two-a-day" in vaudeville. For our second show that day we moved on to Ubon, and I continued my geography lesson.

★

Thailand is owned by Hertz Rent A Snake. It's about the size of Texas, and the reason you're here is that Lyndon Johnson thought it was.

Most things here are exportable; some are even curable.

★

Though weary, the troupe put on quite a show. The Ding-a-Lings danced a funky chicken that was finger-lickin' good, and even Johnny Bench had those guys cheering for his comedy-singing routine. Gloria Loring was the real darling of the show, though. Her warmth and sincerity went rolling over the footlights in waves. When she led the singing of "Silent Night," it brought a catch to my throat. All of a sudden the real show was out there in the audience, in the faces of the men.

USS John F. Kennedy, *Souda Bay, Crete, 1970.*

The next day we flew into Vietnam to entertain that elite unit, the Screaming Eagles—the 101st Airborne Divison.

★

Here I am at Camp Eagle. I was here last year and I came back to hatch the egg I laid.

This is the home of the famed 101st Airborne. They've seen more action than a traffic cop on the Ho Chi Minh Trail.

★

I meant it, too. Commanded by Major General John J. Hennessey, the division was responsible for protecting the heavily populated regions of Thuathien and Quangtri provinces. From the spring of '65 on, they had waged battles from Dak To to the A Shau valley. After driving the Cong out of Hue following the 1969 Tet offensive, they had made nearby Camp Eagle their home.

★

This has been a great trip. We've been to England, to Germany, then to Crete, then to Thailand—and we're going to keep on going until we find Howard Hughes.

I guess you read that Howard Hughes has disappeared. The next day Jack Benny showed up at the police station claiming to be his only son.

They say that Hughes went to the Bahamas, but they don't know how he got there. The last they saw of him he was walking across the Gulf of Mexico.

The mosquitoes here at Camp Eagle are so big, one of them is going steady with a chopper.

But I guess you guys are too busy to be bothered by things like mosquito bites. I hear you go in for gardening. The commanding officer says you all grow your own grass.

He seemed a bit upset about it, but I think that instead of taking it away from the soldiers, they ought to give it to the negotiators in Paris.

In one barracks I passed, a group of GIs was watching Twelve O'Clock High *and they didn't even have a TV set.*

★

The weather was so hot and humid at Camp Eagle that Wanda Bailey and another of the Golddiggers, Tara Leigh, fainted during the show. And even though the next day was Christmas Eve, the weather was just as hellish at Da

Osan Air Force Base, Korea, 1970.

Nang, the second largest city in Vietnam. Da Nang had been the scene of the first U.S. involvement in Vietnam, with the establishment of an American advisory team in 1962. Since then, the camp had grown in size and importance as a major U.S. combat support base. I'd been doing shows there since 1966, when they built the Freedom Hill Recreation Center.

That Christmas Eve, the amphitheater was filled to overflowing with 17,500 Marines, GIs, sailors, Seabees, and Army and Navy nurses.

We had a lot of fun with Bobbi Martin. She did country and western that really appealed to a great segment of our audience. And afterward we used to do a hunk together called "Your Cheatin' Heart" that went something like this:

> BOBBI: All these men must get very lonely out here.
> BOB: Bobbi, the military thinks of everything. All the service clubs have ping-pong.
> BOBBI: Well, when they finally get to go home, they must be like strangers.
> BOB: Yes, I imagine that's quite a scene . . . the lonely soldier coming home from the wars into the arms of his loving wife.

Golddiggers at Yonju-gol, Korea, 1970.

The last Christmas show

BOBBI: I'll play the loving wife.

BOB: I'll play what's left.

> (*Bob makes false exit then returns*)

BOB (*to Bobbi*):

Honey, I'm home! Your loving hubby is home from the wars! All these long months I've been waiting for this kiss.

> (*Bobbi gives him a slap*)

BOB (*takes it, then to audience*): What we have here is a breakdown in communication.

> (*to Bobbi*)

What's this all about?

> MUSIC: *"Your Cheatin' Heart"*

BOBBI (*sings*): Your cheatin' heart—

BOB (*speaks*): Me???

BOBBI (*sings*):

Will make you weep.

You cry and cry

And you try to sleep

BOB: Who's thinking about sleep?

BOBBI (*sings*):

But sleep ain't gonna come

The whole night through.

Your cheatin' heart

Is gonna tell on you.

> MUSIC: *Continues under softly*

BOB: So that's it! You think I've been cheatin' on you! Whatever gave you that idea?

BOBBI: That lipstick mark on your collar.

BOB: It's not lipstick . . . It's ketchup.

BOBBI: I'd like to meet the tomato it came from.

BOB: I swear to you you're the only one I ever thought of.

BOBBI: Yeah? Then who's that "Sylvia" you were always talking about in your letters?

BOB: Sylvia? That's my sergeant!

> (*beat*)

Sylvia's his *last* name.

BOBBI: Oh? What's his first name?

BOB: Shirley . . . his mother wanted a girl.

BOBBI: I suppose he tucked you in and kissed you goodnight?

BOB: Yes, he did. They'll do anything to get you to reenlist.

> MUSIC: *Up*

BOBBI (*sings*):
When tears come down
They're gonna come like pourin' rain.
Yeah, and you'll toss around
And you'll call my name.
 MUSIC: *Under*

BOB: Honest, honey, you got it wrong. I spent all my free time in the library with my nose stuck in a book.

BOBBI: Ha! Your nose was like that before you left.

 (*beat*)

You in a library! You need subtitles to understand the comics.

BOB: Well, I have improved my mind.

BOBBI: That's good, considering what you had to work with.

BOB: Are you sure you're my wife?

BOBBI: You mean you don't remember me?

BOB: After two years, all you round eyes look alike.

BOBBI (*indicating*):

What's that medal for?

BOB: I saved a girl from drowning.

BOBBI: But you can't swim.

BOB: This was in a bathhouse.

 MUSIC: *Up*

BOBBI (*sings*):

You're gonna walk the floor

The way I do.

Your cheatin' heart

Is gonna break the news to you.

 MUSIC: *Under*

BOB: But honey, how can you accuse me of cheatin'?

BOBBI: You went out with other girls, didn't you?

BOB: Yeah.

BOBBI: And you danced with 'em, didn't you?

BOB: Yeah.

BOBBI: You hugged 'em and kissed 'em, didn't you?

BOB: Yeah.

BOBBI: Well, what do you call that?

BOB: Striking out!

BOBBIE: Oh sure. I *heard* about those girls over there. They're all petite and beautiful.

BOB: That's true.

BOBBI: They treat a man like a god . . . wait on him hand and foot.

BOB: That's true.

A few folks at Da Nang, Vietnam, 1970.

BOBBI: They make any shnook feel like he's Richard Burton.

BOB: That's true.

    (*starts to move away*)

I'll be seein' ya.

BOBBI: Where're you going?

BOB: I just remembered. I left my toothbrush in Da Nang.

    MUSIC: *Up*

BOBBI (*sings*):

I said your cheatin' heart

Is gonna tell on you.

    MUSIC: *Playoff* (*applause*)

During mail call, I got one of the soldiers, Bob Mansee, up onstage. His mother had written him saying that his grandmother had played a part in my formative years back in Maple Heights, Ohio. She'd caught me trespassing and had chased me over a fence with a broom. I remembered it, all right . . . After a few gag exchanges, I turned and chased Mansee right off the stage with a prop broom.

We finished our stay in Vietnam with a Christmas Day show at Curry Amphitheater in Long Binh. Again, we'd chosen a big day for a big place. Located seventeen miles northeast of Saigon, Long Binh covered more than nineteen thousand acres, had over twenty-seven miles of perimeter to patrol, and with twenty-seven thousand military personnel and twenty thousand civilian workers, was the largest single military installation in Southeast Asia, even though the troop withdrawals had begun.

General Frederick C. Weyand did my warm-up for me, and Lieutenant General William McCaffrey did the introduction. My response came naturally:

★

With all the troop withdrawals, I'm surprised to see anyone here.

It was nice of you guys to stick around just for me.

General McCaffrey has three stars. When you get to be that important, they ought to give you a war of your own.

In fact, I'm amazed at the number of generals here. Who's minding the store? Somewhere, there's a private answering the phone: "Hello, Vietnam War."

★

After I wisecracked that Long Binh sounded like Dean Martin's wine cellar, a soldier was brought onstage to hug Gloria Loring. When he was all through, I asked him how he felt. "Like I'd only had one potato chip," he fired back. That was enough for me; I've been in the business long enough to know that there's no percentage in staying too long on a stage with a boy with natural lines like that. I not only left Long Binh, I left the country.

We flew back to Bangkok after the show in a C-130, singing Christmas carols all the way, with Les Brown conducting. The big part of the tour was over, though we still had three shows to do, two in Korea and one in Alaska. It turned out to be a great way to beat the heat, even if it did mean spending three nights on the plane before hitting home.

Christmas Day we were sweltering in hundred-degree heat at Long Binh. Five hours later we were at Yonju-gol in Korea putting anti-freeze in our deodorant. Les Brown warmed up the audience, but they were still sitting in subfreezing temperatures when I trotted out. "What a thrill to be here. Yes-

Signs on 1970 tour.

terday it was a hundred. Today, here I am with my suntanned goose pimples."

If there are two things that every GI will remember forever about Korea, they're kimchee and "slickey boys." Kimchee is a local delicacy, a pickled or fermented mixture of cabbage, onions, and fish, seasoned with garlic, horse-radish, red peppers, and ginger. It takes a lot of getting used to. Slickey boys are the local thieves, and they take a lot of getting used to too, particularly when you go to take a shower and find that they've taken it first. If they'd ever been let loose in North Korea, there never would have been any war. In fact, there never would have been any North Korea.

The pot boils over   309

So, my monologue veered away from the weather for a minute:

★

No, it's wonderful to be in Korea when the kimchee and the slickey boys are in bloom.

Hey, I finally found a way to beat the slickey boys. I hired a six-foot MP with a red mustache. Now I am offering a fifty-dollar reward for a six-foot MP with a red mustache.

And stepping off the plane was a big surprise—somebody had stolen the ramp. Fortunately, it wasn't too big a drop: they got the landing gear before that.

Still, weather gags touched the boys where they were living—on an ice cake. The next day I told the Air Force guys at Osan that:

The weather this morning was brisk. That's a Korean expression that means "Chop me a glass of water."

What a morning! I bumped into the sink and broke my pajamas.

At least I got to do my monologue sitting down; the guys at Osan pulled me onto the stage in a two-wheeled cart. I was wearing an old Korean warrior's costume, as much for warmth as for laughs.

This is the only base I've seen where there are guys so cold they're standing at the end of the runway hitchhiking to Vietnam.

★

I tried to brace the audience for the appearance of Miss World by telling them she had a penny in her back pocket and you could see Lincoln smiling. I never had such an attentive audience, and I must say they looked very hard—especially when I mentioned that her measurements were 37–23–36.

I would have been happy if any one of those numbers matched the temperature when we got to Elmendorf Air Force Base in Alaska. But it was eleven degrees below zero when the plane pulled in, and with the wind-chill factor, it felt like thirty-five below. In a moment of wild abandon I let them talk me into doing all the things tourists do in Alaska—skiing, snow-mobiling, getting bitten by a sled dog. I told the airmen in the audience that:

★

It was so cold our plane refused to put its tail down.

But it's nice to be here in Alaska where men are men and women are women—but it's too darned cold to do anything about it.

Golddiggers at Camp Eagle, Hue, Vietnam, 1970.

Johnny Bench at Camp Eagle, Hue, Vietnam, 1970.

Gloria Loring at Long Binh, Vietnam, 1970.

Ding-a-Lings at Da Nang, 1970.

I liked the weather this morning. I took a brisk walk. It made me feel so good, tomorrow I may try it outside.

Nobody catches cold here, though. It's hard for a germ to get into your system when it's wearing mukluks.

I tried a couple of topical lines, particularly in view of the fact that President Nixon and Interior Secretary Walter Hickel, formerly the governor of Alaska, were feuding over conservation programs.

★

Actually, this isn't the coldest place in the world. That honor goes to the spot in Washington were Nixon and Hickel pass each other on the street.

★

Although jokes about marijuana got some of the biggest laughs I heard on the entire trip, they caused quite a stir when we got back home and put together the annual ninety-minute television special.

The job of putting a television show together from our 170,000 or 180,000 feet of rough film is an infinitely complicated one.

Just viewing the film takes twenty-four hours or three working days. Then it has to be coded and catalogued (we have a superb librarian named Barry Parnell who handles this).

The picture and sound have to be synchronized, no simple job, as we may have from one to six cameras in any given scene. The film has to be edited and reedited and reedited; physical effects and dissolves have to be added; titles have to be specially made; narrations have to be included.

The entire picture has to be scored with both music and sound effects; the sound has to be mixed and balanced—a job which has been superbly handled for us by Jimmy Stewart at Glen Glenn Sound.

The negative has to be cut and processed and color-corrected—most often in all-night sessions for which we are indebted to Consolidated Film Labs. And when I say indebted, it's in more ways than one. Fortunately they have a time payment plan and we should be out of debt by the bicentennial.

In a movie this entire process would take from about six months to a year. We manage it in exactly fourteen days. A great tribute to Igo Kanter, who's the supervising editor and coordinator for our entire post-production. Igo is a superb editor and a wonderfully warm, enthusiastic person. He has a great post-production firm with many tireless and dedicated assistants. If ever I go into independent film production I intend to have an affair with Igo.

In 1970 under a lot of pressure from NBC press we let a few newsmen take an advance look at some of the footage. Associated Press columnist

Bob Thomas immediately grasped the fact that he had a controversy by the tail. He interviewed me, then put the following story on the wire:

> HOLLYWOOD (AP)—Bob Hope to baseball star Johnny Bench: "It's a great sport, baseball. You can spend eight months on grass and not get busted."
> Vietnam audiences of American servicemen roared with laughter, and the evidence can be seen on Hope's television special Thursday night.
> Bob Hope doing marijuana jokes for the troops?
> "Yes, I know a lot of people are shocked," said the comedian during a break in editing the NBC show down to ninety minutes.
> "I didn't talk to the military brass about doing it; I just went ahead. I think it's better to get this thing out in the open. Then it can be treated as the problem it is."

A Hope aide remarked that one general was queried for his reaction. "This man deals in the news," said the general, "and pot smoking in Vietnam is news."
"Sure, they smoke pot in Vietnam," Hope commented. "But it was never a problem until this year. That's because the guys have nothing to do. Before, when soldiers got bored they said, 'Let's have a drink.' Now they sit around the fire and light up.

> "But look—when I was a young man, we'd go knock on a door on Fifty-seventh Street in New York and go into a speakeasy to get a drink. Liquor was illegal then, and that was our kick."
> Does that mean Hope favors legalizing pot as well as liquor?
> "Oh no!" he replied quickly. "I've talked to too many doctors about it. I know it's not good for you."
> He even admitted to having smoked pot himself.
> "It was when I was in vaudeville," said Hope. "I tried it and it scared me. It made me sexier—and I thought I was already sexy enough."

I meant what I said, but the powers that be at NBC didn't see it that way. When they got wind of the pot that was going to be on the air, they took a look at the show and then told us to cut the grass. That bothered me a bit—I always hate to lose a laugh—but let's face it, it's their network. If they figured that the national airwaves weren't ready for pot jokes, that was their business. Still, it smacked of censorship, and that stirred up such a storm that I went on the Johnny Carson show to talk about it.

That may sound like a contradiction in terms; NBC wouldn't let me do pot jokes on my show, but they would let me talk about pot jokes on "The Tonight Show." Still, they had a rationale, which went something like this: The network didn't think it was wise to make a laughing matter of the use of drugs within the context of an entertainment show; if it gave comedians a green light to joke about marijuana, TV might be accused of making pot a household word and encouraging its acceptance as a fact of life. Talking about it with Johnny Carson was a different matter. For one thing, the show was late at night, when presumably the audience was mostly adult. For another, the context of the Carson show was different; we were talking about pot and censorship as controversial issues, not just joking about them.

On the Carson show, I repeated a few of my pet pot jokes that had been cut out of the Christmas special, and Johnny and I talked about the censorship. I said I hadn't really objected, but Johnny saw it a little differently. There was nothing like shielding the folks back home from the dark thought that their boys would try the weed, he said, and that it must be some other person's loved one who was getting stoned in Vietnam.

After the show was aired, the New York *Times*'s TV columnist, Jack Gould, had a few thoughtful words to say about the controversy in a long Sunday piece entitled "Some Like It Pot and Some Don't":

> One must wonder if Hope's annual Christmas trip falls within the strict definition of entertainment. Admittedly, the prime purpose of Hope's travels is to bring diversion to troops scattered around the world but, whether so designed or not, his program is also something in the nature of a quasi-documentary if only because much of the film footage is focused on the soldiers, sailors and aviators watching Hope and his coterie of pretty girls.
>
> . . . Hope told it as he found it during his conversation with Carson: the troops in Vietnam did respond to quips on pot, which even the Pentagon admits is heavily used there, and everyone did want peace and wanted to come home . . . But more by manner than word, he left no doubt of the war's unpopularity among the troops he encountered.
>
> Humor, or the reaction to it, often can tell much about the state of culture. If the GIs responded more heartily to Hope's pot jokes than to his traditional patter devoted to putting down the brass, wisecracking about the chow or local references to recreational tedium, doesn't it say rather a good deal about the attitude of the soldiers?
>
> . . . In the case of the Christmas tour, Hope is not only an entertainer and his trip not just a show in the usual sense. He also

SRO at Long Binh, Vietnam, 1970.

doubles as a reporter, a journalist in greasepaint, and the public would seem entitled to share in what he found out.

Because of Hope's unique rapport with enlisted men, stemming from his long-established generosity in making trips to overseas bases, his presence among the military is a special opportunity for them to give vent to their feelings in the form of laughter and applause. Accordingly, the network's argument for censorship of Hope's overseas show seems altogether weak where it might be reasonable in the case of a Hollywood studio audience.

How the men in the field feel about the war involves much more than a 90-minute TV special. Probing jokes that win a hand often can be immensely revealing of attitudes that should be imparted to those at home. In press interviews, Hope has openly worried about the lack of sufficient activity and diversion for troops, the marijuana problem, and the strain of being in uniform in a war that nobody wants.

As a patriot and performer, Hope's credentials are impeccable. It is not unimportant, therefore, that his Christmas tours accurately reflect what he may find out, if only because he has the knack of shedding substantive light through humor rather than preachment. The country needs such a distinctive liaison man between those at home and those overseas. No one would want Hope's TV special to be stripped of its vital elements of humor, but if in his own way he can also incorporate the accompanying elements of significance, *sans* strictures by either NBC or the Pentagon, he could be even more of a national asset than he is.

Thanks, Jack. I'm with you all the way—though I'm far from an expert on the weed. The only pot we knew about when we were kids was under the bed and we damn well didn't smoke that.

Don Ho at Schofield Barracks, Honolulu, 1971.

CHAPTER 22

Hanoi says no

After twenty-five years of last-minute scrambling for planes, I thought that by 1971 I'd finally learned my lesson. I packed early, ate supper early, went to bed early, got up an hour early—and went to the wrong airport. There I was at L. A. International and there was everybody else at Van Nuys Airport keeping General Westy Westmoreland company. I hotfooted it over there just in time for a quick handshake from Westy, a kiss from Dolores and the kids, and a wet buss from the growing gaggle of grandchildren.

As I watched the seventy-eight troupe members file aboard for the fifteen-day, thirty-thousand-mile round-the-world tour, I knew it was going to be a good one. All the gang had to do was live up to the preview we'd done the night before at the Century Plaza Hotel to raise a million bucks for a new USO building in Hollywood. At $500 a plate, the audience laughed with a sneer on their faces. Since our boys overseas were getting it for free, they should really lap up the likes of Brucene Smith, Miss World-U.S.A., a green-eyed, long-stemmed rose of Texas; the beautiful blond star of the supper club circuit, Jan Daly; singer-dancer Suzanne Charny, back for an encore from the 1969 trip; and eleven beautiful Deb Stars, who were picked by the Hollywood Makeup Artists and Hairstylists as "the girls most likely." They were: Lezlie Dalton, Kathy Bauman, Cheryl Davis, Brenda Jackson, Jayne Kennedy, Debbie Lough, Patricia Mickey, Leanna Roberts, Sue Plumber, Chris Calao, and Sissie Tindall. Right now they were all unknowns, but they sure looked to me as if they were going to follow right along in the footsteps of some previous Deb Stars who'd made it big—Raquel Welch, Jill St. John, Anne Francis, and Susan St. James.

In addition to this baker's dozen of cream puffs, I'd signed on Sunday's Child, three beautiful, brilliant singing sensations. Two of them were sisters, seventeen-year-old Eileen and fifteen-year-old Mary Lou Anderson, and the third was a friend of theirs from Portland, Oregon, Renee Woods. They'd

Hollywood Deb Stars, Guantánamo, Cuba, 1971. (U. S. Navy)

performed in Las Vegas with Jack Benny and at the Now Grove in Los Angeles with Sammy Davis, Jr. Despite their ages, I wouldn't have to worry about losing them in the crowds overseas. Eileen, whom I dubbed "Stilt Mama," stretched up as far as the eye could see: 6 feet 2 inches.

We were lucky to augment this show with the great country-and-western balladeer Charley Pride. With four gold LPs to his credit, Charley had become one of the best-selling artists at RCA. He wasn't exactly born with a golden record in his mouth, though; one of eleven children, he'd spent his youth choppin' cotton around Sledge, Mississippi.

Since baseball was Charley's first career, I thought he'd be good company for my other superstar, the dynamic southpaw pitcher Vida Blue of the Oakland As. Only twenty-two years old, Vida had just led the As through a sensational season of wins. He was only the seventh pitcher in the past forty years to win the American League's Most Valuable Player award and I knew the guys overseas would really dig him. They keep up to the minute on big-league sports through *Stars and Stripes* and the games-of-the-week films which are sent overseas to them.

I explained to Vida that on the 1970 Christmas tour Johnny Bench had a great time on the trip and before the plane had left the runway he had three Golddiggers sitting on his lap. Vida took a long look at me and said, "Records are made to be broken."

I'd signed Jim Nabors up months before, right after I saw a tough night-club audience give him a standing ovation. His combination of hillbilly comedy and powerful baritone singing was hard to beat. Thanks to his five-year TV series, "Gomer Pyle, USMC," he was as familiar to the gyrenes in our audiences as the halls of Montezuma.

With memories of our 1970 ladies' man, Johnny Bench, still fresh in my mind, I decided that Charley and Vida and Jim were odds enough, so I rounded out the cast with an acrobatic roller-skating duo, Louise Edwards and Bob Bell. Calling themselves the Blue Streaks, they performed spins and lifts atop a six-foot circular table two feet in the air. I was sure the guys would like this great novelty act.

We were met at Hickam Field in Hawaii by a show almost as big as ours—dancing girls, dignitaries, and military band, complete with the best and and brightest rainbow I've ever seen for a backdrop. I didn't get to see it long, though. They heaped leis around my neck till only my eyebrows were visible, then hustled me off to the Cinerama Reef Hotel to spruce up for a reception at Admiral John S. McCain, Jr.'s quarters. Clare Boothe Luce was one of the guests, and she lived up to her reputation as one of the world's most sharp-tongued women. "I notice you have a publicity man in your group," she said. "Why would anybody like you *need* one?" Suddenly the room became very quiet. All paused in their chitchat, waiting for my answer. I did my best: "He goes ahead of me and hums *'Thanks for the Memory.'* "

Around noon the next day we boarded choppers to fly to Schofield Barracks and thirty minutes later we were on stage before twenty thousand sailors, Marines, Coast Guardsmen, and soldiers of the 25th Division:

★

I'm happy to be here at Schofield. I'm a little late—the invitation read "December 7." That's an inside joke for those of you who remember Pearl Harbor.

The guys in the control tower have a great sense of humor. They gave us our landing instructions in Japanese.

The last time we worked for the 25th Division was at Cu Chi in Vietnam, and the guns were firing. I'm delighted to be here today working above *the stage.*

Don't let anybody kid you, this is a vital base. Schofield was activated to keep the world safe for surfing.

I've met many a brave man here—including one who got the Silver Star for an incredible feat: leading a convoy through Honolulu traffic.

★

I finished up by introducing the guest star for the show. "One of our nicest surprises is a visit by the Hawaiian Perry Como, the fabulous Don Ho, who very generously brought his band and his hula wahines along." Little did I know what I was letting myself in for. Part of Don's act includes stripping audience participants of their shirts—and pants. I knew that during the show he was going to have his grass-skirted dancing girls do the shirt-stripping bit with the unsuspecting GIs. Well, halfway through their number they turned on me. They got my shirt and T-shirt halfway off before I managed to escape.

We took off that evening for Okinawa, but stopped on the way for refueling at Wake Island. When it comes to gas stations, Wake is pretty stupid. It doesn't understand that it is just a gas station; it thinks it's a show site. We tried to sneak past in the middle of the night, but when we walked into the terminal, every man, boy, pilot, and iguana on the island was waiting patiently for a show. We stumbled hastily into and out of the rest rooms, then climbed onstage and did the best we could without benefit of costumes, music, or cue cards. An hour later we had to beg those six hundred fans to let us go; the C-141 was fueled up and ready to go to Okinawa.

Well, the Japanese had finally got their way; they were about to take over Okinawa and this looked like our last show there. Some of the troupe members were half expecting trouble. Betty Lanigan announced, "We've given them foreign aid and we've given them back their island. What more do they want?" "A receipt," said "Sugah" Daniels, our assistant director. Despite our forebodings, we've never had a warmer welcome on Okinawa— and I don't just mean that it was a nice, sunny day. More than nineteen thousand roaring Marines, soldiers, and sailors had gathered at Sukiran Stadium to greet my sallies:

★

So this is the place my Prudential agent meant when he offered me a piece of the rock.

*I asked General Smith if I could come back to Okinawa in 1972.
He said, "That depends on how funny you are in Japanese."*

*We've had this place for about twenty-five years. I forget now
whether we fought for it or whether it was sold to us by a used-
island dealer.*

*It's sad to think that we're giving back all this loveliness, but I
guess it's a fair swap. We're getting three transistor radios.*

★

Next day we flew from Okinawa to our familiar "home base," the Erawan
Hotel in Bangkok, Thailand. Except for a rehearsal and a few receptions,
we had the rest of the day and the next day off. I got my old room back
at the hotel, which was lucky. The basket of fruit they'd put there the
year before was getting ripe, and so were the socks I'd left under the bed.

Actually we got to the Erawan Hotel by accident the first time. It was
the only place that was big enough to accommodate the large troupe we
had. But the number of times we've been back since then is certainly no
accident. It's a lovely hotel, very tropical in appearance with open hallways.
The room service has long since learned patiently to accommodate itself
to our weird Western demands. And they have wonderful reserve and diplomacy—never once have they asked the band to return the towels, the
silver, or the chambermaid.

We did two shows that day in Thailand, Utapao and Ubon, where a
game group of U.S. airmen were keeping the B-52s flying. This was the
year President Nixon was freezing prices and wages to stop inflation, so I
brought Brucene Smith on by announcing, "I don't care *what* the President
froze, this'll thaw it out: Miss World-U.S.A., Brucene Smith!"

(*applause, and you'd better believe it.*)

BOB: At ease, men. Dream if you like.

BRUCENE: Thank you. Say, Bob, the military sure are health-minded.
Every time we get to a base, they give me a physical.

BOB: Tell me. How does a gal get to be Miss World-U.S.A.?

BRUCENE: I don't really know. The judges just looked me over
and I was picked.

BOB: When you're ripe, you're ripe. By the way, how'd you get a
name like Brucene?

BRUCENE: Well, my folks wanted a boy.

BOB: They didn't even come close.

BRUCENE: Really, Bob, in Texas I'm just another girl.

BOB: Yeah, well, if you're just another girl, the Astrodome is just
another pup tent.

We caught a little shut-eye at the Erawan that night, then flew to Da Nang for our first show in Vietnam. The Army called the camp Freedom Hill, but the soldiers still called it Dodge City, for reasons that became obvious as soon as a new arrival experienced his first incoming mortar round. We were hoping for some sunshine, but no luck; we landed in a dense fog. It had been raining there for forty-eight hours, and we were afraid we wouldn't have much of an audience. We were wrong. Those doughfaces may have been sodden lumps of humanity, but there were more than twenty thousand sodden lumps sitting on that hill. They'd been waiting for six hours, and I had to work fast before they began to mold.

★

Here we are at Da Nang, ladies and gentlemen. Da Nang: that's Vietnamese for "We never promised you a rose garden."

You know, according to the papers, the war's over. Now if they can only get somebody to tell the Cong!

Actually, you guys are lucky. You know you're going to get home. But what hope is there for our men at the Paris peace talks?

I want to say I do appreciate you fellas hanging around here just for me. It's wonderful to be working for you leftovers.

★

I have to admit that I caught a little good-natured booing when I called those guys leftovers, but it was more than made up for by the standing ovation they gave the show after the closing speech: "You know, a couple of jerks had the guts to ask me if the guys in Vietnam still like my show. When guys like you will sit out in the rain for six hours, I'm never gonna stop coming here because you're my type—I'll tell you that."

After the show, there was a brief news conference. Since I'd been entertaining servicemen for over thirty years, the big question was whether I thought today's GIs were different from the GIs of World War II. That was easy: "I don't think so at all. I think they're the same. They'll laugh at the same kinds of jokes, and they'll cheer the same kinds of gals, and they still like to hear what's going on back home."

Next we were supposed to copter out to the USS *Coral Sea* in the Gulf of Tonkin. As we were packing up, the monsoon winds and rain got worse and worse. Finally we were told that it would be impossible to land on the *Coral Sea* that day, so for the first time in eight years I had to cancel a show. I did manage to work to the crew of the *Coral Sea*, even if it was in a roundabout way. The Army arranged a phone hook-up that went from Vietnam to the Philippines to Guam and finally to the carrier in the China Sea off Vietnam. I did the monologue on the telephone and they piped

Jim Nabors, U.S. naval base, Rota, Spain, 1971.

it all over the carrier. I don't know how the crew liked it but I got a couple of fair giggles from the long-distance operator.

We had the next couple of days off, but everyone managed to stay pretty busy—or sound asleep. Those perky Hollywood Deb Stars paid their first visit to a military hospital and returned still in good enough spirits to attend the American Teen Club's annual Christmas dance. Almost all the teen-age youngsters whose parents were stationed either in Bangkok or in Vietnam belonged, so it was quite a blast.

Hanoi says no   325

The time off gave me a chance to do a little thinking. Before I'd left California, I'd got hundreds of pleas from concerned Americans about the prisoners of war. Wasn't there *anything* I could do to help them? I was asked the question over and over, and I turned it over and over in my mind. It looked hopeless—if the State Department brass couldn't get those POWs home, what on earth could I do? While I was sitting around the Erawan, it occurred to me that maybe I could at least do a show for them. All I had to do was get permission to go to Hanoi, and if I couldn't bring those guys home, at least I could bring a little bit of home to them.

I called in Bill Faith, my PR man, and we secretly arranged a meeting with the U.S. ambassador to Thailand, Leonard Unger. Ambassador Unger was all for the idea, and he arranged for me and Bill to fly to Vientiane, Laos, to meet with the North Vietnamese consul there, Nguyen Van Thanh. If I was going to get into Hanoi, Thanh was the best bet for getting a visa. The whole thing was very hush-hush. No one in the troupe—never mind any of the bigwigs back in the States—knew I was going. I wanted to do the whole thing strictly as a private citizen.

When Bill and I got the word from Ambassador Unger, we went out to the airport. We were already aboard the plane when we were told that our meeting with Thanh had been canceled. After a little talk with our pilot, General Evans, head of the U. S. Air Force in Thailand, we decided to go anyway. General Evans was in mufti, and the small Army plane was unmarked, so we figured we couldn't get into too much trouble. As it turned out, I'm glad we made that decision. Half an hour after we were airborne, word came through that the meeting was on again.

When we landed in Vientiane, there was a group of civilians on hand to meet us. At least I *thought* they were civilians. After a good hard stare, I realized that one of those men in street clothes was none other than the head admiral of the Pacific command, my good friend John McCain, Jr. The sight of him really gave my heart a tug. Knowing his son was a POW, I suddenly realized that to him, this was a very, very important trip. He wasn't allowed to wear his uniform, but it made no difference if there was any possibility that he could do something to help get the POWs out.

Along with Admiral McCain were some American embassy officials and the Reverend Edward Roffe, a Canadian who'd been serving in Laos for twelve years as a Christian Alliance Church missionary. The Reverend Roffe was going to serve as the interpreter during the meeting with Thanh in case he spoke French the whole time. We drove from the airport to a little house that had a wire fence around it, and in a small living room I was introduced to Thanh.

My jitters disappeared as soon as we shook hands. He was a very personable guy, a young fellow· of about thirty-one. It turned out that he'd really been looking forward to meeting me because he'd seen so many of the

Guantánamo, Cuba, 1971. (U. S. Navy)

Road pictures I'd done with Dorothy Lamour and Bing. His favorite was the one in which Bing and I befriended a Vietnamese child. Thanh went on to say that his country had been at war for twenty-six years and that the people were suffering, especially the children. That gave me an idea, and while we were being served tea and cookies I said, "Wouldn't it be great if the children of our country could help the children of North Vietnam in exchange for the release of the prisoners? If our kids could raise some money, they could donate it to your children to help rebuild their homes, their schools, their hospitals."

Thanh warmed to the idea and was speaking English by now. I showed him a picture of my grandson Zachary and reminded him that the North

Hanoi says no   327

Vietnamese children were the real victims of this war. They eventually were going to have to put the pieces together; they were going to suffer because the schools had been razed; their future had been impaired by the destruction of Vietnam.

I said it would be a wonderful thing for the kids of our country to contribute their nickels and dimes to get the POWs released. But every time I mentioned the prisoners, Thanh made the same answer: "Nixon could get the prisoners of war freed tomorrow if he would listen to the seven points our [the North Vietnamese] negotiators at the Paris peace talks put forth months ago."

Of course, President Nixon had listened to the seven-point peace plan advanced by the Communist side—and had rejected it. The first point said that all U.S. prisoners would be released if the U.S. government would unilaterally set a terminal date for the withdrawal of troops from South Vietnam, and that was unacceptable.

I couldn't do anything about that, so I ended up by telling him that I would be in the area until December 26 and was willing to do anything to help our boys. We went outside and had our pictures taken. Then Thanh said, "Wouldn't it be nice if you could put on a show in Hanoi?" and promised to let me know in a few days if any of my proposals were okayed by the North Vietnamese. He was so polite and so friendly that I really felt good as we headed back toward the American Embassy. The Reverend Roffe raised my spirits higher still when he told me that the consul had never posed for a photograph with anyone before and that meetings with Thanh usually lasted twenty minutes and ours had lasted eighty-five. I was feeling so good I did a spur-of-the-moment minishow for the four hundred English-speaking employees of the U. S. Embassy. Then I winged my way back to Bangkok.

Bill Faith and I thought our trip had been kept a secret—we certainly hadn't told anybody—but when we arrived in Bangkok, newsmen were clamoring to be told what I was going to do in Hanoi. It seems some Associated Press man had spotted me in Laos and had tipped them off. When I told them I was trying to negotiate with the North Vietnamese for the release of the POWs, they wanted to know if I'd talked money, and if so, how much. I hadn't really given the total of all those nickels and dimes much thought, so I said, off the top of my head, "Oh, ten million bucks. We could raise that with no trouble at all."

A postscript to that. Last year I attended a dinner at the White House for the returned prisoners of war and one of them told me that the way they heard about the event over their prison grapevine was that I had offered ten million *ducks* for the release of the POWs. In their cells they pondered the matter and decided that I must have a poultry farm in California and was going to send food in the form of ten million ducks for their release.

I put the whole thing out of my mind and tried to get some sleep. I had to be up early the next morning for the trip to Camp Eagle, home of those famous Screaming Eagles, the 101st Airborne Division. I'd gotten so used to flying into Camp Eagle that I almost fell asleep aboard the C-130 cargo plane that was carrying us in. Then, as we approached Hue, the sky was streaked with F4 Phantom jets strafing the Vietcong forces on the ground. Smoke rising from hit vehicles obscured the view a bit as we peered out the portholes, but something sure was going on down there.

When we landed at Hue, the officers who met us said that just hours before a Cong convoy had been captured only fifteen miles from the show site at Camp Eagle. True, the war was still miles away, but we all began to feel uneasy when a paratrooper colonel began giving orders on how to disperse in case of a mortar attack. Renee Woods, fifteen, the unrelated member of Sunday's Child, asked the question that was on everyone's mind: "Which way do I run to keep from getting killed?" A nearby GI answered that one: "Just follow me. I know a good foxhole."

For the third time on the trip, Admiral McCain was on hand, this time to welcome us to Camp Eagle. When I brought him up onstage, he got a big ovation from the GIs. It was a bit surprising; the soldiers didn't usually cheer too much for a Navy man. But the boys all loved McCain; he was a feisty, ornery old bantam cock of a man, and the fact that his son was a POW won him a lot of sympathy.

So I already had the audience with me when I waded into my monologue:

★

This is the home of the 101st Airborne; they've seen more action than a towel girl in a bathhouse.

Last year our show was interrupted by some shelling. I asked the general about it and he said, "Don't worry, Bob. It's outgoing." I asked, "How can you tell?" And he said, "Just watch the smile on my face. When it's replaced by my feet, then it's incoming."

The infiltration rate is pretty high here. If you're sitting next to somebody in black pajamas, move. He's either one of theirs, or he's got a lot to learn about laundry.

★

After the show we made a quick chopper run across the paddy fields and then flew by plane over the mountains of northern Quangtri and Thua-thien provinces back to Bangkok. Since it was Christmas Eve, I treated everyone to a fancy sit-down dinner before midnight Mass at the Crown Bowl Army Chapel. From the pulpit, the priest asked for prayers to help me on my POW Mission Impossible, saying, "It is a noble effort he is making in his own way." Jim Nabors, who was getting better and better with each passing show, stood up and sang the Lord's Prayer. He apologized for his laryngitis later, but to tell you the truth, I never even noticed it. All the cast members agreed: we'd never heard the prayer sung more beautifully.

Then back to the Erawan and a few hours' sleep before our long foray into Vietnam for Christmas dinner and a show for the fighting men at Long Binh. It's still the largest military base in Vietnam, and about thirty thousand GIs were on hand to cheer us through the ninety-two-degree heat with humidity to match. The troops had been trucked and flown in from all the surrounding bases—everywhere from Camranh Bay to Bienhoa. We wanted to be at our best, especially since the show was going to be aired that night on Armed Forces TV for eighty thousand more troops in Indochina. Someone even promised to airlift a print out to the USS *Coral Sea* to make up for the show that had fallen afoul of the weather.

General Frederick Weyand handled the warm-up. "I just want to ask you one thing," he said. "Did you guys come here to see me?" The soldiers let out with a solid and thunderous no, and I walked on as the general said, "All right, let's hear it for Bob Hope!" And you could hear it. What a wild audience. They were sitting out there in the blazing sun, bare chests as far as the eye could see, hanging from trees, strapped from telephone poles, sucking on beer, laughing and scratching—having a time.

★

Here we are at Long Binh. Long Binh—that's the name of this place, and it's also the principal topic of conversation: "How long's it been?"

Hot pants isn't a fashion here, it's a weather report.

No one knows what the temperature is; the thermometer went over the hill.

This is the biggest installation in Vietnam. Eighteen thousand men with but a single thought: "Who's got the Right Guard?"

★

The heat even got to me, and when the show was over I was so exhausted I could barely stand up. While everyone else packed up, I went and took a catnap in the senior commander's quarters. After an hour of that, I bounced up from my beauty rest like a new man, all set for the flight back to Bangkok.

The cast had found other ways to beat the heat, mainly by soaking hand towels in cold water and burying their faces in them.

330   *The last Christmas show*

Charley Pride, Guantánamo, Cuba, 1971. (U. S. Navy)

When the towels warmed up too much to be any good, people began wadding them up and flinging them playfully at each other. Mort Lachman's assistant, Milton Justice, inadvertently hit Vida Blue with one of the towels. Vida wound up to return it, and suddenly everybody in the game realized that a real pro was on the mound. The thought of the impact of Vida's high, fast ball—even with a wet towel—put a quick end to the towel tossing.

The Long Binh show was our last one in Vietnam that year. Before we left Bangkok, though, I got word that Hanoi had turned down my application for a visa. I'd known all along that my chances were slim, but it was depressing just the same. I couldn't help feeling that all the talk in the press might have had something to do with Hanoi's negative reaction. Bill Faith and I had tried hard to keep it secret, but when news like that gets spread all over the papers, it tends to upset even the best-laid plans.

I never got any direct word about my attempt from anyone in the U.S. government, but the President did have a few kind words to say about it at a press conference: "I can only say that the efforts that he makes, that anybody makes, are deeply appreciated." Nixon went on to say that his government would continue its efforts to seek the release of the prisoners and to obtain more humane conditions for them.

I did hear from some ordinary folk back home, though. Representatives of the Boy Scouts and some Catholic youth organizations phoned to say their kids were enthusiastic about helping release the prisoners. Some Americans who were big in the automotive and oil industries also said they were willing to support the project by helping to raise money for it. Terence Cardinal Cooke, of course, was anxious to help out, and Texas multimillionaire H. Ross Perot came up with an alternate plan. He offered to pay for the removal of all the bodies of U.S. soldiers who had died in North Vietnam. That, at least, would have ended the anxiety of all the POW families who didn't know whether their kin were dead or alive.

The next morning it was back to business, and we climbed into our big bird to settle down for the big sleep: the fifteen-hour flight to Vicenza in northern Italy, where we were doing a show for our boys in the Sixth Fleet. We had to stop somewhere en route to refuel, and that isn't as easy as it sounds; there aren't too many pit stops in the desert.

Fortunately they turned on the Shell sign for us in the capital of Iran, Teheran. The Shah was out of town but he sent his personal representative to greet us. While the plane and the band were being loaded with jet fuel and the cast with souvenirs, pistachio nuts, and Iranian Coca-Cola, I said to the Shah's representative, "I'd love to get some Iranian caviar."

He said, "We'd like to accommodate you, Mr. Hope, but we're like . . . out."

"Like . . . out? You ran out of caviar? That's like Saudi Arabia being out of oil."

He just shook his head and I had to forget about the caviar.

A month later, back in Los Angeles, I received an apologetic note from the Shah that said how sorry he was that he hadn't been in Teheran to greet us and with it a giant package of Iranian caviar—enough caviar to feed a Solzhenitsyn press conference. You wanna know what rich is? Forget gold and silver bars. With a small jar of caviar under your arm you can get a table at Chasen's.

At thirty thousand feet over the Gobi Desert, I got a message that Vicenza was socked in. The fog was so thick, there was no way we could land. We'd already lost one show on the *Coral Sea,* and our egos couldn't take another loss.

We landed at Torrejón Air Base near Madrid, Spain, and sat around our quarters brooding about what to do. The commander of the Torrejón Air Base, Colonel Rafael Lorenzo, said, "There's a lovely golf course nearby. Maybe you could play golf tomorrow."

I stared at him and in a rare moment of truth said, "I can't even play golf when I'm home. Look, we got eighty people here. We gotta do a show. A troupe without a place to do a show is like a guy without a girl." That they understood. We got out a map and started shopping.

Our project officer, Colonel Joe Smith, said, "Let's get Captain McQuill-kin down at Rota Naval Base."

Sil Caranchini called and asked him if he'd like to have the Bob Hope Show there tomorrow morning. And the captain said over the phone, "What is this, some kind of a trick . . . an obscene phone call! I'm gonna report you!"

It took a while to explain to him that it really wasn't a trick and that we really wanted to do a show there. And finally, to convince him that it wasn't a trick and that it was really me, I had to get on the phone and do two choruses of "Buttons and Bows." That was at two o'clock in the morning—four hours later we were on our way to Rota.

As soon as they had received our telephone offer, the men at Rota had started scurrying about to build a stage. They'd really wanted us, but had no place for us to play but an athletic field. Well, they got the stage built in record time and we got all our equipment set up when it happened—a cloudburst. There was no way we were going to cancel another show, so our stage crew, Al Borden, Ray Brannigan, and Earl Elwood, started racing around covering everything in sight with sheets of plastic. Beautiful, white-haired Bobby Comer went around putting tarps on the electrical junctures, knowing if he missed we'd go up in smoke. I looked up on the camera platforms and I saw Allan Stensvold, Harlow Stengel, and Jack McCoskey protecting the cameras with their bodies. Les Helhena, who's one of the great documentary photographers, was shooting in the rain trying to capture a picture of the mess for our television show. If it moved, it got a raincoat. The slickers made things pretty rough on everyone—especially the dancing girls and the band—but when I stepped onstage, the clouds parted and Barney held up the first idiot card:

★

Buenos días, señors y señoritas . . . and a Happy Enchilada to you all.

Don't fool with me. I've been to Tijuana.

It's a pleasure to be here in Frito Bandito's home town.

I'm delighted to be here at Rota Naval Base, wherever that is. I'm not sure of the exact location. I asked the captain but he's very busy guarding the girls' dressing room.

Today we were supposed to be at a missile base in the Italian Alps, but while we were thirty-five thousand feet over the Gobi Desert we received a message from Vicenza saying that the airfield was socked in zero zero and that we could not land. Actually, we were not sure whether the field was socked in or some rat fink turned off the landing lights.

You don't know what it's like flying around at thirty thousand feet begging somebody to let you land. We were turned down more times than a motel bed.

We finally called Captain McQuillkin here at Rota and asked him if he would accept a show from our troupe. He didn't believe it was us. We had to show him our Diners Club card before he'd talk.

I don't blame the captain for being nervous about strangers dropping in. He was the radar man at Pearl Harbor.

I never thought I'd have to travel three quarters of the way around the world to end up as a Rota-Rooter man.

This is the first time I ever played to a bay full of submarines. It's great. If they like your jokes here they just leave the periscopes up.

It's a typical beautiful Rota day here. The sunshine is coming down in buckets.

Of course, these guys don't mind the rain here . . . They're used to living underwater.

I never saw so much mud. As soon as we touched down, a huge crowd came out to the landing strip and tried to find the plane.

I stepped off the plane and sank so deep in the mud, my alligator shoes thought they were coming back to life.

Every time you lift your foot in this mud it sounds like Martha Raye kissing a water buffalo.

They run a tight little base here. We had to circle the field three times while they took down the tennis net on the runway.

The last Christmas show

You know how they get excited over very important personages and give a twenty-one-gun salute? Well, when I landed today the duty officer yawned and cracked his knuckles.

I love Navy lingo. It's so colorful. "Secure the hatches" . . . "Man the pumps" . . . Isn't that exciting? All it means is—"Grab a Jonny Mop, there's a leak in the head!"

★

The rains in Spain continued to fall mainly on the plane—our plane. It was still coming down the next day when we did our scheduled show for ten thousand men at the Torrejón Air Force Base outside Madrid. Here Jill St. John dropped in to join the show. And what a drop-in. She dropped in like Phileas Fogg happened by India. When we first tried to get Jill she was up on the expert's slope in Aspen, Colorado, skiing. When we finally managed to reach her, we were in Bangkok and she was in Beverly Hills, so we agreed to rendezvous in Vicenza in northern Italy.

Jill couldn't get a direct flight to Rome so she left that night and started out for New York. In New York she waited three hours at the airport and boarded a plane for London. In London she toted her wardrobe cases from airline to airline. No airline went to Vicenza, but she did manage to grab a plane to Rome. She'd now been up twenty-four hours.

There was a plane from Rome to Vicenza, but it was socked in so she raced from the airport to the train station and managed to catch the last train, the slow, creaky local from Rome to Vicenza. If all went well, she would just make it to Vicenza an hour ahead of our landing. A very charming Air Force officer and his wife met her at the train and drove her to the airport to meet us. We were at the airport, not on the ground but about thirty thousand feet over it.

When we arrived in Spain we couldn't reach Jill by phone but we were able to wire her through military channels, begging her to hurry to Madrid.

In the fog there was no way she could get a plane. The next train was twelve hours away, but the Air Force officer and his wife had fallen in love with Jill—she was their first celebrity. So they not only insisted on driving her to Rome, but they put Jill in the back seat of their Fiat with their two little children and a small dog.

This eight hours *en famille* to Rome almost finished Jill off. Up to her eyebrows with family, Jill staggered out of the car and grabbed the first Iberian biplane out of Rome. And that's how she happened to just drop in in Madrid . . . after fifty-six hours on the road.

I don't know what it is. She either has great bounce or a masterful will, but when she walked on that stage she looked as if she'd just stepped out of the beauty salon at Vidal Sassoon. And what a reception she got.

Vida Blue, Da Nang, Vietnam, 1971.

Admiral Alan Shepard,
Guantánamo, 1971.

336   *The last Christmas show*

JILL: Oh, what a marvelous reception. Was all that for me, or for your jokes?

BOB: Both, Jill. These men are just crazy about great lines. I certainly was thrilled when you agreed to go with us.

JILL: You thrilled? Listen, I know about those glamour girls you've taken on all those other trips. Raquel Welch at Tan Son Nhut Air Base, Ann-Margret at Okinawa Air Base, Romy Schneider at Rhine-Main Air Base. Gee, you really lead an exciting life.

BOB: Oh, I don't know. When you've seen one air base, you've seen them all. Besides, I really need you on this show.

JILL: How do you mean?

BOB: Well, it's very tough on me being both star and sex symbol. Now, tell me. You've played passionate love scenes with Frank Sinatra, with Sean Connery, and with me.

(*the audience howled at this*)

Cool it. We allow no individual sniggering.

(*back to Jill*)

How do we compare?

JILL: Well, Bob, Frank is a typical Italian. He's passionate, fiery, always the lover. And Sean Connery, well, he's a typical Welshman. He's savage, untamed, primitive, forceful. You know, he's all man. And you—you're a typical Californian.

BOB: Wait a minute. A typical Californian?

JILL: Uh huh. Nothing will move you but an earthquake.

That night we skimmed three thousand miles across the Atlantic for our next show at Guantánamo Naval Base in Cuba. I spent the whole night humming Desi Arnaz's hit, "I'll See You in C-U-B-A," trying to fight off the wild thought that the USO was hijacking me. It was a beautiful day for our last show. And what a turnout! Eight thousand sailors, Marines, dependents, and native Cubans. In fact, we had two hundred more people at the show than were supposed to be on our side of the fence from Castro's Cuba.

In Guantánamo we were joined by Rear Admiral Alan Shepard, who . . . well, the script kind of tells the story:

BOB: You know we're very honored to have in our audience today one of our great heroes. Really our first American to journey into space . . . space commander of Apollo 14 . . . the first man to hit a golf ball on the moon . . . chief of our astronauts . . . and a delegate to the twenty-sixth session of the United Nations General Assembly . . . Rear Admiral Alan Shepard . . . right here.

MUSIC: "*Fly Me to the Moon*" (*standing ovation*)

ALAN: Nice to see you, Robert.

BOB: Thank you, Alan. What brings a famous astronaut like you to Gitmo?

ALAN: Well, Bob, when you've spent as much time as I have on the moon you get homesick for dull and lonely places.

(applause)

BOB: Tell me, do you think there are people on other planets?

ALAN: Oh, of course there are.

BOB: Well, how do you know?

ALAN: I never miss "Star Trek."

BOB: Do you think you'll find life on your next trip?

ALAN: Listen, I'm hoping to find a little life on this one.

BOB: But you have a great distinction. You're the first man to play golf on the moon. Why'd you do it?

ALAN: The bowling alley was closed.

BOB: When I heard . . . I just didn't believe that you hit a golf ball up there on that thing. I just couldn't believe . . .

ALAN: Bob, I'll tell you what I did for you.

BOB: What?

ALAN: For the first time in public I brought the golf club that actually hit the shot on the moon. I'm gonna show it to you today.

BOB: I gotta see that.

ALAN: Would you believe this is a golf club?

(shows Bob weird club)

Normally, we use this for scooping up lunar dust. There's a little cup that fits on the end . . . and this six iron head fits right on here. There you are. That's the club that actually hit it on the moon, right there.

BOB: Hey, that's wild. I may take that with me when I go. I'm going as soon as they get a bigger capsule. I don't wanna go with two fellas because people talk . . .

(applause and music playoff)

En route to Los Angeles we received the sad word that retired Air Force general and head of the USO "Rosy" O'Donnell had died. We stopped en route at Colorado Springs at the Air Force Academy, where Rosy was buried with full military honors. That year we dedicated our television special to Rosy with these words:

★

We'd like to dedicate this show not only to our servicemen and women all around the world, but also to a distinguished American,

*General Emmett "Rosy" O'Donnell, who passed away while we were
overseas.*

*Rosy's untimely death was not only a personal loss to many, it was
deeply felt by GIs everywhere who benefited from his concern and
dedication.*

*When age forced his retirement after thirty-five years of service,
he eagerly accepted the job of heading the USO, to which he
brought his vigor, his wisdom, and his innate talent for leadership.*

*Rosy played Santa Claus for our troupe a few years ago . . . He
made the entire trip with us to inspect USO facilities around the
world.*

*And so we said good-by to Rosy. I'm sure that where he is now
there are more than just four stars on his shoulders . . . I'm sure
they're all around him.*

The flight back to Colorado Springs to attend Rosy's funeral at the Air
Force Academy's Catholic chapel and the flight from there back to Van
Nuys in California gave me plenty of thinking time. And I plainly had
plenty of thinking to do. I couldn't get the faces of all the POW wives and
mothers out of my mind. I just had to do something to help those boys out.
I came up with the idea of having a telethon; I could probably raise $50
million that way. After all, the Olympics telethon with Bing had pulled in
$51 million. I decided to keep thinking about ways to help those POWs, and
I stepped off the plane brimful of enthusiasm.

The press asked me about the prisoners of war and I said that I was
willing to go back to Vietnam if necessary to help free the American
prisoners. "It was a try, and we haven't had an official turndown from the
North Vietnamese yet," I said. "It's a long shot, but we're not giving up.
The North Vietnamese haven't closed off conversation, so it's not ended.
We intend to talk again." I went on to tell them that things were okay
with our boys overseas: "This is the best Christmas trip in fifteen years.
Morale is high, and I don't know whether it's because they know they'll
be coming home soon or what."

I decided I'd better try to get hold of Secretary of State William Rogers
and see what I could do through official channels. I asked Bill Faith and
Betty Lanigan to help me draft a formal proposal to our government out-
lining what I thought I could do for the POWs.

It took a long time and a lot of asking for us to get an answer to that
proposal. The answer was no, and it came accompanied by a lot of hemming
and hawing. Rogers let it out that the North Vietnamese had turned down

General Emmett "Rosy" O'Donnell's funeral, Air Force Academy, Colorado Springs, Colorado, 1971.

my visa application. The official position was that the only person who could effect any kind of release was President Nixon. Sure enough, after I'd been back a week or two, Nixon and Kissinger unveiled a $2.8-billion appeal to the North Vietnamese.

I didn't know anything about their plan while I was proposing mine. It gave me quite a jolt, as if money—particularly the amount of money offered —was the crux of the issue. It wasn't. The amount was negotiable, and not my point at all. The real issue was our boys, and I tried to tell them so at the close of the televised version of my 1971 Christmas show:

"This time in Vietnam," I said, "we ran into a situation that would ordinarily take the heart out of any performer, but which to us was reason for rejoicing. I mean the clusters of empty seats during our shows at Da Nang and Camp Eagle. Every empty seat meant a guy who'd returned home, a GI who'd gone back to the world.

"But the empty seats were just one indication of the change that's taken place in Vietnam over the past year. The men are more relaxed, quicker to laugh, and far more optimistic about their immediate future. I've been making these trips for years, and sometimes the job ain't pretty. There are a lot of forgotten people in this war, which has eroded so deeply the fabric of our society. I'm not talking about just the POWs, but the guys in hospitals and burn wards too. People meet me at airports and ask, 'Can you do something?' The real question is, how can you stand by and do nothing? All any of us ever wanted to do is make the burden lighter for those guys who are making the sacrifices. Maybe we don't all demonstrate or join parades,

340   *The last Christmas show*

but we're all anti-war. Especially these guys right up close to it, the guys who do the miserable business.

"A peaceful world, in which armies are no longer needed, has been man's dream for centuries. Unfortunately, that is still a long way off, so we must face the world as it is—divided, hostile, and menacing. Our servicemen know that we must be strong as a nation, equal to or better than any other force on earth, forces that may not have the same ideas we have about each person being allowed to do his own thing. That's why these fellows think that the United States is still a pretty decent country to defend. They've been a lot of other places and they know what they're fighting for.

"We had a great Christmas with them. They make you feel like you're doing something big for them when, really, they're laying it all on the line for us.

"God bless 'em."

By way of thanks
to the superb crew who made the 1972 show possible:
Written by Charles Lee and Gig Henry/Mort Lachman/Lester White and Mel Tolkin/Raymond Siller
Consultant   Norman Sullivan
Assistant to the Executive Producer   Sil Caranchini
Choreography   Jack Baker
Unit Manager   Ed Kranyak
Assistant Director   Clay B. Daniel
Technical Adviser   John Pawlek
Director of Photography   Allan Stensvold, A.S.C.
Sound   Dave Forrest
Costumes   Kate Drain Lawson/Charles Solomon/Rose Weiss
Make-up   Mike Moschella
Hair Stylist   Marlene Kolstad
Editors   Igo Kantor/Donald W. Ernst/Christopher Holmes/Graham Lee Mahin
Assistants   Richard P. McCarty/Matin Deffke/Kent Shafer/Gary Kemper
Librarians   Barry R. Parnell/Michael O'Shea
Negative Cutters   Kay Suffern/Toby Morgan/Marge Sokolow
Cameramen   Les Helhenna/Jack McCoskey/Ralph Gerling/Richard Vanik
Aerial Photography   Woody Mark
Production Secretary   Susan Simons
Production Assistant   Joni Rhodes
Coordinator   Onnie Morrow
Assistant to the Director   Milton Justice
Directed by Mort Lachman

Merlin Olsen as Santa Claus, Van Nuys, California, 1972.

The last Christmas show

1972

The last Christmas show

My last Christmas show—you can't imagine what emotions those words stir in me. I guess the strongest feeling is gratitude—gratitude that the painful war was winding down to the point where the trips were becoming less necessary, gratitude that my strength and the need for me were coming out about even, gratitude for the good and faithful band of troupers who stuck with me to the end, gratitude for the tough job being done by those lonely GIs who kept writing me to visit them, gratitude for those audiences that responded as they always had.

I think it was Mr. Chips who said that it wasn't that he was getting older, it was just that the youngsters were getting younger. I understand exactly how he felt, but at the same time I had the distinct impression that if that war kept going, and I kept going, that it wouldn't be too long before I looked out at the audience and saw nine- or ten-year-olds in battle fatigues.

I decided well in advance that the 1972 tour would be my last, but I planned the trip just as carefully as all of the others. We were going to Vietnam and Thailand for the ninth time, of course, and I also wanted to touch down at a couple of tiny, out-of-the-way bases, as I had in the past. It may be hammy of me, but I always loved the welcome our gang got when we swooped down out of the sky at some of those forgotten outposts where the only living creatures besides our boys were gooney birds and walruses.

One kid wrote from Camp Shemya, which was on an island four miles long and two miles wide in the Aleutians. He said that they had no trees, no native population, just eight hundred guys and one female. And that female was a dog. I wrote back that if it was okay with the Defense Department it was okay with us. The next thing I knew, it was on our schedule.

And then there was Diego Garcia, a flyspeck of an island nine hundred miles south of India in the Indian Ocean, where a few hundred Seabees were building a communications center. I not only got letters from the kids there but from all their relatives here, asking me to go visit them. The letters said that the Seabees didn't have anything; it was just rock down there. It turned out to be a beautiful rock, like a set from *South Pacific*. I kept waiting for Mary Martin to walk out from behind one of those palm trees. When we wrote that we were coming, they started working round the clock to build an airstrip long enough for our jet to land on.

Just because it was our last trip it didn't mean it was the smallest. We took along eighty-seven people, all our C-141 Starlifter could lift, and eighteen thousand pounds of equipment, including Rudy Cardenas' equipment. Rudy has one of the greatest juggling acts in show business. But it was all worth it—he can keep more in the air at one time than Boeing—and on a carrier yet with that ocean sway.

To me, the most important performer along was Dolores Reade, the classy chanteuse I first heard in a New York nightclub when I was appearing in *Roberta*. You know the one: she later became Mrs. Leslie Townes Hope. After our first Christmas tour in 1948 she made the trip with us three times, but the times I remembered most vividly were the ones when the plane was ready for boarding at Los Angeles and we walked to the gate together. I would kiss her, and we'd look at each other. She would say, "Well, take care of yourself."

And I'd say, "Well, I will. And you take care of *your*self." And then I'd take off. This time, she took off with me, and the song she sang was one of the hits of the show.

I remember that last Christmas tour in lots of ways. I remember traveling out to the private island of my old golfing friend, Thai Air Marshal Dawee Chulasapya, and pressing my footprints into some cement alongside those of the Duke of Edinburgh, Lady Bird Johnson, Edwin Aldrin, and Neil Armstrong. I remember the eight hundred Seabees on Diego Garcia, sitting patiently through what seemed like a typhoon, waiting for the show to begin. We put it off as long as we could, but finally there was nothing to do but go on. When I went out to do my monologue the rain stopped and the sun broke through—a final stroke of the old Hope luck.

Another thing that made the trip for me was the fact that we couldn't play Long Binh. Once upon a time we'd entertained thirty thousand troops at one sitting in Long Binh, but now there was nobody there. That's the best kind of audience of servicemen—the kind that doesn't exist because their part of the war is over.

We also played to the worst kind of audience that last year—the airmen at the B-52 base at Utapao in Thailand. When we got there, we were told confidentially that they had just lost fifteen planes. The commanding officer was a General Sullivan whom I'd known at March Field, and he was really uptight. It's a terrible thing to lose just one man, but when you lose the crews of fifteen planes it's truly a disaster. If they ever needed a morale boost, it was then, because I believe that those fliers were the guys who

First stop—Wake Island, 1972.

got the job done, who really helped write finish to the war. I don't think Hanoi would have ever listened to any offer if we hadn't rocked them a little, because otherwise they had it going pretty good—we had excused them from any kind of shock for so long.

They asked me to brief the B-52 crews before they went out that night, so I went and talked separately to the pilots, the navigators, the gunners, and the radar men. It was an amazing thing: the pilots all laughed at the jokes, but the radar men almost never cracked a smile. They were preparing for a mission and they weren't going to get to see the show, so I told them all of my monologue jokes. Before they left, they did me the honor of naming their mission the Bob Hope Mission. They were bound for Haiphong, a very dangerous target, and I found out about three weeks later that they didn't lose a single plane.

But these are all snapshots, not the whole picture. The way I remember that 1972 Christmas tour best is the way it played on NBC-TV when we

The last Christmas show   345

got back. Somehow, being the last one, it summed up all the twenty-one tours that went before it. So here's some of our last Christmas show, just as it appeared in our script, even the monologue our B-52s interrupted at Utapao.

THE BOB HOPE CHRISTMAS SHOW
NBC-TV
January 17, 1973

Starring

REDD FOXX

LOLA FALANA

ROMAN GABRIEL

FRAN JEFFRIES

RUDY CARDENAS

BELINDA GREEN-MISS WORLD

DOLORES READE (MRS. BOB HOPE)

12 AMERICAN BEAUTIES

and

LES BROWN AND HIS BAND OF RENOWN

TITLE: Wednesday Mystery Movie Title Slide

FRANK BARTON (*voice over*): NBC Wednesday Mystery Movie will not be seen tonight, but will return next week at its regular time.

FILM: Peacock

ANNOUNCER: Now, a special program in living color on NBC.

fade out

MUSIC: *Tympani roll*

FADE UP ON: Shot of Shemya

BARTON (*voice over*): From Shemya Island in the Aleutians

FILM: Yakota, Japan

From Yakota, Japan

FILM: Camp Casey

And from Camp Casey

FILM: Osan

And Osan in Korea

MUSIC: *Tympani accent*

FILM: Udorn

From Udorn

FILM: Utapao

Utapao

FILM: Namphong

And Namphong in Thailand

FILM: Tan Son Nhut

And from Tan Son Nhut Air Base in Vietnam

MUSIC: *Tympani accent*

FILM: Diego Garcia

From the island of Diego Garcia in the Indian Ocean

FILM: USS *Midway*

And from aboard the USS *Midway* off Singapore

MUSIC: *Tympani accent*

FILM: Subic Bay

And from Subic Bay in the Philippine Islands

FILM: Guam

Anderson Air Force Base in Guam

FILM: Wake

And from Wake Island . . .

MUSIC: *Tympani accent*

TITLE CARD: The Bob Hope Christmas Special

BARTON (*voice over*): It's the Bob Hope Christmas Special!

MUSIC: *"Thanks for the Memory"*

Starring . . .

FILM: Redd Foxx

Redd Foxx . . .

FILM: Lola Falana

Lola Falana . . .

FILM: Roman Gabriel

Roman Gabriel . . .

FILM: Fran Jeffries

Fran Jeffries . . .

FILM: Rudy Cardenas

Rudy Cardenas . . .

FILM: Miss World

Miss World . . . Belinda Green . . .

FILM: Dolores Hope

Dolores Reade . . .

FILM: American Beauties

Plus twelve American Beauties . . .

FILM: Les Brown

And Les Brown and His Band of Renown.

Sailor doing impression of Mae West on USS Midway, *Singapore, 1972.*

The last Christmas show

Lola Falana at Camp Casey, Korea, 1972.

Finale, Namphong, Thailand, 1972.

BILLBOARD

MUSIC: *Air Force theme*
FILM: Air Force guys loading equipment
FILM: Army guys loading the plane with baggage
FILM: Rear end of plane starts to close, pan up to tail
FILM: Up shot to Bob and Santa with beard on
FILM: Jim Nabors joins group
FILM: Long shot over crowd to Bob in doorway
FILM: Bob on steps of plane, girls in back of him
(*shot of plane taxiing*)
FILM: Plane heading into camera from moving point of view
FILM: Side angle as plane comes into camera and leaves the ground, pan it into the sky

HOPE: Well, like they say in show business—One More Time! Here we go . . . seventy-eight of the faithful for our twenty-second annual overseas junket.

That big stack of Santa Claus turned out to be Merlin Olsen of the Los Angeles Rams. If you follow the Rams you know why Merlin was wearing the beard.

And there's a fellow who looks a lot like Jim Nabors . . . oh . . . no wonder. Hi, Jim.

Get a load of those American Beauties. They told me to limit my baggage to sixty-five pounds . . . but . . . I know how to pack.

Every time we start down the runway I ask the same question— "How do they know this monster can fly?" Okay, suck in your breath and lift up your legs, we need all the help we can get.
(*shot of C-141 just as it lifts*)
HOPE: Made it!

MAP: Los Angeles to Shemya
FILM: Deplaning at Shemya
HOPE: Next stop Shemya in the Aleutians . . . eight hours away . . . seven if we make all the lights. Shemya is a wind-swept rock in the North Pacific with eight hundred Air Force men clinging desperately to the tundra.

And we're here because Colonel Donald Jolly convinced the Defense Department that this remote, out-of-the-way base was actually a short cut on the way to Tokyo. Colonel Jolly oughta have a magic act. There's Colonel Hooper out there doing my warm-up.

FILM: Shemya monologue
HOOPER: You know, we're pretty fortunate in having Bob Hope

and the show come to Shemya. It was quite a last-minute deal for them to work it into the program but nonetheless they're here. You know most of us were keeping our fingers crossed all day long to see whether that wind would hold so that they could get in . . . and they made it.

HOPE: Thank you, thank you . . . thank you very much.

Ladies and gentlemen . . . Here we are at Shemya Air Force Base. The Defense Department got a letter from up here signed by three hundred GIs, two seals, and a misplaced gooney bird, and Colonel Jolly.

This is the truth . . . The letter said how lonesome everybody was and how they all loved the Bob Hope Show and how much they wanted to see me. And one snow job led to another.

They've got snow, rain, hurricanes, sleet . . . I feel like I never left California.

They tell me they had a lovely day here year before last. Sun came out and it was so pretty, they quick-froze it and haven't seen it since.

And you can tell what time it is just by holding a finger up. If the wind blows the first two knuckles off, it's time to get inside.

They call the wind "williwaw" . . . Which is an old Eskimo word meaning "Forget your zipper, your underwear just went!"

MUSIC: *Air Force theme*

FILM: Production shots various angles: Rudy, Fran, Lola with GI

HOPE: We were just scheduled for an impromptu gas-stop show but everybody did a big act . . .

MUSIC: *Oriental music*

MAP: Shemya to Yakota

FILM: Sign on street . . . traffic moving in background. A policeman directing traffic . . . Sign saying "Bob Hope Show"

FILM: Establish huge audience

HOPE: It's only a four-hour flight from Shemya to Yakota Air Base outside Tokyo but we lost a whole day when we crossed the international date line. Try explaining that to your stomach or your wife . . . they both grumble a lot. In Yakota we played to one of our biggest audiences, eleven thousand Air Force, a couple hundred Marines, and thousands of wives . . . and get a load of all the kids . . .

FILM: Audience with lots of kids

HOPE: Someone must have told them I was the big bird from Sesame Street.

The last Christmas show   351

Fran Jeffries on USS Midway, *Singapore Harbor, 1972.*

352   *The last Christmas show*

Redd Foxx at Subic Bay, Philippine Islands, 1972.

The last Christmas show   353

And dig this little number I picked up in Oleg Cassini's Ginza branch.

FILM: Bob enters in samurai armor. Yakota monologue
MUSIC: *"Thanks for the Memory"*

HOPE: Hey, you all . . . Isn't this a wild outfit? . . . I look like I'm playing in the Rams backfield. This thing weighs five thousand pounds . . . Get it off.

(*audience shot*)

HOPE: Okay, take that back to the plane. I'm gonna wear that the next time I play with Agnew.

Yes, sir, here we are at Yakota Air Base, Japan. We had to come here . . . I needed new batteries for my Sony.

What about this . . . Is this great . . . We were here four years ago and we had to come back. The band needed another bath.

And I wanna tell you . . . the Japanese really went all out with their reception. They carved "WELCOME BACK PAPA-SAN" in the smog.

This is the only base in the world where you can get a Purple Heart for breathing.

I went shopping today and the prices here are wild. Anything you've got a yen for you haven't got enough yen for!

But the department stores are just like ours . . . everything "Made in Japan!"

And when they serve you dinner in Japan, they seat you on the floor. I practiced this at home last week. I sat on the floor and ordered my wife to serve my dinner. She brought me chopsticks and a bowl of Alpo.

(*voice over audience applause at end of monologue*)

Here's Rudy Cardenas, a guy who stopped the show everywhere we went. I haven't seen juggling like this since my tax man left for Tijuana.

MUSIC: *"Mexican Hat Dance"*
MUSIC: *"Caissons Go Rolling Along"*
MAP: Yakota to Korea
SOUND: Helicopter
FILM: Aerial view of crowd at Camp Casey
FILM: Point of view through window of chopper landing
FILM: Lots of troops marching to show
FILM: Pictures of trucks and troops crossing bridge with sign in foreground "Weak Bridge"

HOPE: Better button up whatever it is people button up these days because it's twelve degrees below freezing here at Schoonover Bowl in Korea. This is our coldest show of the trip but one of our hottest audiences . . . eleven thousand guys from the 2nd Infantry and the 73rd Armored. They've been perched here on this frozen hillside for the last four hours. I better hustle. Our landlord, four-star general Donald Bennett, is out there doing my warm-up.

FILM: Camp Casey monologue

MUSIC: *"Thanks for the Memory"*

HOPE: Look at this mob—isn't it beautiful! Very happy to be here at the Rose Bowl.

Ladies and gentlemen, this is the 2nd Infantry Division, occupying Korea . . . Except on Saturday night, and Saturday nights they occupy Seoul.

Yes, sir, on Saturday night these fellows all go to town for a little Seoul food.

Nah, but it's wonderful to be here, this is my eighth trip to Korea. After eight trips to Vietnam the Defense Department figured I earned a trip to this glamour spot.

Eight trips . . . I like it here. Don't stare at me . . . That line kept me a civilian.

FILM: Audience at end of monologue

HOPE: When you want to warm up an audience, there's no one better than Fran Jeffries. When she'd finished, Schoonover Bowl was a rice paddy.

INTO: Fran Jeffries song

SOUND: Helicopter

FILM: Girls cross airstrip carrying luggage on board

FILM: Back of large chopper

SHOT: Air view out of chopper over encampment and show site

FILM: From inside chopper as the girls leave it

HOPE (*voice over*): From Schoonover Bowl in Camp Casey to Osan, Korea, is just a short chopper jump. But it was a big change in weather. That beautiful warm sun brought out twelve thousand Army and Air Force guys from all over southern Korea. When I asked the CO, General McNeil, if there was anything we could do for him, he said, "You might just mention to the folks back home that we're still here." Confucius, the famous oriental philosopher, once said, "When in doubt change hats." Was it Confucius or my wardrobe man, Charlie Solomon?

FILM: Osan monologue

HOPE: Here we are at Osan Air Base, Korea. Osan . . . That's Korean for "Don't just sit there . . . call Dial-A-Prayer."

(*puts on new hat*)

You *like* that? It's got a part missing or something, hasn't it?

But I got a typical Osan welcome. The cockroaches got in formation and spelled out "Thanks for the Memory." Yeah.

The last Christmas show   355

Fran Jeffries, Yakota, Japan, 1972.

(*puts on new hat*)

Man, I've never had this many hats . . .

(*reads sign*)

Koon-Ni Range . . . Never heard of that . . . Where have you been, folks?

(*adjusts mike*)

What are you, a spy? To keep entertained when I got here Colonel Kirkpatrick gave me a shotgun and told me to go pheasant hunting. I think I'm in trouble. I thought he said peasant hunting.

(*puts on new hat*)

Just my size . . . It's not easy duty here. That's why it's listed as a hardship base. You have no idea how tough it is for a round eye to look an almond eye in the eye and be sincere.

MUSIC: *Thai travel music*

MAP: Osan to Udorn, Thailand

FILM: Line of military personnel and red carpet to plane

FILM: Then Bob, all military personnel salute

FILM: Bob is walking with astronaut

FILM: American Beauties leave plane

FILM: Officers putting leis around the girls' necks

FILM: Weapons carrier moves toward camera with sign: "Hope Special"

HOPE (*voice over*): And now let's jump from bleak Korea to steaming Thailand. Our next gig was an old stand for us, Udorn Royal Thai Air Base, four hundred miles north of Bangkok on the Laotian border. Here we are joined by two gypsies, astronaut Donn Eisele, who is now the head of the Peace Corps in Thailand, and an exotic singer named Dolores Reade, who moonlights as my wife. We came to the Far East hoping to join in the celebration of peace, but instead the action was hotter than the weather.

Did you ever try to get off the ground with a monologue while fifty Phantom fighter jets are trying to do the same?

FILM: Udorn monologue

FILM: Planes taking off

MUSIC: *Air Force theme*

HOPE: Thank you very much. We passed the line . . . There they go . . . All right, stop this stuff, colonel, or I won't go on.

FILM: More planes taking off

. . . passed the line there, and a kid said, "I'll be watching from Hanoi. You couldn't schedule the show for one o'clock, huh?"

Anyway, we're happy to be here at Udorn, Thailand. Udorn . . . that's a native word meaning "Keep the motor running."

The last Christmas show　357

There goes another one . . .

It's nice to be here. This is the "Home of the Hunters" . . . That name certainly fits this base, but what are they going to call it when you get indoor latrines?

How many are gonna take off?

Nah, this is the busiest base in Thailand. It must be . . . You have to wait three weeks to get a reservation at the bathhouse. If you can't get into the bathhouse, you guys manage to stay clean anyway. If it isn't the bathhouse, it's the crap games.

Really, you men have a very important mission here. Somebody's gotta protect all these Seiko watches.

MUSIC: *"Caissons Go Rolling Along"*

COLONEL SCOTT: I want you to know we got another outfit here, the 7th RFS Ramason Station. Sign's out there, Bob.

FILM: More planes taking off, louder

HOPE: How about that . . . Reminds me I got to send a Christmas card to Don Rickles . . .

Here's a girl who joined us two years ago on our annual resort trip. When you see her you'll know why she's such a hit. She's made it big in nightclubs and concerts. And now she's made it big as a regular on the Bill Cosby show. Here she is—Miss Lola Falana.

Lola Falana song

MUSIC: *"She's a Lady"*

MUSIC: *"Washington Post March"*

MAP: Udorn to Utapao

FILM: American Beauties get on float with Santa at Utapao, Thailand

FILM: Wide-angle shot of flashbulbs going off

HOPE (*voice over*): And now it's back to two-a-day. This is our first night show, which took us to Utapao on the Gulf of Siam. Home of the B-52s. This was one of our most challenging shows because that day a lot of B-52s had been lost over North Vietnam and morale here really needed a boost . . . although it's hard to tell from this reception . . . How about this for an opening night!

FILM: Utapao monologue

MUSIC: *"Thanks for the Memory"*

(*Bob enters riding golf cart*)

HOPE: Yes, sir. Thank you very much. Here we are in Utapao, the gateway to beautiful downtown Satahip. Satahip . . . Sounds like a Greyhound rest room stop.

Good evening, fellow Utapaoans . . . I'm getting nervous. I'm learning to pronounce this place. When I first came here I thought it was You-Tapioca.

Boy, I wanna tell you, this place is really something else. It isn't often you have to fly this far to work in an Air Force ghetto.

There are also some tremendous tankers here with an almost unlimited capacity. You can see them any night at the bar in the officers' club.

(*voice over audience applause at end of monologue*)

HOPE (*voice over*): At every base, we picked one lucky serviceman from the audience to come up and sing to our beautiful Miss World—Belinda Green.

FILM: Miss World with GI

HOPE: Belinda, I want to thank you for coming along with us, and before you go there's just a few words I'd like to say . . .

MUSIC: *Arpeggio*

(*Hope sings*)

You're just too marvelous
Too marvelous for words
Like glorious, glamorous
And that old standby, amorous.

(*Hope speaks softly under the music*)

And I'm not the only one that feels that way . . . Look at those faces out there . . . How 'bout . . . How about that one? Right there.

(*Hope points*)

(*camera cuts to GI with glazed look in his eyes*)

(*cut back to Bob and Belinda*)

HOPE: There's a kid who looks like his transfer just came through! Hey, come up here.

(*GI mounts stage*)

HOPE: What's your name? I say . . . say . . . hey! . . .

(*The boy is staring at Belinda. He doesn't answer*)

(*Hope turns his head toward him*)

Hey . . .

(*Hope whistles at him*)

Try to read my lips . . . What's your name?

GI (*reacting*): Oh . . . Oh . . .

(*he pulls his dog tag out from his shirt and reads his name*)

Daniel.

HOPE: Really? Daniel Foy, this is Belinda Green.

GI: Sure is.

HOPE: Don't you want to shake hands?

GI: I'm shakin' all over.

HOPE (*to Belinda*): What do you think of this fellow, Belinda?

BELINDA: I think he's so charming . . . He's so polite . . . He seems like a perfect gentleman.

HOPE: Perfect gentleman! (*to GI*) Are you sure you're on our side? This is Miss World, Foy . . . She's from Australia.

GI: Oh, uh—*Parlez-vous français?*

HOPE: Boy, he's officer material if I ever saw one. *Parlez-vous français.* Hey, soldier, would you like to sing a few bars to Miss World?

GI: Sure.

HOPE (*to camera*): Okay, hold it . . . hold it . . . get your hook off her. I have a terrible feeling we may be unleashing another Engelbert Humperdinck. Go ahead—sing it with feeling. Get in there.

(*GI takes Belinda's hand in his. Hope slaps it away*)

GI (*sings*): You're just too wonderful,
　　　　　Too wonderful for words

HOPE: You got him up to here. Stay in there and fight. Go, Foy!

GI: Like glamorous, glamorous
　　That old standby amorous . . .

HOPE: I may go on sick call . . .

GI: You're just too glamor . . .
　　I'll never find the words

HOPE: Just look at the cards. You'll find them all right.

GI: That say enough, tell enough,
　　I mean they just aren't swell enough . . .

HOPE: What sincerity . . . I didn't know Chet Huntley had a son.

GI: You're much too much
　　And oh so very very . . .

HOPE: Yeah . . . how about that?

GI: To ever be
　　In Webster's Dictionary.

HOPE: I think his tonsils struck oil . . .

GI: And so I'm borrowing . . .

HOPE: Stay in there, Foy.

GI: A love song from the birds . . .

HOPE: Sell it, man, sell it. Give me a finish.

GI: To tell you that you're wonderful . . .

HOPE: Your voice is changing.

GI: Too wonderful for words!

　　(*applause*)

HOPE: That will be three dollars, man. Okay, baby, that's Miss World . . . right here . . . Miss Belinda Green.

MUSIC: *Playoff*

(*fade up*)

MUSIC: *Air Force theme*

FILM: Utapao to Saigon

FILM: Emphasizing huge audience

FILM: Ambassador Ellsworth Bunker

FILM: Ambassador Bunker's wife

HOPE (*voice over*): Next stop the Pentagon East, Tan Son Nhut Air Base, Saigon. There's a lot of VIPs in our audience today, including Ambassador to Vietnam Ellsworth Bunker. If he laughs we get our passports back, and here's his lovely wife, the ambassador to Nepal, Carol Laise Bunker.

SHOT: General Weyand onstage, Bob shakes his hand

And here's a very good friend, the fellow who runs the store, four-star general Fred Weyand.

GENERAL WEYAND: C'mon now, and let's welcome Bob Hope.

(*applause*)

MUSIC: *"Thanks for the Memory"*

HOPE: I'm very happy to be here at Tan Son Nhut, Southeast Asia's biggest rocket base . . . mostly incoming . . .

I played golf here this morning. When we started out it was an eighteen-hole course. When we finished it was a fifty-four-hole course.

Tan Son Nhut is the busiest airport in the world. You usually have to stay in the holding pattern for hours. But I came right on in. That Henry Kissinger impersonation works every time . . .

Great to see you. Here we are Christmas Eve in Saigon for the trimming . . .

This is my ninth trip to Vietnam and my last. It has to be . . . The chicken with my blood type died.

And I'll miss Saigon . . . It's such a friendly city. I'll never forget the time a total stranger walked up to me and handed me a grenade.

(*hears jets overhead*)

Are those ours? They're bringing my laundry in.

It's hard to believe . . . this is the last time we'll be playing this base . . . And this is the last time you out there in the audience will be seeing us here. Try not to cry.

We figured it would all be over when we got here, but no luck. Not only did they fail to reach an agreement in Paris . . . now they're fighting over the hotel bill.

HOPE (*voice over audience applause shot at end of monologue*):

The last Christmas show 361

Here's what it's all about . . . and this is where it's at. Here are twelve of the most beautiful girls in the world and certainly twelve of the most charming . . . the American Beauties.

MUSIC: *Beauty medley*
"Today We Love Everybody"
MUSIC: *"Song of the Seabees"*
MAP: Saigon to Diego Garcia
FILM: C-141 in flight
FILM: Aerial of Diego Garcia
FILM: C-141 landing
FILM: International Airport sign
FILM: Los Angeles and New York mileage sign
FILM: Jeep in the rain
FILM: Rain shots at site

HOPE (*voice over*): We started out early Christmas morning to pay a visit to twelve hundred Seabees stuck in the middle of the Indian Ocean on a flyspeck called Diego Garcia. This 2200-mile detour was a command performance. Our answer to a lot of requests from the Seabees and their relatives. Finding it was only a minor triumph . . . we were the first jet to attempt to land there. As we swung into final approach they were still finishing the runway. The Seabees had worked feverishly the last two weeks to make this possible. Then we were greeted by a torrential tropical wind and rain, but these Seabees were determined to have a show. They waited through the downpour . . . Nobody budged. Finally, after an hour or so, it cleared enough. I better go out there and get to work before they mildew over.

FILM: Diego Garcia monologue

HOPE: Where are we? Diego Garcia, huh. It's a little embarrassing because we started out for Honolulu.

But we're awfully glad they slid the island under us when we dropped in. I'd like to thank you for inviting us here and the flies for giving us permission to land.

Our Seabees here share this base with the English. They coexist beautifully in spite of the language barrier.

Some of these Seabees have been over here a long time. I asked one guy why he doesn't quit. He said, "Somebody's gotta stop the Kaiser."

It's nice to be with ya on this Christmas Day. And it's a little different. Really. I've never seen a land crab playing Santa Claus before.

HOPE (*voice over audience applause at end of monologue*): Last month in Burbank Redd Foxx told me he wanted to make the Christmas trip. I thought he was kidding. Fortunately for a lot of GIs he meant it. Here we go with our fatigue version of "Sanford and Son" . . . and son??????

FILM: Bob/Redd sketch

(*Scene is a section of barracks somewhere overseas. Bob enters, pushing broom and singing. He's dressed in bedraggled fatigues, with hash marks the length of his arm*)

HOPE: What kind of fool am I?

I'm stuck here with this broom.

They told me I'm the only one

Who knows how to clean up this room.

What kind of shnook am I?

Fine work for an aerospace engineer!

(*calls offstage*)

All right . . . what am I doin', a solo out here?

(*Redd Foxx, another bedraggled GI, enters holding pail and dragging mop*)

REDD (*singing to "It's a Great Day"*):

Oh, it's a great day for having' a ball,

And it's a great day for going AWOL . . .

(*to Bob*)

Did you call me, Sylvester?

HOPE: That's right, Spiro. C'mon, crank it up. Let's get started.

REDD (*pitifully*): Okay, if you want to work a man who is old and tired and sick.

HOPE: If you're sick, how did you get in the Navy?

REDD: Instead of a physical they gave me an autopsy.

HOPE: Hey, can you imagine giving a man with my IQ a job like this?

REDD: What's your IQ?

HOPE: Twenty-three.

REDD: Twenty-three. I didn't know you were a college man.

HOPE: This is no life. I want to tell ya that.

REDD: Yeah . . . sure gives you the miseries . . . being ordered around, never havin' a mind of your own . . . being told don't do this and don't do that.

HOPE: War is war . . .

REDD: I'm talking about marriage . . . I never even got a three-day pass from her.

HOPE: Yeah, and they get mad if you send for replacements. What are you goin' to do when you get out?

REDD: I got it all planned. I'm gonna cash in on everything they taught me in the Navy.

HOPE: How?

REDD: I'm gonna open a chain of washrooms.

HOPE: How long we been sweeping?

REDD: About three, maybe four minutes.

HOPE: We better rest before we get promoted.

(*both sit down*)

REDD: What's wrong? You look down in the mouth today.

HOPE: I got a "Dear John" letter today.

REDD: So what? So she found another guy?

HOPE: Another guy? This was mimeographed.

REDD: Forget it. This place is crawlin' with groovy chicks. I had a wild date last night. Smooth skin, real slinky, and she couldn't let go of me.

HOPE: That was no chick . . . that was a water snake.

REDD: No kidding? You think she'll give me the ring back?

HOPE: Who cares? Find out if she's got a sister.

REDD (*takes out envelope*): Well, look. This is the kind of letter I get—with a hole in front! See that!

(*opens, reads*)

It's from my wife . . . uses the envelope from the gas bill . . .

HOPE: How romantic can you get?

REDD: Look at it! Her cousin Harold's livin' with us! I didn't know she *had* a cousin Harold!

HOPE: You got a problem. You ought to tell it to the chaplain.

REDD: I *did* that.

HOPE: What did he say?

REDD: He said I must make a mature adjustment to environmental factors beyond my control.

HOPE: What does that mean?

REDD: I don't know, but they usually serve it on a shingle.

HOPE: C'mon, we better hurry. Boy, I wish our replacements would get here.

REDD: There's some new guys in today.

HOPE: How can you tell they were new?

REDD: You can tell they were new—they were smiling.

VOICE (*offstage*): Now hear this . . . Now hear this . . . Report to quarters and pack your gear, we're going home. Repeat, we're going home.

(*Hope and Redd throw down mops, head for exit. Inga and Margy enter. They pick up mops and start cleaning. Bob turns and returns*)

Herb Ball, Alan Satterwhite, Shirley Eder, Frank Liberman, Betty Lanigan, Jim Bacon, Bill Faith, press at Tan Son Nhut, Vietnam, 1972.

HOPE: Wait . . . wait . . . wait . . . You're our replacements.
GIRLS: That's right.

> (*Redd rushes back . . . tugs at Bob*)

REDD: Let's go. We're leaving this war.

> (*Bob doesn't budge . . . Redd pleads*)

You're the fellow that hates war. You're against war . . . You don't want no more to do with war . . . What did you say?

> (*Bob puts arms around girls*)

HOPE: Full speed ahead and damn the torpedoes.
REDD: Some sneaky way to get you to reenlist.
HOPE: You're a beauty, Redd!

> (*applause*)
>
> MUSIC: *"Dolores"*
>
> (*over audience applause at end of sketch the camera brings Dolores out of audience onto stage*)

HOPE: Dolores Reade joined us for our very first visit to Vietnam. There was no way we could turn her down when she volunteered for this one.

> (*Dolores sings*)
>
> MUSIC: *"But Beautiful"*

Love to be here with you guys,
Time is short I realize,
Quick hellos and quick goodbyes
But beautiful.

Beautiful, to share with you
This season of good cheer,
There's no place we'd rather be
Than here.

You stand out in any crowd
With your head high and unbowed,
What you've done here
Makes us proud
You're beautiful.

Cause you're bringing
A lasting peace,
Good will to men again,
And that would be
But beautiful . . . Amen.

> MUSIC: *Playoff*
> (*applause*)

MUSIC: *"Marine Hymn"*

MAP: Bangkok to Namphong

FILM: Guard tower and sign: "MCAS Rose Garden, Crash Crew, When in Doubt, Call Us"

FILM: Moving point of view past MP, who waves, then past tents and small buildings

FILM: Rudy Cardenas practices in front of men's john

FILM: Mike makes up Miss World

FILM: Someone going through Bob's trunks backstage, straightening out clothes

HOPE (*voice over*): Our next spot was a new one for us, Namphong. That spot on the map is just a guess. This base is so secret the Defense Department first found out about it in *Time* magazine. There are very few comforts at this remote Marine salt mine. It's sixty miles of jungle to the nearest anything. Several hundred of these two thousand gyrenes camped out all night waiting for the show. Let's have at 'em.

FILM: Namphong monologue

HOPE: Great to be here in beautiful Namphong, Thailand. Namphong . . . that's a Thai expression meaning "You only have one so keep it close to the ground."

I bring you greetings from America . . . You remember that. It's a big piece of land across the ocean complete with plumbing and everything.

They conned me into coming here. I thought a "six-holer" was a golf course.

How do you Marines like it here? Bet you never thought you'd be homesick for Da Nang, huh?

You know, I knew this was a Marine base. I saw a guy wearing a cobra to keep his pants up.

And it's nice to be working in snake country. It's the first time I've been hissed before I did my act.

But this is a lovely place to be stationed. If you think the guys are happy, you should see the CO. I've never seen a paper hat with gold braid on it before.

(*applause shot end of monologue*)

FILM: Onnie and Rose handing out wet towels to American Beauties

HOPE: The guy who wrote "When You're Hot, You're Hot," must've got the idea in Namphong. We had to put iced towels on the American Beauties so they wouldn't dissolve before they went on.

(*Hope brings girls out*)

These gals all volunteered to come here because they wanted to do a show for you guys, and I think you deserve finding out who they are, don't you?

MONIKA: Hi. I'm Monika from Illinois. I'm Miss Illinois World. And I want to say Merry Christmas from the Windy City.

MARGUERITE: Hi. I'm Marguerite and I'm from New York. Yeah . . .

INGEBORG: Hi, you guys. I'm Ingeborg Sorensen. I'm Miss Norway. I'm Miss World runner-up.

HOPE: I'm convinced that in Norway, sardines aren't the only thing they pack.

CINDY: Hello, I'm Miss Kansas, Cindy Lee Sikes. Merry Christmas. I'm eighteen and I won the swimsuit contest in the Miss America pageant.

MELANIE: Hi, you all. I'm Melanie, Miss Georgia World. Anybody from Georgia? Any of you all like to try a little southern comfort?

HOPE: What did she say? Try what? I like southern gals . . . by the time they say you can't, you have.

THE TWINS: Hi. I'm Patricia Barnstable from Louisville, Kentucky. And I'm Pris Barnstable, her twin sister, and we just want to know if there is anybody out there who thinks he can handle two?

HOPE: Hey, all at once this turned into an all-volunteer audience.

JACKIE: Hello. I'm Jackie Berhendt, Miss Texas World. I just want to say the eyes of Texas are upon you. Are the eyes of Namphong on Texas?

SANDY: Hello. I'm Sandy from Florida. Where we make the freshest orange juice in the whole world.

HOPE: We make the freshest orange juice in the whole world . . . Crosby, eat your heart out. Here goes Frances.

FRANCES: Hi, you all. I'm Frances Adams from the Bluegrass State, Kentucky. And I just want to know if any of you guys have seen any of our bluegrass lately?

HOPE: Next, c'mon, Pat.

PAT: Hi, I'm Pat Price, Miss California. I live in San Diego, where all the big boys are chargers. How about you guys?

GAIL: Hi. I'm Gail and I'm the former Miss Polish America from New Jersey.

HOPE: Isn't she beautiful? She was with National Airlines and she came to me in Miami and said, "I gotta go on the trip with you" . . . and she just wanted to come. There you are, baby. How about these gals . . . thank you, gals.

MUSIC: *Playoff "Jay"*
MUSIC: *"Anchors Aweigh"*
MAP: Zoom into Singapore
FILM: Bob and driver with black fez
FILM: Leading cast on barge
FILM: Singapore harbor
FILM: Waves breaking over windshield cleaning revealing *Midway*
FILM: Boarding USS *Midway*

HOPE (*voice over*): Here I am back on the road to Singapore. So *that's* Singapore harbor. I prefer the *real* one back at Paramount.

Here we are boarding the USS *Midway*, better known by Navy men as "the Whale." The name fits . . . it's no anchovy. We did the show for five thousand sailors and Marines, including those from the USS *Rich*, the *Fresno*, the *Cleveland*, the *Tucare*, and the *Inchon*.

INTO: *Midway* monologue
FILM: *Midway* monologue

HOPE: Thank you very much. Isn't this beautiful? When's the tornado come in? Here we are aboard the USS *Midway* . . . pride of the fleet and home of four thousand gooney birds. No, it's good to be here. I'm the Jolly Green Giant's surfboard.

Imagine the job it must be to clean the deck? You couldn't swab this down with Howard Cosell's tongue.

The home station of this floating crap game is Alameda, California . . . Yeah, Alameda. All you Alamedians . . . No, this ship is lucky to be from Alameda . . . When they have to take evasive action they can always bring a California driver behind the wheel.

The *Midway* is parked just outside Singapore, the cleanest city in the world . . . And after three days' shore leave, so is the crew. I hope you had luck with the Singapore ladies . . . Better known as Yankee clippers.

I'm really delighted to be here. You know, it's an extra kick for me because one of the first pictures Bing and I made was called *Road to Singapore*. It was the first of the *Road* pictures and I've been waiting for twenty-two years to come back here and apologize.

We had some fun last night in Singapore. The drummer in our band wandered down a dark street and some girl asked him if he'd like a Singapore sling. He said, "Sure" . . . so she broke his arm.

HOPE (*voice over audience applause at end of monologue.*): On the *Midway* Fran Jeffries proved she's not only beautiful and talented, she's also brave. Here she is risking her career by doing a number with me.

FILM: Bob/Fran duet
HOPE: Fran, you know how I feel about you . . .
    MUSIC: *"When My Sugar Walks Down the Street"*
    MUSIC: *"Anchors Aweigh"*
    MAP: Singapore to Subic Bay
    FILM: Big audience
HOPE (*voice over*): And here we go headed toward home. Destination Subic Bay, the largest naval base in the western Pacific. And we drew pretty good, eleven thousand Navy, five hundred Marines, one provincial governor, two mayors, and a water buffalo. But more about that during my monologue.
    FILM: Subic Bay monologue
HOPE: Here comes my cab. Bring him through. He wouldn't come up the steps so we're just wheeling him by. There you are. That's fine . . . Looks like one of Crosby's horses. Take him back. Take him back and put him on the plane. We'll take him right in. We can get about one dollar a pound for him in North Hollywood. Yeah, we'll wear a Marine cap later . . . we integrate.
    FILM: Audience applause at end of monologue. Go to Hope
    live onstage for his intro of Miss World
HOPE: You know, through the years we have had the privilege of bringing you many of the Miss World winners . . . She won it in London a few weeks ago. This year I think we have one of the loveliest young ladies ever to win that contest. She is from Sydney, Australia, Miss World . . . Belinda Green.
    MUSIC: *"The Most Beautiful Girl in the World"*
    (*Belinda Green parades*)
    (*applause*)
    (*cheers, whistles, etc.*)
HOPE: Isn't that nice?
BELINDA: Thank you, fellows!
    (*blows them a kiss*)
  Gee, is this what's known as a standing ovation?
HOPE: No, I would call it more of a crouching ovation.
BELINDA: Are they always this demonstrative?
HOPE: Oh sure. You should hear them applauding their chief in the shower!
BELINDA: Bob, I really appreciate the way you've been looking after me on this trip.
HOPE: Please, Belinda . . . no details . . .
BELINDA: I mean, who else would take the time to come to my room each night and knock on my door and ask, "Is it locked? Is it locked?"

HOPE: Well, that's the wonderful kind of person I am.

BELINDA: You know it's strange, Bob, but everybody looks after me.

HOPE: Well, that's as good an angle as any, I guess.

BELINDA: I mean, wherever I happen to be, there is always some kind of gentleman there offering to carry my luggage for me. Has that ever happened to you?

HOPE: Once, and I'm still looking for the guy and the luggage. Hey, Belinda, how does it feel to be Miss World?

BELINDA: I can't believe it. When I heard them announce my name, I just swelled up with pride.

HOPE: I'm not gonna fool with that line at all. Tell me, Belinda, four years ago, we had a Miss World who was also from Australia. Why do you think your country produces so many beauties?

BELINDA: Who can say, Bob. Maybe it's because we're descended from the British and they're handsome people.

HOPE: Well, *I* was born in England.

BELINDA: Really? Maybe it's the fresh air and sunshine.

HOPE (*to camera*): How did I get whiplash this far from the freeway? Well, I'll tell you, it must be exciting to be Miss World.

BELINDA: It is, Bob. But I can't help looking ahead to a year from now when all the glamour and adventure is over and I'm back home in Australia . . . just another girl.

HOPE: Just another girl . . . If you're just another girl, then Liberace is the Godfather. Tell me, how do you feel about a man's age? Is that important?

BELINDA: Why do you ask?

HOPE: Well, I don't know. I'm a glutton for punishment, I guess.

BELINDA: Well, Bob, today it's impossible to tell a man's real age. They wear girdles and toupees, they have face lifts and transplants . . .

HOPE: Yeah, it's so disgusting. (*to camera*) Is my head on straight?

BELINDA: It's true, Bob. It's the *men* who lie about their age.

HOPE: I know. That David Cassidy's sixty if he's a day.

BELINDA: You're not like that, Bob. You've retained that youthful enthusiasm. You still have that spring in your walk.

HOPE: What spring? That's Supp-Hose!

(*bow*)

HOPE (*voice over audience applause shot at end of Miss World*): Here's a guy that had a rough football season with injuries and illness. But in this post-season appearance for the GIs, he gave an All-Pro performance. Here's Roman Gabriel, the mightiest Roman of them all.

FILM: Roman Gabriel spot

HOPE: Here's a man who went through all sorts of obstacles to be with us today . . . and you'll know what I'm referring to when I tell you he's the quarterback of the Los Angeles Rams . . . Roman Gabriel . . . right here . . .

MUSIC: *"Football Hero"*

(*applause; Roman enters*)

HOPE: Roman, I think we all appreciate the sacrifice you made in turning down the playoff to be with us.

ROMAN: Well, it was nothing, Bob. I just threw an interception and here I am.

HOPE: Gabe, when you were working out strategy to beat Detroit, didn't you try to get expert advice?

ROMAN: We sure did, but the President had bigger things on his mind.

HOPE: It's no secret, Roman, that you've had better seasons.

ROMAN: Yes, and I don't understand it. I . . . I use . . . I shave with Gillette, I use Desenex, I eat Wheaties, I comb my hair with Vitalis, I gargle with Listerine, and I wear Fruit of the Loom shorts.

HOPE: Well, what about the huddle? Have you tried Binaca? How's your arm this year?

ROMAN: I sure wish I knew.

HOPE: I understand you tried acupuncture for your elbow.

ROMAN: Right. They put so many holes in me I could have worked as a sprinkler.

HOPE: Well, did it help? Did the pain go away?

ROMAN: Yeah . . . Soon as they took the needles out. Did you try acupuncture?

HOPE: Well, not in the arm.

ROMAN: Where did you try it?

HOPE: And it wasn't called acupuncture.

ROMAN: What was it called?

HOPE: Overseas shots. Roman, this is the season of the running quarterback . . . You know, Bobby Douglass and Greg Landry ran for a lot of yardage.

ROMAN: What yardage? They ran for their lives.

HOPE: I know what you mean. Having Godzilla on your tail can really get you out of neutral.

ROMAN: I used to scramble a lot, Bob, but I got discouraged . . . Now I'm trying a new strategy.

HOPE: Is that right. What's that?

ROMAN: Prayers.

HOPE: Well, does it do any good?

ROMAN: No, they're intercepting that too.

HOPE: I tell you, Roman, you've been a great top football star for a lot of years. You must have done very well with the bread, huh?

ROMAN: I have no complaints, Bob, but I just love football and money is unimportant.

HOPE (*to audience*): And Jim Brown thinks *he* can act. (*to Roman*) But really, Roman. Pro football players today earn every penny they get. The game today is so rough, the Dallas Cowboys have a combination coach and chaplain.

ROMAN: Joe Namath has so many wires in his knees, he can pick up two channels in Philadelphia.

HOPE: Well, you know Joe. He's never had trouble picking up anything. Have you thought about going into coaching?

ROMAN: No, I'd like a steady job.

HOPE: So would Nixon's Cabinet. Gabe, before you go, is there any word of advice you care to give the young people who may follow in your footsteps?

ROMAN: Well, Bob . . . I would say, respect your body, and keep it strong and healthy . . . and don't abuse it.

HOPE: Well, I'll try to cut down.

ROMAN: And when you play the game, play hard . . . and above all play clean . . . especially if the referee's watching.

HOPE: Roman, thanks for joining our taxi squad and we all wish you and the Rams a great football season next year. Roman Gabriel . . .

> MUSIC: *Playoff "Football Hero"*
>
> (*applause*)
>
> MUSIC: *Air Force theme*
>
> MAP: Subic Bay to Guam
>
> FILM: Shots of Guam
>
> FILM: Audience applause

HOPE (*voice over*): Last stop. All out for Guam. We always get a special kick out of Guam because it's a final stop, but this time it has special significance—it's the last show on our last trip.

> FILM: Bob's entrance and standing ovation

These weeks of base hopping were having some effect on my constitution. Here you see me taking my medicine . . . that sound may be applause to you, but to me it's therapy. I look like the man from Glad!

> FILM: Guam monologue
>
> MUSIC: *"Thanks for the Memory"*

HOPE: Here we are on Guam, or as it's known down at the enlistment office, fungus a go-go. Actually, Guam is a beautiful place. It's turning into a mecca for honeymooners. It's sort of a Niagara Falls with coconut crabs.

One hotel offers breakfast in bed, but the breakfast is wild pig. The waiter brought up breakfast to one couple and knocked on the door. The groom said, "What is it?" The waiter said, "It's your wild pig." The groom said, "One at a time."

(*applause*)

HOPE (*voice over audience applause at end of monologue*): Here's Lola Falana foolishly trying to keep up with "the Fred Astaire of radio."

FILM: Bob/Lola duet

HOPE: Les . . . go—take it.

MUSIC: *"Cabaret"*
(*4-bar intro*)
(*16 bars both tap*)
(*16-bar soft shoe*)
(*dance to end*)
MUSIC: *Playoff*

HOPE (*voice over applause*): Well, this is it . . . this is where we say our farewells and acknowledge the work and dedication of a lot of people who've made these shows possible for so many years . . .

FILM: Cast bows with Hope

FILM: "Silent Night"

HOPE: Let me just say one thing about these fellas . . . All these cats out here . . . Doing this work here . . . All these camera guys and all these sound guys . . . Let's give an extra hand for them, huh?

(*applause*)

Fran is going to sing a chorus of "Silent Night" and we want you all to join us in the second chorus and if you can't think of the words, move your lips and we'll dub in something from some other base, huh? Okay, here we go.

MUSIC: *"Silent Night"*

FRAN: Silent night, holy night
    All is calm, all is bright
    Round yon virgin, mother and child
    Holy infant so tender and mild
    Sleep in heavenly peace
    Sleep in heavenly peace

FILM: Audience shots from all the bases
    Silent night, holy night
    All is calm, all is bright

Round yon virgin, mother and child
Holy infant so tender and mild
Sleep in heavenly peace
Sleep in heavenly peace

HOPE: Have a great '73 and pray for peace. God bless ya!

MUSIC: *Playoff*

FILM: Getting off plane at Wake

(*couple of shots in Wake showing audience and acts*)

HOPE: Well, that's it. That's the end of the line except for a stop at Wake Island to refuel the band. Wake Island, where all the GIs jammed the island and we did a stand-up show at midnight. Pretty good laughs for that hour.

I hope I can be excused a little sentimentality as I look back over twenty-two of these Christmas trips and the millions of servicemen and -women who responded to our efforts with warmth, enthusiasm, and affection.

FILM: Audience applauding . . . Large shots at Da Nang . . . guys in show

FILM: Audience with signs . . . Eating Xmas dinner with boys . . . cakes . . . etc.

(*still pics, Jinx, etc.*)

HOPE: Actually, my romance with the GIs started way back in 1941, at March Field, California. And I still remember fondly that first soldier audience. I looked at them, they laughed at me, and it was love at first sight.

(*close-up: happy, smiling audience faces*)

And now here we are thirty-two years and three wars later and we're still going steady.

(*more audience shots*)

Over these past three decades, we've been around the world several times, gone from Thule, Greenland, to Diego Garcia in the Indian Ocean, heard many languages and seen some strange customs. But all that seems to recede in the face of the grim reality of Vietnam.

(*Greenland, 1954 . . . Berbers in Morocco . . . camels . . . elephants . . . Pleiku . . . montagnards*)

When we made our first trip to Vietnam in '64, we never dreamt we'd be making eight more. We saw a lot of courageous fighting men from our country being baptized in guerrilla warfare, a very treacherous business.

Yes, we saw mountains of men . . . Guys who lived with that murderous heat, who tasted the dust, or sloshed through the jungle mud in search of a cunning and resourceful enemy.

The last Christmas show   375

Roman Gabriel and American Beauties on arrival at Guam, 1972.

SHOTS: Tough-looking soldiers . . . soldiers in the heat . . .
River Rats . . . pilots . . . jets taking off

We'll never forget them . . . the "River Rats" at Dong Tam, the "Jolly Greens" and the "sandys" at Nakhon Phanom, the "grunts" at Pleiku, the Marines at Da Nang and Chu Lai, and all the fighter pilots on the carriers on "Yankee Station" in the South China Sea. And just a couple of headlines ago the B-52 pilots and crewmen who braved the flak-filled skies over North Vietnam. They all met the challenge with fantastic courage and good humor.

SHOTS: Guys in audience who are pilots; Guam

Over the past nine years, we've seen the number of men in Vietnam dwindle dramatically from a high of 500,000 to about 25,000 still there.

LONG SHOT: Long Binh Bowl jammed with 28,000 servicemen waiting for Hope Show

Remember this scene? This is how we saw Long Binh a year ago. They were wonderful audiences . . . They waited for us in the rain and the heat . . . But nothing could dampen their spirits . . .

SHOTS: Servicemen reacting, laughing at jokes, using cameras to snap shots of performers, etc.

Well, this is how Long Binh looks now . . .

376   *The last Christmas show*

SHOTS: Same long shot . . . stadium now empty, deserted . . . weed-choked, desolate expanses of empty seats

And this is how it should be. All those happy, smiling, beautiful faces are gone . . . But most of them are where they really belong . . . home with their loved ones.

SHOT: "Silent Night" audiences

SHOT: Hospital ship. Children and doctors

All of us who've been on these trips have many vivid memories of Vietnam, the heartbreak of our visits to the hospitals—and witnessing the incredible fortitude of the wounded.

We remember the hospital ship off Da Nang where Vietnamese children suffering from all the ailments that come with war were given expert care and treatment by our doctors and nurses.

Everywhere we witnessed the kindness and humanity of our GIs. They went out of their way to help the civilian population with their time, their money, and their good will. I can tell you that they are more concerned with building and healing than destroying.

SHOTS: Adopting kid . . . orphanage in Korea . . . two kids who turned in Cong

We'll always be grateful to the many people who made these shows possible. Men like Senator Stuart Symington, who started the whole thing . . . the late, beloved General "Rosy" O'Donnell, who as head of the USO kept us safe and comfortable and smoothed out all the rough spots . . . Neil Armstrong, who was a living reminder to our GIs of the greatness America can achieve.

SHOTS: Symington and Rosy bowling . . . Armstrong . . . President Nixon . . . Westmoreland . . . Abrams . . . McCain at Cu Chi

President Nixon and Mrs. Nixon for launching one of our Christmas shows. General Westmoreland cheering us on at Saigon. General Creighton Abrams giving the peace sign. And we'll never forget Admiral John McCain for his inspiring visits at Cu Chi and Da Nang.

And of course we owe a great debt to the many talented performers who made these trips. All of the Miss Worlds from around the globe. And of course the greatest band in the world . . . Les Brown and His Band of Renown.

And also to Dolores Hope, who was always nice about giving me a pass over Christmas.

To the Military Airlift Command, Tactical Airlift Wing. To my travel agents at the Pentagon . . . to the USO . . . Howard Miller . . . Harvey Firestone . . . And to all those who toiled behind the scenes . . .

(start plane shots)

And to the sponsors who picked up the tab for these pictures that we've brought to the families of all these great Americans we've met on these trips, my eternal gratitude.

And especially to the millions of guys we played to in every latitude and every longitude around the world. Thank you for Christmases I'll never forget. Good night!

Les Brown, Dolores Hope at Diego Garcia, Indian Ocean, 1972.

CHAPTER 24

That's a wrap

In show business "that's a wrap" means just that. Time to wrap up the cameras, pack the lights, and strike the scenery.

Nineteen seventy-two really was the last Christmas show and I must say it was a strange feeling. For twenty-five years I was late for Santa Claus. When I got home all I ever found was a few reindeer hairs and a note that said "Sorry you blew it again." I have the only kids who never saw Mommy kissing Santa Claus.

The Christmas of '73 I was almost lonesome without the cheers, laughs, and wolf calls of 150,000 young Americans. Dolores was very understanding. She said, "I bet you miss those Christmases with Zsa Zsa, Joey Heatherton, Jill St. John, Ann-Margret, and Raquel Welch."

"Of course not," I sobbed.

During the holidays we visited Letterman Hospital, Long Beach Veterans Hospital, Walter Reed Hospital, and Bethesda Hospital and we saw a lot of kids. Every time we'd walk up to a bed a kid would stick his hand out and say, "Long Binh," or "Da Nang." For most of us the war is over. For many of these kids it will never end.

Over the years I've seen a lot of Christmas trees in a lot of remote places. You might even say godforsaken places, except that they were filled with the kind of men who carried their own particular sort of God with them wherever they went.

Some people wondered whether that last Christmas trip, the trip of 1972, was necessary. The war was coming to an end, they said, and besides a lot of people had gone very sour on our involvement. I felt the last Christmas trip was almost more important than the previous ones, if only because our troops were so aware of the mixed feelings back home.

They had read about the anti-war protests in the papers, and they'd heard about them in letters from home. A lot of them had started to wonder whether they were headed in the right direction, whether they were really

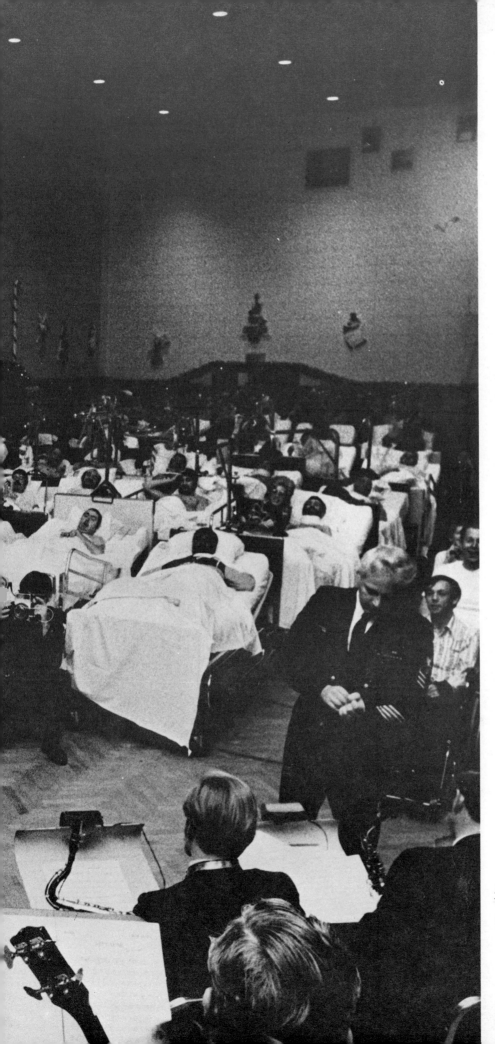

Long Beach, California,
Veterans Hospital, 1973.
(*Los Angeles* Herald-Examiner)

fighting for their country, whether what they were doing was right. They began to wonder whether all the political fighting back home had cost their country the strength and unity it needed to support their fighting in Vietnam. Because of this, it was clear to me that those kids needed a Christmas show more than ever.

We were lucky. We circled the globe backward and forward, we crossed oceans, we flew in every kind of plane, we traveled in everything from a limousine to a jeep. We waded through snow, plodded through mud, found our way through fog, smog, and smoke. We had a lot of laughs and a few tears and we made it back safely. No injuries, except possibly a few bruises to the ego, a couple of pounds around the pot, and a few extra wrinkles that make-up will have to worry about.

That's it, Colonel Woody Mark. We've borrowed you from the Air Force for the last time. You're a brilliant cameraman, but it's all over. Pack your clapboard and head for Big Sur. We've made our last take.

That's the past and all I see in the future is a lot of work at Lakeside Golf Club on the driving range. And just enough television shows and personal appearances to support my lost ball habit. On the other hand, don't bet on it.

This morning I got a call from Margaret Wilson at the Defense Department. There's a batch of guys in Korea who haven't had a show for a long time. "Out of the question," I said. And I meant it. Not a big show with the band and the Golddiggers and the cameras, etc. I could go alone and tell a lot of jokes . . . of course, on the other hand, I could call up Joey Heatherton and see if she's between gigs. Ann-Margret might have time before her next special. Tony Romano had his nose fixed—I don't think that will affect his guitar playing.

And let's see, for the monologue I could open with:

★

Thank you. It's a pleasure to be here with all you papa-sans.

There's been some changes in the White House. Your commander in chief just got promoted to civilian.

The new Prez couldn't sleep that first night in Lincoln's bed. There were fourscore and ten lumps in it—for a while he thought that's where the tapes were.

The President's hobby is swimming. He swims like a fish. When he gets out, he doesn't even use a towel, just flips himself dry!

The Prez is a water freak. Our new Vice-President could be Mark Spitz!

Of course, it hasn't been all smooth sailing. This morning he had his first real crisis. He ran out of instant pancake mix.

But he's very handy in the kitchen. He may be the first President to win the Pillsbury bakeoff!

Incidentally, there's no truth to the rumor that he's appointing Sinatra ambassador to Australia.

Everyone seems to like him because he's a regular guy and has the common touch. He's the kind of man who would take the Shah of Iran to McDonald's.

I see where the President picked Rockefeller as his VP. That's one Ford that's never gonna run out of gas.

Isn't that something—picking Rockefeller as Vice-President? What a sneaky way to balance the budget.

You know, with inflation he's just what we need—a back-up Fort Knox. But how's the White House gonna look with all those Standard Oil pumps in front . . .